A DARK HISTORY:
THE
KINGS & QUEENS
OF EUROPE

A DARK HISTORY:
THE
KINGS & QUEENS
OF EUROPE

FROM MEDIEVAL TYRANTS TO MAD MONARCHS

BRENDA RALPH LEWIS

METRO BOOKS

NEW YORK

© 2008 Amber Books Ltd

This 2008 edition published by Metro Books
by arrangement with Amber Books Ltd.

Metro Books
122 Fifth Avenue
New York, NY 10011

Editorial and design by
Amber Books Ltd

Project Editor: James Bennett
Designer: Zoe Mellors
Picture Research: Terry Forshaw, Kate Green

ISBN-13: 978-1-4351-0209-5
ISBN-10: 1-4351-0209-6

Printed and bound in China

1 3 5 7 9 10 8 6 4 2

CONTENTS

Introduction   6

CHAPTER 1
Philip IV of France and the Knights Templar   8

CHAPTER 2
Elizabeth Bathory: The Blood Countess   26

CHAPTER 3
Two French Royal Rakes: Louis XIV and Louis XV   42

CHAPTER 4
The King and the Vamp: Ludwig I of Bavaria and Lola Montez   58

CHAPTER 5
Castles in the Air: The Tragic Story of Ludwig II of Bavaria   74

CHAPTER 6
The Mayerling Tragedy   94

CHAPTER 7
Madness in the Spanish Royal Family   112

CHAPTER 8
More Madness in Spain   130

CHAPTER 9
Queen Christina of Sweden: A Question of Gender   148

CHAPTER 10
Haemophilia: The Royal Disease   164

CHAPTER 11
Kings and Communists: Carol II of Romania   178

CHAPTER 12
The Netherlands: A Royal Family in Trouble   196

CHAPTER 13
King Leopold II and the Belgian Congo   214

CHAPTER 14
The Grimaldis of Monaco   232

Map of Key Locations   250

Index   252

INTRODUCTION

History can be dark in many ways, and the royal history of continental Europe is no exception. For example, in the fifteenth and sixteenth centuries, Elizabeth Bathory and Gilles de Rais were mass murderers. De Rais and the horrors he perpetrated at his castle entered French folklore in tales of the barbaric Bluebeard, who murdered seven wives and hung their bodies in a blood-drenched cupboard. In the nineteenth century, King Leopold II of Belgium reduced the population of the Congo, in Africa, by 70 per cent, through the appalling punishments and brute exploitation practised in his colony, the Congo Free State.

◆

Vlad III Dracul, a fifteenth-century Prince of Wallachia (now part of Romania), also entered the shock-horror annals of Europe. He was probably the model for Count Dracula, the blood-sucking vampire in Bram Stoker's famous novel *Dracula*, published in 1897. The real Vlad Dracul went a great deal further: he specialized in impaling his enemies by having stakes driven through their bodies, and afterwards leaving them to die a slow, horrifically agonizing death.

Several kings of France appear in the cast list. The most notorious was the fourteenth-century King Philip IV, who coveted the wealth and feared the power and influence of the Knights Templar, the most prestigious of the crusader military orders. Philip devised a truly evil plot to destroy them. Hundreds of Templars died or were crippled after being tortured to confess.

Two later French kings, Louis XIV and Louis XV, were more civilized, but still reprehensible. They

specialized in debauchery. Louis XV had his own private brothel near the Palace of Versailles where he regularly serviced a bevy of young girls. In the seventeenth and eighteenth centuries, kings were expected to have a mistress as a consolation prize for their duty to enter an arranged marriage and produce heirs to the throne. Both Louis XIV and Louis XV gained a great deal of 'consolation' by way of this tradition.

> Not all the dark history in this book deals with barbarity, wickedness or immorality. Some royal lives were ruined by the insanity that ran in their families because of the unwise practice of inbreeding.

This was supposed to keep the dynastic line 'pure' and retain royal power, wealth and influence within the family. But inbreeding ran too close to incest and produced monsters so damaged in body and mind that their families dared not reveal the truth about their condition.

'The Family of Louis XIV' painted in 1711 by Nicolas de Largillière. The picture shows some of the legitimate heirs of King Louis (third from left) but his many illegitimate children were not, of course, included. The small child pictured was the King's great-grandson and successor in debauchery, the future King Louis XV.

The Spanish Hapsburgs and the Wittelsbachs of Bavaria were riddled with insanity and its appalling manifestations. They suffered lifelong torment, which included morbid fears, hallucinations and murderous violence. The pity of it was that some of them knew they were losing their minds, yet were inexorably swept on into the maelstrom of madness. Another scourge, haemophilia, the dreaded 'bleeding disease', wrecked two European royal families and ruined many lives.

Scandal, of course, proliferates in dark history. King Ludwig II of Bavaria was revealed as a hapless old fool over his infatuation with the femme fatal Lola Montez, who cost him his throne. Queen Christina of Sweden, whose gender was uncertain, scandalized Paris and Rome with her eccentric behaviour. The royal families of Netherlands and Monaco, together with King Carol II of Romania, provided years of salacious copy for the intrusive modern media. This is not a book for the faint-hearted. It took a strong stomach to write it. It could require another to read it.

En lan de mre seigneur mil Φ
v lix templiers a pare Φ
le moulin abrent apro leo

PHILIP IV OF FRANCE AND THE KNIGHTS TEMPLAR

Grand Master Jacques de Molai had nothing to lose when he appeared before an assembly of French prelates to confess, yet again, to a roster of terrible charges first laid against his Order of the Temple of Solomon in 1307.

✦

The accusations, which were entirely bogus, were the work of the Grand Master's implacable enemy, Philip IV of France. They included denying Christ and his apostles, blasphemy, sodomy and other homosexual practices that were said to be rife within the Order, which was better known as

Left: Falsely accused of crimes by King Philip IV of France, the Knights Templar burn while Philip (on horseback) looks on. Above: Jacques de Molai became Grand Master of the Templar Order in 1295.

the Knights Templar. It was now seven years since these accusations had first been made against the Order, but whatever happened on this day – 18 March 1314 – de Molai knew that the least he could expect was to spend whatever remained of his life in the stinking holes that served as prisons in medieval times.

LAST-MINUTE RESOLVE

De Molai was about 70 years old, what in his times was considered extreme old age. He was deeply ashamed because, terrified of the agonies of torture and death by fire at the stake, he had already confessed to some of the charges against him. Now, de Molai was required to reaffirm his 'guilt' and do it before the crowd of onlookers gathered around a scaffold before the Cathedral of Nôtre Dame in Paris. This time, though, he had found a latent courage and, though well aware of the consequences, he was resolved to recant.

'It is only right,' he told the crowd, 'that at so solemn a moment, when my life has so little time to run, I should reveal the deception that has been practised and speak up for the truth. Before Heaven and Earth and all of you … I admit I am guilty of the grossest iniquity. But the iniquity is that, to my shame and dishonour, I have suffered myself … to give utterance to falsehoods in admitting the disgusting charges laid against the Order … I declare, and I must declare, that the Order is innocent … I disdain to seek wretched and disgraceful existence by grafting another lie upon the original falsehood.'

This pronouncement by the most senior of all Templars created uproar and dismay, all the more so because de Molai was backed by another prominent Templar, Guy de Charnay, Preceptor of Normandy. Before de Molai could say anything else, the two men were summarily seized and dragged back to prison. Two other Templars, Hugues de Rairaud and Geoffroi de Goneville, were either less courageous or less despairing; they distanced themselves from the Grand Master and Preceptor. The damage had been done, however, and the Order of the Temple of Solomon and its Grand Master stood on the brink of ultimate punishment.

All that was left after de Molai and de Charnay were burned at the stake in 1314 was blackened bones and ashes, and nothing could have symbolized more starkly the tragedy and ruin that overtook the Knights Templar between 1307 and 1314. King Philip IV's revenge was complete.

AN ORDER OF PROTECTION

The Templars had been among the first of the military and religious orders formed to manage the new situation in the Holy Land that followed the brilliant

PHILIP'S LONG-AWAITED REVENGE

King Philip IV had waited a long time for this moment, the moment when he could destroy the Templars once and for all. His motives included greed for the Templars' wealth and fear and jealousy of their power. His method was accusation of the worst possible kind. Now, after a seven-year campaign of lies, fake evidence and false witnesses in court, Philip was not going to let de Molai, his prize captive, get away with uncovering his duplicity. A few hours after the Grand Master made his recantation, he and de Charnay were taken to the Ile-des-Javiaux, an eyot in the River Seine that lay between the royal gardens and the convent of Saint-Augustin. They were tied to stakes, the wood beneath them was lit and the two men burned to death. According to witnesses, de Molai and de Charnay met their terrible end with dignity, calm and courage. To many who saw them die, they became instant martyrs. Some waited until the ashes had cooled in order to sift through for bones that they could keep and revere as holy relics.

Philip IV, nicknamed The Fair, became King of France in 1285. Apart from the Knights Templar, Philip also quarrelled with Pope Boniface VIII, installing in 1305 his own rival pope, Clement V, at Avignon.

success of Christian arms in the First Crusade of
1095–1099. The Muslim forces were decisively
defeated, and Crusader realms were set up in Tripoli,
Antioch, Edessa and, most prestigious of all,
Jerusalem, which had fallen on 15 July 1099 after a
long and bloody siege. The new Christian acquisitions
needed defence and succour; for this purpose, military
and religious orders of chivalry were created soon after
the end of the First Crusade.

These included the Knights of the Holy Sepulchre,
whose task was to defend this most important centre of
Christian worship in Jerusalem; the Orders of the
Hospital of St John of Jerusalem, known as the Knights
Hospitaller, who provided medical services; and the
Knights Templar. Like the Hospitallers, the Templars,
who formed in 1118, were mainly composed of
Frankish knights. Their task was to provide armed
escort and protection for the pilgrims who made the
long and arduous journey to the Holy Land.

Jerusalem was the emotional focus of these
pilgrimages, which were large-scale events even before
the Muslims captured the city in AD 638. But travelling

This painting by the French artist François Marius Granet depicts the inauguration of a Knight Templar. He painted many scenes inside churches and monasteries and, like many, was fascinated by the Templars.

to, or merely being in, the Holy Land could be a
perilous business. Unarmed pilgrims were ambushed,
robbed, killed, kidnapped and even sold into slavery by
bandits who specialized in swift hit-and-run tactics, then
melted away into the desert landscape. The first Knights
Templar who volunteered to guard and protect the
pilgrims against such merciless enemies were only nine
in number, but were otherwise well suited to the task.

NOBLE KNIGHTS
All of the Templars were of noble birth, all well
connected to powerful families. All came from the area
around Champagne and Burgundy in northeast
France, and their leader, Huges de Payens, who was
born near Troyes, was probably a cousin as well as a
vassal of Hugh, Comte de Champagne. The comte was
one of the mightiest and most prestigious magnates in

This painting shows the inauguration in 1295 of the 54-year old Jacques de Molai as Grand Master of the Templar Order. We know very little about de Molai's life up to this point, but he has become the most famous of the Templars' Grand Masters.

France, devoted to the cause of crusade and virtually independent of the French king. He was undoubtedly his cousin's richest and most powerful patron, but the Knights Templar did not take their cue from his kind of eminence. Instead, they opted for the poverty, chastity, obedience and humility of monks, willing to beg for their food and lead pure, exemplary lives. Their original name, the Poor Knights of Christ and the Temple of Solomon, said a great deal about them.

CHANGING FOCUS

In time, however, the realities of life and the nature of Christian society in the Holy Land worked together to change this emphasis. The Templars retained their martial identity and were, in fact, the most effective of all the military orders in the field. But though they exemplified the two great passions of medieval times – fervent faith and fighting prowess – they soon became celebrities, thrilling the popular imagination as valiant champions of Christ, with God undoubtedly on their side. They also attracted rich, powerful backers, including the Pope himself. Only 10 or 12 years after the Order was founded, prominent magnates such as Fulk, Count of Anjou (afterwards fourth Crusader King of Jerusalem) and Thibaud II, a later Comte de Champagne, both became Templars and gifted large sums of money to the Order. Fulk's contribution alone was 30 pounds of silver a year.

Other, rich revenues together with fine properties were lavished on the Templars by aristocrats and churchmen on a scale that gave the knights a status they had neither sought nor envisaged. They became wealthy, privileged and both politically and diplomatically significant. Eventually, it was reckoned that the Templars owned 900 estates, many of them donated to the Order by new recruits from prominent families, who were not allowed to own personal property. In time, the Order

A Knight Templar in action on horseback, from a fourteenth-century manuscript.

King Philip IV of France seated 'in majesty' on his throne, flanked by two lions. Philip was killed when he was mauled by a wild boar during a hunting trip. All three of his sons eventually became kings of France.

established itself in Britain, Italy, Cyprus, Germany and France, where it owned a total of 870 castles, schools and houses. In addition, the Templars established major castles in the Holy Land – at Jaffa, Acre, Sidon, Safed and elsewhere. But the favours the Templars attracted went beyond the merely material.

> Muslim forces successfully challenged crusader power in the Holy Land, sending crusading zeal into decline.

They were given special papal protection, and a Bull of 1139 issued by Pope Innocent II declared them exempt from any other jurisdiction, whether Church or government. The properties the Templars acquired were tax-free: they did not even have to pay the usual ecclesiastical tithes.

HONEST MONEY MEN

Possibly the most significant concession Rome made to the Templars was to exempt them from the ban on usury, which had long ago acquired a bad name in the Christian world. This enabled the Order to set up banks and other financial institutions which eventually embraced most of the banking functions common today – current accounts, safe deposits, loans and credit, international money transfers, trustee services, strongholds for keeping secure jewellery, gold or other treasure, and armed guards when it was in transit. The Templars inspired such trust in their honesty and efficiency that several European princes and even some wealthy Muslims allowed them to handle their not insubstantial treasuries.

PHILIPPE   LE BEL ·

Still, the picture was not all glorious. The lavish favours, the special treatment, the mass of wealth and the extraordinary privileges the Templars acquired meant that they were soon regarded as spoiled darlings and were, of course, deeply resented as such. Already, by 1295, when Jacques de Molai became Grand Master of the Order, the Templars were being regularly accused of loving luxury, glorying in wealth and fame, and encouraging the sin of pride, and even arrogance. In 1307, de Molai was personally attacked for failing to emulate the self-denial practised two centuries earlier by Huges de Payens. In the demanding world of Christian piety, these were very serious accusations. What is more, they arose in full force at a time Muslim forces successfully challenged crusader power in the Holy Land, sending crusading zeal into decline. The

This medieval manuscript depicts the destruction of the Knights Templar and the death of King Philip IV, who survived martyred Jacques de Molai by only eight months.

Muslim forces reoccupied the Crusader kingdoms and other territory in 'infidel' hands and, by 1303, had the last Crusaders confined to the tiny island of Arwad, some three kilometres out in the Mediterranean Sea. There was talk in Europe of another crusade, but it failed to arouse sufficient interest.

DECLINE OF CRUSADERS

This ignominious failure badly damaged the standing of the military orders which had been an integral part of the crusading scene for more than 200 years. It was far worse than simple loss of face. The success and glory, and the certainty that God approved crusader endeavours, had gone as well. Inevitably, to the superstitious mindset of medieval times, their place was filled by fears that the devil and all his works had

Two Knights Templar, tied back to back, are burned for heresy. This was a scene which occurred in several parts of France, and was normally attended by large crowds.

TORTURE AS AN INTERROGATION METHOD

Medieval torture had numerous refinements. Prisoners were stretched on the rack, so dislocating their joints. Thumbscrews, toe-screws or foot-crushing boots were used to shatter their bones. Their mouths were forced open so wide that their jaws cracked. Their teeth or fingernails were pulled out. Their legs were immobilized in iron frames and grease spread over the soles of their feet and set on fire. The agony was so intense and the damage so great that the heel bones of one priest, Bernard de Vado, dropped out through his scorched skin. De Vado confessed, but later retracted his confession and gave his flame-blackened heel bones to his inquisitors as a memento.

Although many Templars died under torture, still stoutly proclaiming their innocence, de Vado's brand

Torture by burning the feet persisted even beyond the medieval period. In this painting, an Aztec priest is horrifically tortured by Spanish conquistadores, in the early 1520s.

of impudent courage was not all that common and the confession rate was high. All but four of the 138 Knights Templar interrogated in Paris confessed to the charges against them, perhaps taking their cue from Grand Master de Molai whose arms, legs and testicles were flayed before he gave in and signed. Other high-profile Templars, including Guy de Charnay, Preceptor of Normandy, and Huges de Pairaud also capitulated. De Piraud was in a particularly invidious position, for several of his fellow Templars had named him as the man who led them astray.

wormed their subversive way into the Church. In fact, the failure of the Crusades and the decline of crusading gave King Philip IV of France just the opportunity he needed to strike at the two most prestigious institutions of the Christian world: the papacy and the Templars.

THE BEGINNING OF THE END

King Philip's first target was Pope Boniface VIII, who had declared in 1301, 'God has set popes over kings and kingdoms.' This was a direct attack against the growing self-confidence which European monarchs

One of the many forms of medieval torture was strappado, seen here being applied to a prisoner while his inquisitor looks on. Strappado involved tying up a victim's hands with rope behind his back, then suspending him in the air, dislocating his arms.

> The Templars, King Philip contended, were not only guilty of blasphemy and homosexuality, but also of cannibalism, infanticide and child abuse, and dabbling in witchcraft and the supernatural.

had in their own glory and greatness. In response, Philip sent in the 'heavy mob'. On 7 September 1303, French troops headed by Guillaume de Nogaret, the king's chief minister, appeared at the Pope's private retreat in Agnani, near Rome, and demanded that Boniface resign. When Boniface refused, Nogaret is said to have beaten him up and threatened him with execution, although there appears to be little hard evidence for this. The Pope was released after three days, but never got over the shock. Whatever Nogaret did to him was more than enough for a man of 86 who probably thought his person was sacrosanct. Boniface died a month later, on 11 October 1303.

VICIOUS ASSAULT

Conditions were now ideal for King Philip's assault on the Knights Templar, and he pulled no punches, couching his accusations, issued on 13 September 1307, in the language of overkill.

'A bitter thing, a lamentable thing, a thing which is horrible to contemplate, terrible to hear of, a detestable crime, an execrable evil,' was how the King described the 'abominable work' of the Templars, whom he claimed surpassed 'unreasoning beasts in their astonishing bestiality (and) exposed themselves to all the supremely abominable cries which even the sensuality of unreasoning beasts abhors and avoids'.

This statement, with its blatant appeal to medieval superstition and fears of depraved sexuality, set the stage for the accusations finalized in the summer of 1308. The Templars, King Philip contended, were not only guilty of blasphemy and homosexuality, but also of cannibalism, infanticide and child abuse, and dabbling in witchcraft and the supernatural. It was also alleged that they worshipped the Baphomet, the devil in the form of an embalmed head or idol with a goat's beard and cloven hooves.

King Philip IV watches as Knights Templar are led to their deaths. The stakes on which they will be burned are shown top right.

After this, Philip spent the next month organizing mass arrests. On 13 October 1307, all over France, some 15,000 Templars and others associated with them – servants, tenants, farmers, shepherds – were seized and thrown in to the royal dungeons or imprisoned in castles. Subsequently, friars were dispatched to churches all over France to preach against the Templars and so rouse popular fury against them.

The proportion of senior Templars detained was relatively small, only around one in 20: they comprised 138 knights and some 500 sergeants and other 'brothers' of the Order. King Philip had, however, apprehended the most important leaders, including Grand Master Jacques de Molai who, only the day before his arrest, had been in high royal favour, serving as pallbearer at the funeral of the king's sister. Philip lost no time appropriating Templar land and property, which he had ordered to be surveyed before the arrests were made. But he never got his hands on the Order's records: despite intensive searches, the documents disappeared, either burned, hidden or spirited away by some 50 knights who were apparently forewarned of the arrests and made their escape by sea from the port of La Rochelle.

The lack of documentary evidence that the records might have provided was not a problem for the prosecution. Prosecutors in medieval courts relied on confessions extracted from the accused or from witnesses willing to fill in the fine detail of the charges. Not all of them were honest, and some had their own agendas. For example, the first allegations of Templar misconduct to reach King Philip, in 1305, came from one Esquin de Floyran, a criminal who purported to be a one-time member of the Order and clearly harboured a grudge against the Templars. Philip was de Floyran's second try: his first bid to poison the Templars' reputation, at the court of King James II of Aragon, failed to convince. Whether King Philip was seeking a cover to conceal his intentions or was more susceptible than James is not precisely known, but he was certainly willing to act on information received.

INCREASING MACHINATIONS

The king also sent agents to locate other dissident Templars. Among several malcontents, Brother Etienne de Troyes and Jean de Folliaco proved particularly useful: both of them alleged that they had been forced to deny Christ and his apostles. De Troyes went further: he recounted how he was forced to spit upon the cross, receive homosexual attentions and venerate an idol in the form of a severed head. Dramatic testimony such as this, designed to shock and awe a courtroom, gave impetus to the guilt by accusation that underlay trials of this nature.

Likewise, torture to extract confessions was a recognized procedure, quite probably on the premise that the devil could be encouraged by pain to disgorge his evil secrets. The Roman Inquisition set up in 1231 by Pope Gregory IX was permitted to use torture in 1252, but, short of that, psychological pressure was exerted. Prisoners were kept awake and starved on bread and water. Only if they refused to confess at this stage did the Inquisition proceed to the next level and begin the torture.

Ultimately, King Philip's inquisition extracted confessions from most of the Templars in France, in exchange for promises of pardon and freedom. The victims soon discovered just how cynical these promises were. When the torture ceased, they were invariably taken back to their icy, unhealthy cells, where there was no straw to lie on and no covering to keep out the cold.

'The human tongue,' an anonymous, pro-Templar chronicler wrote in 1308, 'cannot express the punishments, afflictions, miseries, taunts and dire kinds of torture suffered by the … innocents…. The truth kills them, and lies liberate them from death.'

A few Templars were displayed for propaganda purposes. They were sent to repeat their confessions before tribunals. Others, however, reneged, including Huges de Pairaud and Grand Master de Molai. In 1309, both Pairaud and de Molai withdrew their confessions in the presence of two cardinals sent to Paris by Pope Clement V to report on the Templar trials. The Pope was initially minded to protest against the persecution of the Order, but later changed his mind in the face of threats from King Philip, including hints that his life would be in danger if he refused to toe the royal line.

> The Templars had no hope of just treatment, for Philip did everything possible to 'fix' the final judgment against them. Anyone who confessed, then withdrew his confession could be condemned to burn as a lapsed heretic.

That line was profoundly cynical. The Templars had no hope of just treatment, for Philip did everything possible to 'fix' the final judgment against them. Anyone who confessed, then withdrew his confession could be condemned to burn as a lapsed heretic. Philip's sinister protegé, the lawyer Guillaume de Nogaret, circulated anti-Templar rumours even while the accused were still giving evidence in court. The king packed the courtroom with hostile witnesses and brought in theologians from the University of Paris to trumpet his credentials as a champion of Christ and the Church, valiantly fighting the 'depraved' Templar Order.

THE FINAL BLOW

At last, in 1310, King Philip took steps to bring the cycle of confession and retraction to an end. On 12 May of that year, 54 Templars, all lapsed heretics, were taken to open country near the Pont St Antoine des Champs, outside Paris, and were burned at the stake by slow fire. Another 67 died the same way by the end of the month.

SLAUGHTER IN THE CASTLE: GILLES DE LAVAL, BARON DE RAIS

Outwardly, Gilles de Laval, Seigneur de Rais (1404–1444), gave no sign of the murderous nature that would one day appall the whole of Christian Europe. Instead, he appeared to be a valiant warrior and a generous patron of music, literature and art. He was also renowned for his religious piety and his charity towards the poor. Yet beneath this prestigious mask lay an undercurrent of extraordinary sadism.

After the death of his parents in 1415, Gilles de Laval was brought up by his godfather Jean de Craon. While in de Craon's indulgent care, Gilles developed into a spoiled brat, intent on having his way in everything. No one, it appears, attempted to rein him in. When he was 16, Gilles kidnapped a rich heiress whom he afterwards married. In time, he squandered both her fortune and his own. His conduct in battle was also less than honourable, for he showed an early taste for bloodletting and pillage.

CHILD SACRIFICE

The symptoms of depravity went unrecognized or perhaps ignored for several years, until Gilles retired from military service and took up residence at the castle of Tiffauges, near Nantes in western France. At Tiffauges, Gilles began experimenting with the occult and was persuaded by a Florentine sorceress that he could regain his lost fortune by sacrificing children to a demon called Barron. Before long, children, most of them young boys who had been sent to Tiffauges to beg for money, were failing to return home.

In time, fearful stories began to filter out of Tiffauges, stories of sexual orgies as well as allegations of torture, sodomy and black magic. At first, given Gilles's heroic reputation, these stories were dismissed as mere gossip and impossible to believe when they involved so illustrious a figure as the Seigneur de Rais. Until the Seigneur made a big mistake.

On 15 May 1440, he had an argument with a clergyman, Jean le Ferron, over the ownership of a château. In a rage, Gilles de Laval seized le Ferron and held him captive. This was so much out of character for a much-respected, devout and chivalrous

Giles de Laval, Seigneur (Lord) de Rais seen seizing a young boy, doubtless to add to his roster of slaughtered victims.

knight that Jean de Malestroit, the influential Bishop of Nantes, decided to investigate Gilles de Laval's activities. What he uncovered at Tiffauges was utterly horrific and, in September 1440, Gilles de Laval was arrested and threatened with torture. Faced with this ghastly prospect, Gilles preferred to confess to a long list of hideous crimes.

Parts of his confession were so gruesome that, at his trial, many of the details were removed from the record. These and other evidence, which included the bodies of 50 young boys dug up inside Gilles's castle, revealed that the illustrious Seigneur de Rais had committed satanism, heresy, sodomy, apostasy, sacrilege, kidnapping and the torture, murder and mutilation of between 80 and 200 children. The children were usually beheaded, and the court heard how the Seigneur's accomplices, Henriet and Poitou, used to place the severed heads on display so that they could choose which one they liked best.

'CARNAL DELIGHT'

In the courtroom, Gilles de Laval seemed to be two totally contradictory people. One moment, he was the fierce, proud nobleman, insulting the judge for daring to bring him to trial. The next, he would assert his devout Christian faith, then break down in tears. However he behaved, he made no secret of how much he enjoyed watching his young victims die slow, agonizing deaths. When asked for an explanation, he replied that it was for the 'pleasure and carnal delight' the spectacle afforded him. Gilles de Laval, Henriet and Poitou were hung for their crimes in October 1444. Gilles was simultaneously burned.

Those who lived in the harsh, cruel world of medieval Europe did not shock easily, but Gilles de Laval, Seigneur de Rais, had committed so many of the worst possible crimes that he became a universal symbol of evil. His name soon entered European legend and, as so often happens, he was invoked by parents as a bogeyman to frighten children into obedience. The folk tale of Bluebeard, first recorded by Charles Perrault in his *History or Tales of Past Times* (1697) may also derive from the grisly story of Gilles de Laval. Bluebeard was a rich nobleman who murdered seven of his wives and hung their bodies on the walls of a blood-drenched room in his castle. The Seigneur de Rais slaughtered 30 times that number. This dubious achievement enabled him to retain his place among the world's most prolific and horrific serial killers.

The seal of Gilles de Laval, Seigneur de Rais, showing him on horseback, sword in hand. This design was typical of aristocrats who were military leaders as well as feudal lords and great landowners.

Pope Clement V, elected in 1305, collaborated with King Philip IV of France in the destruction of the Templars. Like Philip, he died in 1314 shortly after the Templar knights were finally eliminated.

Others who had always denied the accusations were imprisoned for life. Only those who confessed and stood by their confessions had a hope of escaping prison. Eventually, on 5 June 1311, after sessions lasting more than two years, the trials were brought to a close.

DIVIDING THE LOOT

Eight months later, Pope Clement V issued a Papal Bull formally suppressing the Templar Order. Templar property, which King Philip had been persuaded to relinquish, was handed over to the Knights Hospitaller. Philip kept 10 per cent as his commission on the deal. Some of the property passed into other hands in Germany, Italy and Cyprus, while in England it was initially given to guardians appointed by the king Edward II. Afterwards, Edward, who had a penchant for expensive homosexual favourites, gave it to his boyfriend of the moment, Piers Gaveston. In 1312, however, the year Gaveston was murdered by Edward's infuriated nobles, the pope ordered that Templar lands

should be handed over to the Hospitallers and, despite resistance from the English king, the transfer was duly effected in November 1313.

The following month, Jacques de Molai and the three other senior Templars were again put on trial in Paris, this time before a formidable battery of experts – cardinals, prelates, theologians and lawyers. After a trial lasting three months, fresh confessions were expected, but de Molai refused to deliver. Instead, he stood by his last recantation and died in the flames without flinching, so redeeming himself and his honour in what was his finest as well as his final hour.

Philip IV did not live long to enjoy his triumph over the Templars or the Pope, who learned a salutary lesson about royal egos and never again attempted to place themselves above kings. Philip died on 29 November 1314, eight months after Jacques de Molai. Some said the cause of death was the will of God; others, hardly less judgmental, called it guilty conscience.

Medieval orders of chivalry like the Templars expressed their military ethos in mighty castles that exuded an air of power. This impressive castle was built by the Knights of St. John Hospitaller on Rhodes after they subjugated the island in 1309.

ELIZABETH BATHORY
THE BLOOD COUNTESS

Elizabeth (Erzsébet) Bathory (1561–1614) belonged to one of the richest and most influential families in sixteenth-century Hungary. Members of this powerful Protestant family had been rulers of Poland and Transylvania – warlords, political leaders, clerics, judges and landowners on a vast scale. One of them, Stephan Bathory, fought with Vlad III Dracul (the model for Count Dracula) during his wars against the Turks. Elizabeth, who was born in 1560 or 1561, was herself a niece of another Stephan Bathory, who was King of Poland.

✦

With her prestigious connections and the promise of extraordinary beauty she already showed at a very young age, Elizabeth was a great 'catch' for an ambitious husband, and several suitors showed an interest after she was placed on the

Left: A portrait of Stephan Bathory, King of Poland from 1576 to 1586, the uncle of Elizabeth Bathory.
Above: Elizabeth Bathory looks innocent in this portrait but she was one of history's most infamous torturers and serial killers.

'marriage market' in around 1570. The successful suitor was Count Ferenc Nadasdy, aged 25, who sought to increase his renown through his marriage: this was why he took the unusual step of adopting the Bathory surname as his own, rather than Elizabeth adopting his.

All the same, Nadasdy possessed his own prestige. He was wealthy, a famous war hero and an athlete, although even his mother admitted that he was 'no scholar'. Elizabeth, by contrast, was well educated and able to read and write Hungarian, Greek, German and Latin. This disparity was of little consequence in an age of political marriages, when royal or noble males earned renown by their exploits on the battlefield and literacy was regarded as an inferior activity fit only for clerics and women.

What Elizabeth and Nadasdy shared, though, was much more important to the events that marked their marriage, which took place on 8 May 1575, when she was aged 14: both of them were sadists.

AN INHERITED EXCESS?

Nadasdy had a furious temper which, when roused, prompted savage beatings and floggings, and earned him the nickname of the 'Black Hero of Hungary'. Nadasdy's cruelties, however, paled beside his wife's, which afterwards led to the most horrific scandal that ever occurred among the nobility of Eastern Europe. What was more, where Nadasdy had his limits and was disgusted by some of Elizabeth's excesses, her brand of cruelty seemed to know no bounds. Subsequently, she became known as the 'Blood Countess' and, although it was a fearful nickname, it actually understated the nature and extent of her crimes.

One source of Elizabeth's frightening behaviour derived from the Bathory family and their practice, common among European aristocracy, of inbreeding to preserve the 'purity' of the noble line. Both of Elizabeth's parents, György and Anna, belonged to the Bathory family, which produced many examples of mental derangement, including schizophrenia, sadomasochism, bisexuality and the purely sadistic streak which Elizabeth inherited.

Count Ferenc Nadasdy might look like an innocent young man here, but his horrific crimes, carried out with his wife Elizabeth Bathory, make him worthy of infamy.

GRISLY SPECTACLE

As a child, Elizabeth Bathory witnessed a display of public execution that was in many ways typical of the period, one which involved the execution of a gypsy who had been sentenced to death for treason. In the sixteenth century, and for a long time afterwards, gypsies were considered to be barely human and in some places were liable to be shot on sight, like animals. This perception may have explained the unusual nature of the execution Elizabeth witnessed. First, the belly of a live horse was dissected. The gypsy was pushed into it and sewn up inside. The spectacle proceeded as the horse writhed in agony amid blood and gore, while the hapless gypsy struggled in its belly in a hopeless bid to escape. Only when both horse and gypsy lay still, and evidently dead, did the barbaric spectacle come to an end and the onlookers start to disperse. Whether or not this ghastly event triggered Elizabeth's dormant brutality is a matter of conjecture, but it is at least possible that it had some influence on her future actions, which were callous in the extreme.

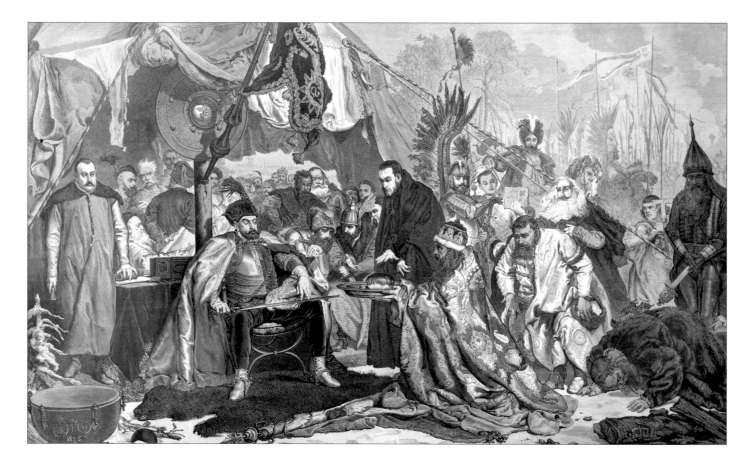

Stephan Bathory, the uncle of Elizabeth, is regarded as one of Poland's greatest kings. He is pictured here at the siege of Pskov, during the Livonian wars of the 1500s.

Elizabeth also displayed dismaying symptoms of her own. At age four or five, she began to have epileptic fits. She became prone to seizures that brought on violent, uncontrollable rages. She suffered extreme mood swings, one moment being cold and aloof, the next changing to murderous outbursts of temper. Elizabeth's instability was not helped by her upbringing. She was badly spoiled as a child, for a girl in her high position was considered too privileged to be disciplined by any of the numerous governesses who took charge of her. As a result, Elizabeth grew up vain, imperious and preoccupied with her own beauty. She was also susceptible to the callous and barbaric nature of the time and place in which she lived. Public executions, for example, were treated as a form of entertainment, which can hardly have helped to curb her instincts for cruelty and callousness.

This callousness was further encouraged by the circumstances of Elizabeth's married life. As a warlord, her husband was frequently absent from their home,

the Castle of Cachtice, high up in the Carpathian Mountains of northwest Hungary. The military campaigns he conducted against the Ottoman Turks were prolonged; in the gloom and boredom of the castle, Elizabeth had plenty of time to develop skills in the 'dark arts' and the finer points of torture. She had

> Where Nadasdy had his limits and was disgusted by some of Elizabeth's excesses, her brand of cruelty seemed to know no bounds. Subsequently, she became known as the 'Blood Countess'.

the opportunity, too, for her companions at Cachtice were her Aunt Klara, a sadomasochist and expert in flagellation, and Thorko, a retainer, who introduced Elizabeth to occult practices. She quickly moved on to experiments with potions, drugs, powders and herbal, possibly toxic brews.

Castle Cachtice, where Elizabeth Bathory committed her crimes, is in present day Slovakia. Built in the mid-13th century, it was a wedding gift from the Nadasdy family on Elizabeth's marriage to Ferenc Nadasdy in 1575.

AN OBSESSION WITH BLOOD ... AND YOUTH

Star-kicking was definitely a depraved formed of torture, but even this was not the ultimate extreme to which Elizabeth was willing to go. As she aged, she became obsessed with preserving her beauty and particularly the creamy smoothness of her skin. One day, a servant girl accidentally pulled Elizabeth's hair while brushing it, and received a slap in the face from her mistress that was so hard it made her nose bleed. As the girl wiped away the blood spots that had splashed her hand, Elizabeth thought she noticed that the skin where it had fallen seemed regenerated. At that, Elizabeth reputedly had the young girl's throat cut. She drained her blood into a vat and bathed in it while it was still warm. This, it seems, became regular practice at Castle Cachtice, with dozens of girls – all virgins – murdered to provide blood baths for the countess. Local gossip whispered that Elizabeth did not content herself with bathing in blood, but actually drank it and even ate the flesh of her victims after she bit their necks and breasts.

Elizabeth's husband, Count Ferenc Nadasdy, shared the gruesome tastes of his wife Elizabeth, but was completely outclassed by her cruelty.

SPIRALLING APPETITES

Somewhere along the line, Elizabeth discovered the delights of torturing the most vulnerable among her servants, the adolescent girls who were the general dogsbodies of their class. They were the least likely, through fear of the consequences, to tell tales about their mistress's behaviour. Elizabeth ensured that they kept their mouths shut about what went on at Castle Cachtice by employing five of her most trusted servants to make certain that they remained silent.

The slightest mistake or omission could be the excuse for excessive punishment. Elizabeth once sewed up the mouth of a girl who talked too much. Girls were beaten until they bled, then thrashed again with stinging nettles. This was nothing, though, to the punishments given servants suspected of stealing; Elizabeth would order them to strip, then torture them by placing red-hot coins on their skin.

Not that misbehaviour was required. Elizabeth would kill, torture and mutilate just for the thrill of it. Reportedly, she would tear the head of a servant apart, by exerting pressure on the sides of the mouth until they tore away and the neck snapped. Before long, Elizabeth had a collection of instruments for inflicting pain. Among them were tongs and pincers which were heated until red-hot, then used to tear flesh; spiked cages for impaling the girls alive; and red-hot irons to brand them. Girls were set on fire and left to burn to death while Elizabeth watched, often squealing with delight at the spectacle. Even Ferenc Nadasdy, no stranger to the horrors of the battlefield where mutilations were common, walked out of the room rather than watch these tortures.

> The slightest mistake or omission could be the excuse for excessive punishment. Elizabeth once sewed up the mouth of a girl who talked too much. Girls were beaten until they bled, then thrashed again with stinging nettles.

Other girls were covered in honey, then left tied to trees, where birds pecked at their flesh and insects devoured them. The 'water torture', another speciality at Castle Cachtice, involved stripping girls naked and leaving them outside in winter on days when the temperature fell below freezing point, until they froze to death. Sometimes their bodies were thrown over the castle walls to be eaten by wolves. One of Elizabeth's favourites was the torture known as 'star-kicking'. Pieces of oiled paper were placed between the girls' toes and set on fire. The victims jumped, jerked and kicked in futile attempts to get rid of the paper, but the oil made sure it remained in place while it burned, and the torture continued.

POWERFUL ARISTOCRACY

By this time, the slaughter and torture at Castle Cachtice had been going on for several years and at some point, despite Elizabeth's precautions, news of her activities was bound to get out. The hundreds of girls who had mysteriously vanished, the mutilated bodies found around the castle, the atmosphere of terror that prevailed in the surrounding countryside – these were

impossible to ignore. And yet for a long time they were.

The power of the aristocracy in sixteenth-century Europe was so great that it was possible for them to frighten witnesses into silence and so escape official detection and, with that, justice. Local peasants dared not speak out for fear of reprisals. Parents who had lost their young daughters were powerless against the mighty Bathory family. The Church kept quiet, fearing Bathory revenge. Other nobles who came to know of the rumours or acquired more solid information from their own grapevines remained silent, rather than

betray one of their own, however bloodthirsty. Besides this, peasants, men and women alike, were serfs and therefore the property of their employers. Nobles such as Elizabeth Bathory could do anything they liked with their property.

THE INEVITABLE END

Elizabeth's 'reign of terror' was bound to end at some time, if only because, in around 1609, after more than 30 years, she ran out of local girls. By then, Elizabeth had managed to extinguish an entire generation of

females in the area around the Bathory estates, and although she was able to 'buy' a few more girls from poor peasants, ostensibly 'for a life of security in the service of the mighty House of Bathory', she needed to extend her reach. Looking further afield, Elizabeth decided on a new approach. At Castle Cachtice, she established a 'school' for girls for the minor nobility, where she intended, she said, to 'teach them the social graces' appropriate to their class.

It was not long before these girls, too, went missing, presumed dead. Istvan Magyari, a priest from a village near Cachtice Castle who had long suspected that a

> Before long, Elizabeth had a collection of instruments for inflicting pain. Among them were tongs and pincers which were heated until red-hot, then used to tear flesh; spiked cages for impaling the girls alive; and red-hot irons to brand them.

nightmare scenario was being acted out within the castle, found the courage to go to the local authorities and tell them what he knew. This time, they listened. They might have been willing to keep quiet about the mass deaths of peasant girls, but now the girls involved were of noble birth – that could not be so easily overlooked.

The Bathory family, who were well aware of what Elizabeth was doing, had worked for years to prevent any enquiry into her activities and labelled any news that *did* get out as local gossip or ignorant superstition. These tactics would no longer work. Magyari's evidence reached the ears of King Matthias of Hungary, who immediately ordered an investigation. This action may have reflected much more than shock and dismay at alleged atrocities. The king, it seems, had an agenda of his own, and saw an

This imagined nineteenth-century illustration shows the depraved Elizabeth Bathory, right, seated in Cachtice castle, commanding her servants to torture a number of local girls who have been stripped naked.

NOTORIETY BEYOND THE GRAVE

Notorious in life, Elizabeth Bathory soon became controversial in death. Her family wanted her buried at Cachtice, but the local populace objected strongly to the idea of her being close to their own homes, and interred in consecrated ground, too. There were also superstitious reasons for wanting Elizabeth buried far away from Cachtice.

Like Vlad Dracul more than a century before her, she was equated by popular myth with witches, warlocks and sorcerers whose black arts endangered the souls of honest Christians. Rather than being buried at the castle, Elizabeth was buried instead at Ecsed, her birthplace in southern Hungary.

It was unusual for the mighty Bathorys to pay so much attention to the opinions of peasants, but quite possibly they realized that, at Cachtice, Elizabeth's grave might be subject to desecration or to satanist rituals, where demons were believed to make sacrifices to the devil. That could have been just as damaging, if not more so, to the Bathory name than the crimes Elizabeth never admitted and for which she never showed any remorse.

opportunity to impose control over his troublesome nobility by revealing dark doings within the powerful and prestigious Bathory family. Matthias ordered Count György Thurzo, Lord Palatine of Hungary, to lead a raid on Cachtice Castle and find out what was going on. Count Thurzo already knew, for he was a cousin of Elizabeth's and, as a Bathory relative, had played his part in the family's attempts to hide the ghastly truth.

But when he reached the Castle on 29 December 1610, Count Thurzo quickly discovered that Elizabeth's crimes were even more hideous than he had imagined. There was a dead girl lying in the main hall. Nearby, there was another girl whose body was full of holes. She was, amazingly, still alive. More girls, dead or dying, were found in cells. In the basement, yet more girls had been hung from the rafters. They had been slit open and their blood was dripping into large vats on the floor below, apparently ready for one of Elizabeth's blood baths. Count Thurzo ordered the basement floor dug up; beneath it, 50 bodies were found. A further search of the castle revealed a register that Elizabeth kept in her desk; it contained the names of some 650 murdered girls.

Countess Elizabeth Bathory, in a contemporary painting. The well-connected Hungarian aristocrat was considered lovely as a girl, but she sought to perpetuate her youthful beauty by bathing in the blood of young virgins.

> They might have been willing to keep quiet about the mass deaths of peasant girls, but now the girls involved were of noble birth – that could not be so easily overlooked.

ARREST AND TRIAL

Count Thurzo arrested Elizabeth and her four accomplices, Dorottya Szentes (known as Dorko), Ilona Jo, Katarina Benicka (a washerwoman), and the dwarf Janos Ujvary (who was also known as Ibis or Ficzko). One servant, Erszi Majorova, a recent addition to Elizabeth's staff, escaped when the others were apprehended at the castle, but was afterwards caught and arrested. While the accomplices were taken away, to be tortured into their confessions, Elizabeth remained at the castle under house arrest. As it was not permitted by law to arrest aristocrats and put them on trial, Elizabeth never testified in court. Instead, her accomplices took the full brunt of the accusations and suffered the penalties.

It appears that Elizabeth repeatedly asked for her case to be presented before the judges, even though in doing so she risked a public scandal and, if found guilty and executed, the loss of her extensive property to the Crown. This was probably why King Matthias, who was anxious to curb the power of the Bathorys, also wanted her to be put on trial, but the family still exerted too much influence to allow the royal demands to be met. They managed to keep her where her cousin Count Thurzo had left her, confined to her castle and beyond the reach of the king.

As far as the trial was concerned, Elizabeth's appearance in court would, in any case, have been superfluous. The evidence against her, drawn from the accounts given by 200 witnesses and the gruesome discoveries made by Count Thurzo, was more than enough to establish her guilt.

The first trial of Elizabeth's accomplices opened on 7 January 1611 and was heard before 20 judges headed by the Royal Supreme Court Judge Theodosius

> While the accomplices were taken away ... Elizabeth remained at the castle under house arrest. As it was not permitted by law to arrest aristocrats and put them on trial, Elizabeth never testified in court.

Syrmiensis de Szulo. The confessions of the accused, obtained by torture, were placed in evidence, and the accomplices were duly found guilty. At the second trial, one of Elizabeth's servants, Zusanna, told the court about the register that listed the 650 victims whose ill treatment and deaths Elizabeth had recorded in her own handwriting.

SICKENING TESTIMONY

Inevitably, some of the testimony given in court was sickening, even by the standards of the early seventeenth century, when casual cruelty and savage punishments were considered justified ways of treating criminals. One young girl, a 12-year-old named Pola, had been abducted and imprisoned in Castle Cachtice, but managed to escape. Dorka and Ilona Jo pursued and caught her, and brought her back to the castle, where she was confronted by an enraged Elizabeth. Elizabeth forced Pola into a cage shaped like a huge

ball. The ball was hauled up by a pulley and, suddenly, dozens of sharp spikes shot out of the sides and into the cage. From down below, the dwarf Ficzko manipulated the ropes until Pola, trapped inside the narrow cage, was caught on the spikes. Eventually, the girl was sliced to death.

Even when she was ill, it seems that Elizabeth's taste for sadistic pleasures was as strong as ever. Once, she ordered Dorottya Szentes to bring a girl to her as she was lying in bed. Elizabeth sat up as Szentes dragged the girl in, and bit her on the cheek. She then tore a piece of flesh from the girl's shoulders with her teeth and next went to work on her breasts.

At their trial, Dorottya Szentes and Ilona Jo were declared to be witches, a 'fact' that was reflected in their punishments. Their fingers, which had 'dipped in the blood of Christians', were torn from their hands with red-hot pincers. The pair was then burned alive. The dwarf Ficzko was considered less guilty than the other accomplices, and he was beheaded before being burned to ashes. Erszi Majorova was also executed, on 24 January. The only accomplice to escape death was Katarina Beneczky, who was exonerated by the other defendants and also by the servant Zussanna. Beneczky was sentenced instead to life imprisonment.

WALLED UP

Elizabeth Bathory received the same penalty, not from any court of law, but at the insistence of her family. They had striven mightily to save her life as well as preserve the family honour, but they still regarded her as a menace and a fearful disgrace to the Bathory name. They determined that she should never be free again, so she was walled up within her bedchamber at Cachtice Castle. Although it would be practically impossible for her to escape from there, guards were placed in the bedroom to make doubly certain. Small slits were left open for ventilation and to allow food to be passed through to her. Elizabeth survived there for more than three years, until 21 August 1614, when she was found dead, face down, inside her narrow prison cell. She was 54 years old.

Victims of Vlad III Dracul, another Wallachian aristocrat and the inspiration for Dracula, are impaled on sharp stakes driven from one side of the body to the other. It is more likely that the agony was prolonged by using the body's orifices to drive the stakes through the internal organs.

VLAD III DRACUL, THE REAL COUNT DRACULA

Vlad III Dracul, meaning Vlad the 'Demon', or 'Dragon', earned for himself a reputation for extreme cruelty that went way beyond that of any other European ruler. Numerous myths, superstitions and horror stories grew up about Vlad, including one tale which told how he invited a crowd of beggars, elderly and sick people to his castle, where he treated them to a big banquet, before boarding up the castle and setting it on fire. All his 'guests' died. This, it seems, was Vlad's way of releasing them from their troubles.

Vlad's influence went beyond mere anecdote. It created a genre of horror stories based, most sensationally, on his rumoured habit of drinking the blood and eating the flesh of his victims. This made him the model for stories about blood-sucking vampires, which proliferated in southeastern Europe in medieval times.

CRUEL SUPERSTITIONS

It was not surprising that the fifteenth century in southeastern Europe was the source for lurid tales and fearsome superstitions. The area was barely civilized. The time and the place were rife with violence. Murderous vendettas were common. Violent crime was an everyday event. So were punishments such as hacking off limbs, gouging out eyes, maimings and mutilations. Vlad's favourite punishment, it seems, was impaling his enemies on stakes. Sometimes, rumour asserted, more than 20,000 men, women and children were impaled at one time. With this, Vlad acquired the nickname of Tepes, meaning the 'impaler'.

Long before the Irish author Bram Stoker is said to have used him as the basis for his novel _Dracula_ (1897), Vlad III Dracul was being identified with the vampire legends that were rife in eastern Europe in medieval times.

Vlad was fairly typical, however, of local rulers who were faced with handling the excesses of a volatile region and often went over the top in their efforts to retain power and see to it that their dignity was preserved. Vlad was definitely one of this kind. On one occasion, he demanded that a group of Turkish diplomats remove their hats in his presence as a mark of their respect. They refused, telling him that it was not their custom to go bareheaded. Vlad made sure that they observed their custom for ever: he ordered their hats nailed to their heads.

Vlad III had no love for the Turks. In his youth, he and his younger brother, Radu, lived as hostages at the court of the Ottoman Turkish Sultan Murad II. The brothers were there to ensure the loyalty of their father, Vlad II, who had fended off a threatened Turkish invasion by agreeing to become the sultan's vassal.

A RECIPE FOR REVENGE

The young Vlad suffered greatly at the hands of the Turks. He was imprisoned in an underground dungeon and was frequently whipped for being rude and stubborn. Then, in 1447, when Vlad was aged 16, his father was assassinated by Wallachian *boyars* (noblemen) on the orders of John Hunyadi, who resented the submission Vlad II had made to the Turks. Vlad III was released and at once set out to avenge his father, and also his older brother Mircea, who had been blinded with hot stakes and buried alive by *boyars*. Vlad raised a Turkish army and returned home to thrash the forces of John Hunyadi and take power in Wallachia. His triumph was brief, for Hunyadi hit back and dethroned Vlad. In the next few years, the two rivals tussled for control, but at last, in 1456, Vlad emerged victorious. Whether he killed Hunyadi in battle or Hunyadi died of plague is not clear. Either way, Vlad's rival was gone and the throne of Wallachia was his.

Vlad then set about wreaking revenge on the *boyars* who had killed his father and elder brother. Apparently, he invited the *boyars* to his castle for an Eastertide feast, but when the meal was over he had them seized and flung into prison. The sick and old among them were impaled on stakes and left to die. The others were taken to a ruined fortress some 80 kilometres away. There, they were forced to build a new fortress, later called Castle Dracula. When it was finished, these *boyars* were in their turn impaled.

King Matthias Corvinus of neighbouring Hungary was so disgusted by Vlad's savagery that, in around 1462, he seized him and placed him under house arrest. But Vlad's imprisonment, which lasted for up to 12 years, failed to cure him of his sadistic habits. While he remained confined, the impaled bodies of rats, mice, birds and other small creatures were discovered all over his palace. Some were beheaded; others tarred and feathered.

INVADING ARMY

Nor had Vlad's reputation for cruelty faded while he was out of the way. Although he was admired by some for defending his kingdom against the marauding Turks, he was also deeply feared. This

was so not only in Wallachia and the surrounding kingdoms, but also among the Ottoman Turks. During his imprisonment, the Turks had seized Wallachia and planted their own candidate, Basarab cel Batrin, as its ruler. In 1475, after his release from house arrest, Vlad gathered a small army of around 4000 men and invaded Wallachia, intent on retrieving his crown for a third time. Although Vlad's army was comparatively few in number, his approach seemed to inspire such panic in the Ottomans that they fled.

Not long afterwards, the Ottoman Turks got their revenge. Vlad was killed in battle against them at Vaslui, near Bucharest in 1476. The Ottomans afterwards decapitated him and took his head back to their capital, Istanbul. There it was preserved in honey and put on display by the Sultan Mehmet II to show that Vlad Tepes, the Impaler, was well and truly dead.

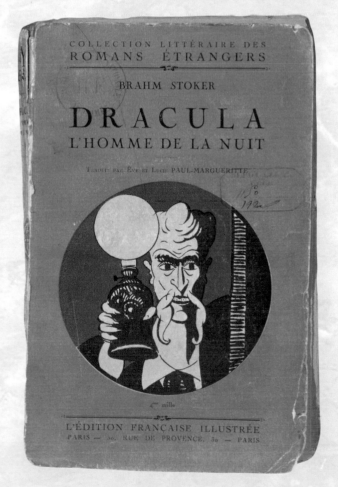

Bram Stoker's novel *Dracula*, published in 1897, was partly inspired by stories of Vlad III Dracul, although there are also similarities to the story of Elizabeth Bathory — both Dracula and Bathory had a fondness for human blood.

TWO FRENCH ROYAL RAKES: LOUIS XIV AND LOUIS XV

King Louis XIV of France, the so-called 'Sun King', and his great-grandson and successor, Louis XV, were the greatest royal rakes Europe ever knew. Of the two, the fifteenth Louis was the more debauched and the less careful of his power and position. His most famous mistresses, the Marquise de Pompadour and the Comtesse du Barry, became influential figures while the king dallied elsewhere.

✦

This was something Louis XIV would never have permitted. The greatest of the absolute monarchs of Europe, he never doubted that power and influence rightfully lay in his hands. He

Left: King Louis XIV, the Sun King, was the most absolute of absolute monarchs and the most powerful king France ever had. Above: King Louis XV matched his great-grandfather only in his appetite for debauchery.

never doubted, either, the truth of the Divine Right of Kings, which was impressed upon him at an early age. 'Kings are appointed by God,' he wrote as a child. 'They may do as they please.'

A later pronouncement, *'L'état c'ést moi!'* – 'I am the state!' – became his unofficial motto, and his greatness was expressed by his magnificent palace at Versailles, which was universally recognized as the most splendid of its kind. Many of the artistic, architectural and design features which Louis approved for Versailles came about through the influence on the king of his first – platonic – love, Marie Mancini, who arrived at Louis's court when she was aged 16. Marie was a niece of Cardinal Jules Mazarin, the king's chief minister during his minority. A bright, well-educated, cultured girl, she introduced Louis to great literature, painting, sculpture, philosophy and other intellectual subjects.

THE EXPECTED POLITICAL ALLIANCE

By 1657, Louis, aged 19, and Marie, 18, had fallen in love and wanted to marry. Sadly, though, Marie was not queen material. The marriage of a King of France needed to have a political purpose that brought his country diplomatic, trade, military or religious benefits. Despite her Mazarin connection, Marie Mancini afforded no such advantages, and that fact doomed any chance of her marrying the young king. Marie was sent away and Louis was heartbroken. The more prestigious union required of a king took place on 9 June 1660, when Louis married the Infanta Maria Theresa of Spain, who, unlike Marie Mancini, qualified as a consort with the 'right' ancestry.

These advantages, it seemed, overrode her rather alarming appearance and personality. Maria Theresa looked like a dwarf and had the overlong jaw known as the 'Hapsburg lip'. She was simpleminded, with no interests beyond cakes and sweets, her pets, her dwarf entertainers, playing cards and praying. But at least she rapidly provided Louis with the male heir all kings desired: the first of their six children, the Dauphin Louis, was born on 1 November 1661.

> The marriage of a King of France needed to have a political purpose that brought his country diplomatic, trade, military or religious benefits.

Louis remained faithful to Maria Theresa during their first year of his marriage, but this fidelity did not last. The chief, and sometimes only, purpose of royal marriage was the provision of heirs. Beyond that, kings chose mistresses for their pleasure. French practice formalized the arrangement. The *maîtresse-en-titre*, the King's official mistress, held a recognized position at court. As such, she could acquire considerable power and wealth, as long as she remained in favour. Louis's first *maîtresse-en-titre* was the artless and adoring Louise de la Vallière. Louise was the stepdaughter of a French aristocrat, Jacques de Courtarvel, Marquis de Saint-Rémy, and this connection enabled her to enter royal circles.

Louise, aged 16, arrived at the court of Louis XIV in 1660 and was soon appointed a maid of honour to the English Princess Henrietta, who had recently married Philippe, Duc d'Orléans, the King's younger brother. Henrietta, sister of the English King Charles II, shared her rakish brother's taste for *amours*. After Henrietta's arrival at Louis's court in 1661, it was only a matter of time before she went to work on the young French monarch. Rumours quickly spread that an affair, and with it a full-blown scandal, was on its way.

The Infanta Maria Theresa of Spain, first wife of King Louis XIV. From her marriage in 1660 to her death in 1683, she remained the perfect consort — uninterested in politics, devout, providing heirs while turning a blind eye to Louis's love affairs.

Louise de la Vallière became Louis XIV's first mistress in 1661 and gave him four children before she was supplanted by the Marquise de Montesan in 1667. Afterwards Louise retired to a nunnery.

... AND A SUITABLE MISTRESS

At that juncture, Louis's mother, Anne of Austria, stepped in and inserted Louise into the picture. Louise's task was to divert suspicion by making out that the young king was smitten by her rather than his sister-in-law. But an unexpected factor was involved: the innocent Louise was already in love with the king, who soon forgot about Henrietta and, instead, fell for her maid of honour. The haughty Henrietta was so enraged that she at once took up with the Comte de Guiche, her husband's favourite.

Louise's attraction for the king was something for which the proud, possessive Henrietta could never have provided. Outwardly, Louise was a very plain

> Louise was a very plain Jane. She was mousy and retiring ... But she scored with the king where it most mattered. She was no artful, self-interested coquette. All Louise wanted was to love Louis, and Louis basked in her adoration.

Jane. She was mousy and retiring, whereas the beautiful Henrietta could enslave men with a glance. One of her legs was shorter than the other, and she had to wear special heels to prevent her limping. But she scored with the king where it most mattered. She was no artful, self-interested coquette. All Louise wanted was to love Louis, and Louis basked in her adoration.

Louis XIV and Louise de la Vallière had four children, the first born in 1663 and the last in 1667. Their relationship lasted for six years, but in 1661 almost foundered because of a fierce quarrel over Princess Henrietta. Despite their enmity, Louise remained loyal to Henrietta and refused to inform the king about Henrietta's liaison with the Comte de Guiche. Louis exploded in fury, and Louise was so frightened that she fled to a convent. Eventually, Louis learned of the affair with de Guiche after le Comte was threatened with exposure. In order to save her lover, Henrietta went to the king and told him everything. De Guiche was later exiled.

Princess Henrietta Anne, daughter of King Charles I of England, was the wife of Louis XIV's younger brother Philip Duc d'Orléans.

A NEW FAVOURITE

Louise remained in place as royal mistress, but by 1666 she was falling from favour. The previous year King Louis had created her Duchesse de la Vallière and gave her the estate of Vaujours. It was a going-away present. This was not just a matter of Louis tiring of a long-term mistress, as kings tended to do. Louise was being undermined behind the scenes, by the venomous Françoise-Athénais, Marquise de Montespan, who was determined to replace her as *maîtresse-en-titre*. That position had far more prestige and offered far more

money and advancement than her marriage to the Marquis de Montespan, a minor nobleman of only modest wealth.

The marquise planned her campaign carefully. Nothing dramatic. Nothing perceptible. Merely a series of apparently innocent moves that got her close

Françoise-Athénais, Marquise de Montespan, achieved her aim of making herself Louis XIV's mistress in 1668, after staging a campaign to ensnare him that was said to include sorcery and witchcraft.

RUMOURS OF THE DARK ARTS

The extraordinary hold the Marquise de Montespan exerted over Louis XIV gave rise to rumours that, even before she became his *maîtresse-en-titre,* she was using black magic, witchcraft and sorcery on him. Nothing was conclusively proved, but it was alleged that during her campaign to ensnare the king, the marquise purchased from the sorceress Catherine Monvoisin love powders containing obnoxious ingredients such as toad's spittle. She was also said to be involved in 'black' masses, which were held over her naked body. Later on, although no evidence was found against her, the marquise was again implicated when members of the aristocracy were, with others, put on trial for witchcraft and poisoning in 1675.

The king, it appears, was completely unaware of any of the rumours that his bewitchment had a darker source. He believed that in the marquise he had found his ideal companion, and lavished jewels, fine clothes and all manner of other luxuries on her. The king's money not only enabled the marquise to live in splendour and make substantial donations to her favourite charities, but also to obtain high positions for members of her family: her father, for example, became governor of Paris.

But talk of sorcery, poison and witchcraft did not go away. When Louis began to suffer from dizzy spells, fainting fits and bouts of uncontrollable shivering, rumour was soon claiming that the king's ardour was cooling and, in an effort to reignite it, the marquise was again plying him with noxious love powders. But the

King Louis XIV never lost his appetite for sex. This made life difficult for his second wife, Françoise d'Aubigné, who wrote in her diary of 'painful occasions'.

marquise, it seemed, chose another way. She decided that a gesture of piety was due. When she went to make confession of her many sins at Versailles, however, the priest, the Abbé Lécuyer, refused to hear it or to grant her absolution. Incandescent with rage, she complained to the king, only to learn that it was the Abbé's duty to refuse absolution to such an inveterate sinner. The marquise withdrew from the court and fasted to confirm her repentance. Louis, too, had been refused absolution in 1675 and went through a similar performance to prove his penitence.

THREE AFFAIRS

At last, in July 1676, the lovers were allowed to meet again. Soon after their reconciliation, the marquise was restored to her position as *maîtresse-en-titre* with all the privileges, such as precedence over duchesses, that went with it. Even so, she was aware that all was not well. Louis was having affairs with three other court ladies more or less simultaneously: one of them, it was rumoured, had given birth to a child by him.

The marquise reacted with predictable rage and also put it about that another of Louis's 'extra' mistresses, Madame de Ludre, suffered from a fearful skin ailment. She need not have bothered. De Ludre was already on the way out after Louis learned that she had appointed her own husband as messenger between herself and her royal lover.

enough to the King for him to notice her. First, the marquise became friendly with Philippe, Louis's younger brother. Next, she moved on to the queen, and put on a mask of piety and virtue which the devout Maria Theresa was bound to appreciate. After that, the marquise became close to Louise herself and, through Louise, to the king. Very little time passed before Louis noticed this witty, strikingly beautiful

> The Marquise could not have been more different from the diffident, devoted Louise. She was a formidable figure – arrogant, sensual, cruel and unremittingly vengeful against anyone who angered her.

interloper. She attracted him so powerfully that, while Louise was giving birth to his son, the Comte de Vermondois, in 1667, the king was dallying with Montespan until early morning.

The Comte de Vermondois was Louise's last child by the king, although she remained at court until 1674, when the official separation of the Marquis and the Marquise de Montespan was announced. Louise's presence as the apparent *maîtresse-en-titre* was camouflage for the king's liaison with his new mistress. By this means, the jealous marquis, who had been attempting legal moves to get his wife back, was left with no real evidence of an affair. In order to maintain this charade, Louise was forced to attend the marquise like a servant, helping her with her toilette. In 1674, she was allowed to enter the convent of Sainte Marie de Chaillot and became a nun. Louise died in Paris in 1710. On hearing the news, King Louis commented that she had been 'dead' to him from the day she left.

By the time Louise de la Vallière escaped from her years of humiliation at court, the Marquise de Montespan had already given birth to the first five of her seven children by the king. The Marquise could not have been more different from the diffident, devoted Louise. She was a formidable figure – arrogant, sensual, cruel and unremittingly vengeful against anyone who angered her. She was a real challenge for Louis, defying him whenever the whim took her, giving as good as she got in violent quarrels, yet also bewitching him with her beauty and her charms.

CHANGING FORTUNES AND CHANGING ATTITUDES

All the same, time was still running out for the marquise to score triumphs over all comers. By 1678, when her last child by Louis was born, she was almost 40 years of age and growing fat and frowsy. She was also being confronted by increasingly younger rivals such as Angélique de Fontanges, a beautiful but empty-headed maid of honour who had been instructed by her ambitious parents to become the king's mistress. The marquise found out, of course, but this time her fury failed to move Louis. Her time was up, but she went on living in her apartments at Versailles for some years. The king visited her there from time to time, but in 1691 the marquise retired to a convent with a large pension of 500,000 francs. She died in 1707. Angélique was discarded in her turn, as Louis tired of her.

This time, the successor to the King's favour was not some ambitious fortune-hunter, but a woman who had been around the court – and the king – for some time. Françoise Scarron, the widow of the writer Paul Scarron, first arrived at court in 1669, to look after and educate the marquise's first child by the king, who was born that year. Later, she also took charge of the six others who followed.

Françoise was an exemplary nurse and governess, and the children quickly came to love her.

This is possibly a portrait of Marie Angélique de Scorraille de Russille, Duchesse de Fontanges, who in 1678 became Louis XIV's mistress.

Louis recognized Françoise's importance to his 'second' family by the marquise and, in 1674, gave her the money to purchase a house from the Duc de Maintenon. With this came a new title, Madame de Maintenon.

Even in the face of this generosity, it took Louis quite a while to appreciate her. At first, he looked on Françoise as a dull, difficult prude who was far too full of *bel esprit* – high moral tone. He knew that she disapproved of the licentious way he led his life and once said, 'To preserve one's honour, the first thing one must give up is pleasure.'

Yet, despite himself, the king could not help noticing how kind she was, how gentle and caring and how comely and pretty she looked, even at age 37. 'She knows how to love,' he remarked. 'It would be pleasant to be loved by her.'

> He looked on Françoise as a dull, difficult prude who was far too full of *bel esprit* – high moral tone ... she disapproved of the licentious way he led his life ...

Louis already knew Françoise well enough to realize that she would never consent to be his mistress. Morality and modesty would not permit it for, in her eyes, sex belonged to the marriage bed and only the marriage bed. The king was, by now, very much in love with Françoise, but could not accept the alternative to an illicit affair – a platonic relationship. The opportunity to solve this problem arrived in 1683, when Queen Maria Theresa died, probably of cancer, aged 44.

Louis summoned Françoise to his presence, and in his arbitrary way informed her that he meant to marry her morganatically. This meant that, as his wife and a commoner, she could not enjoy the honours and privileges usually due a royal consort. Françoise was

Madame de Maintenon was an unusual woman to find at the libidinous French court. During the 32 years that she was married to Louis XIV, she created a more dignified atmosphere at Versailles.

uninterested in honours and privileges, and married the king in secret some time in October 1683. The marriage lasted until Louis's death in 1715 and, during those 32 years, the high-minded Françoise managed, remarkably, to transform him from a licentious rake into a virtuous and faithful husband. Louis seemed to thrive on this new lifestyle and so did his libido which enabled him to make love to Françoise twice a day in 1710, when he was 72 years old.

Five years later, when Louis XIV was dying of gangrene, and his five-year-old greatgrandson was about to succeed him as King Louis XV, he told his courtiers: 'You are about to see one king to his grave and another in his cradle. Always bear in mind the memory of the one and the interests of the other.'

A NEW MONARCH

King Louis XIV, the mighty Sun King, was always going to be a hard act to follow, but for his greatgrandson even the attempt was impossible. Since 1711, the fifteenth Louis had been the 'last-chance' direct heir to the French throne after the deaths of all other males in the line of succession. As a result, he had been so coddled and spoiled that he grew up to be profoundly timid and indecisive. Although he dutifully performed the public role of imperious autocrat with all its pervading pomp, his own lifestyle choice was the quiet existence of a country gentlemen. Louis took little or no interest in affairs of state, became flummoxed when confronted with financial problems and, effectively, did nothing to promote the welfare of his realm or his people. As Louis's foreign minister, René-Louis de Voyer de Paulmy, Marquis d'Argenson, put it, the king 'opened his mouth, said little and thought not at all' when required to attend meetings of his ruling council.

Left: A portrait of King Louis XV. Louis, who became king when he was five, was the only survivor of a family tragedy in which his father, grandfather and all their other children died when an epidemic of smallpox swept through the royal household.

Louis XV greatly enjoyed the thrill of the hunt, but his overriding interest in life was the company of women. By this means, it was said, he sought to fill the gap left by the death of his mother, Marie-Adelaide of Savoy, in 1711, when Louis was less than two years old. The king's quest began in around 1725, shortly after he married his queen, Maria-Catherine Leszczynska of Poland. Within the year, she gave birth to twin girls, the first of her 10 children by Louis, but already the chase was on to find a mistress for the king.

He dallied for a while with an assortment of housemaids and other servant girls. After that, he went through all four of the de Mailly-Nesle sisters in succession.

It was early days, for Louis was only 15 years old when he married. He dallied for a while with an assortment of housemaids and other servant girls. After that, he went through all four of the de Mailly-Nesle sisters in succession. The most ambitious of the four was the youngest, who arrived on the royal scene in 1742. Marie-Anne wanted Louis to be a more active, involved monarch. She forced him to work harder at the business of government, see his ministers more often and attend to more and more detail of public affairs. This was torture for the indolent Louis.

King Louis XV's queen, Maria-Catherine Leszczynska, gave him 10 children, but four of his daughters and both of his sons predeceased him.

Marie Anne de Mailly-Nesle was the youngest of four sisters, all of whom became successive mistresses to King Louis XV. She attempted to make the lazy, self-indulgent king more active, but died in 1744, aged 27.

'Madame,' he protested. 'You are killing me!'

The king was released from his torment after two years, when Marie-Anne died of pneumonia in 1744 aged only 27 years. Her successor was the beautiful, well-educated Jeanne Antoinette d'Etoiles, who initially lacked the basic qualification for the role of *maitress-en-titre*: connections with the aristocracy. Jeanne Antoinette, however, belonged to the more lowly bourgeoisie. Nevertheless, there was a prediction about Jeanne that gave her and her family high hopes of overcoming this difficulty. In 1730, at age nine, she was told by a fortune-teller that she would one day capture the heart of a king. After that, her family nicknamed her 'Reinette' – little queen – in anticipation of the exciting event.

THE RISE OF MADAME DE POMPADOUR

The exciting event took place in February 1745, when the Dauphin Louis, heir to the French throne, married Princess Maria Teresa of Spain. Among the fêtes and celebrations, grand balls were held in Paris and Versailles where anyone who was suitably dressed was invited to attend. Jeanne Antoinette made a special point of attending a masked ball at Versailles, where she manoeuvred her way close to the king and engaged him in conversation, masks off. The signal was quickly understood. 'The handkerchief is thrown,' one of

Jeanne Antoinette Poisson, Madame de Pompadour, was the most able of all Louis XV's mistresses. Her 'reign' lasted 20 years and though not quite as powerful as some historians have made out, she took over much of the running of everyday royal business.

Louis's courtiers remarked in 'court-speak', meaning that an intimate relationship had begun.

A few days later, the king invited Jeanne Antoinette to meet him for a private supper at the Hotel de Ville in Paris. Before long, he was deeply in love with her and afterwards turned her into an aristocrat by giving her the title of marquise and later, Duchesse de Pompadour. Jeanne Antoinette lost no time exercising the power of a *maîtresse-en-titre*. She was not as politically active as some historians have believed, but her influence counted when it came to the advancement of her friends and relatives. For instance, she persuaded the king to champion the candidacy of her friend Voltaire, the brilliant writer and historian, for membership of the prestigious Académie Française.

Her most striking achievements, however, were in the social sphere, where she created a homely atmosphere for the king in which he revelled in the friendly, relaxed company of her family. She also coaxed Louis to interest himself in the theatre, listen to music or appreciate art and design, none of which had places at the trivial-minded, back-biting royal court. For the first time in his life, Louis XV was enjoying

> Her most striking achievements, however, were in the social sphere, where she created a homely atmosphere for the king in which he revelled in the friendly, relaxed company of her family.

himself and, if his snobbish court wanted to whisper enviously that his mistress had him in thrall, it scarcely bothered him.

There was though, a dark lining to this silver cloud. Jeanne Antoinette did not enjoy good health, and she was in constant fear that she would not be able to keep up with the king's more lusty approach to sex. She began to consume vast quantities of aphrodisiacs – vanilla, truffles, celery – but all that did was to make her sick. Her condition was not helped by a series of miscarriages. Eventually, inevitably, Jeanne-Antoinette developed heart trouble, continual headaches, breathing difficulties and, in 1764, congestion of the lungs. She died, aged 42, on 15 April 1764 and was buried two days later in Paris.

As Jeanne Antoinette's health declined, it was likely that her sex life with Louis came to an end. He never ceased to love her, but kept other mistresses in the last few years before her death. He also returned to his servant girls and lodged them in a private brothel at the *Parc aux Cerfs* (Park of Deers), a small villa in Versailles. Louis sometimes visited the Parc disguised as a Polish nobleman, but one of the girls searched through her lover's pockets as he lay sleeping and discovered who he really was. The girl was hauled off to an insane asylum, a move that would certainly invalidate anything she said about the king.

The *Parc aux Cerfs* was the centrepiece of Louis's debauchery, which, by 1764, was profoundly affecting his popularity with his subjects. In 1744, he had been nicknamed *bien aimé* (well beloved) after recovering from a serious illness. Twenty years later he had

The Parc au Cerfs near the royal palace at Versailles was Louis XV's bolt-hole where he could enjoy his energetic sex life in peace. The establishment was very efficiently run for him by Madame de Pompadour.

PHILIPPE, DUC D'ORLÉANS
LOUIS XIV'S 'HOMOSEXUAL' BROTHER

Philippe, Duc d'Orléans (1640–1701), may have been the younger brother of Louis XIV, but their mother Queen Anne treated them very differently. She guarded Louis's rights as king by deliberately making Philippe seem inferior, even ridiculous. That way, he could not challenge his brother's rule. Encouraged by his mother, Philippe pretended to be homosexual when he was, in fact, twice married and fathered several children. He also wore female dress, made up his face and chose handsome young courtiers as his favourites.

Louis was very fond of Philippe, who was known as 'Monsieur' at court, and continually showered him with gifts. Nonetheless, Louis continued his mother's work of distancing his young brother from the sources of power and influence in France. One way was to purchase the beautiful villa of St Cloud, which was close, but not too close, to Versailles, where the business of government was conducted. Philippe was delighted with the villa and the opportunity it gave him to beautify its gardens. More important, however, was St Cloud's function in keeping Philippe away from the centre of royal power, and Louis deliberately saw to it that his brother played no part in French affairs. The king's attitude towards his brother was affectionate, but intensely patronizing.

'Now we are going to work,' he was reported to have told Monsieur before discussing royal business with his ministers. 'Go and amuse yourself, brother!'

King Louis XIV was very fond of his brother Philippe, duc d'Orléans, but he did not consider him competent enough to be involved in state business and excluded him from councils with his ministers.

Marie Jeanne Bécu, Madame du Barry, was the last mistress of King Louis XV, who is shown standing by her bed. She made a tremendous impression when she was presented at court in 1769, and Louis, totally entranced, bedded her within a few weeks.

become 'well hated' for his weak government, his financial incompetence, the disasters France suffered in war and for the excesses of his sex life. But the girls at the Parc aux Cerfs were not as important as lurid tales of orgies made them appear. Rather, they provided Louis XV with a place to play while he waited for his next *maîtresse-en-titre* to emerge from the numerous hopefuls who crowded his court at Versailles.

AMBITION REALIZED

Among the women who aspired to the position occupied by the late Jeanne Antoinette was Marie Jeanne Bécu, the illegitimate daughter of Anne Bécu, a seamstress or cook. In 1758, aged 15, Marie Jeanne, a remarkably good-looking blonde, moved to Paris where she caught the eye of a philanderer, Jean du Barry. Du Barry soon realized that she was royal mistress material and, in 1768, provided her with the required noble title by marrying her to his brother Comte Guillaume. The new Comtesse du Barry was presented at court on 2 April 1769. She made a tremendous impression, with her extravagant gown and the diamonds that adorned her neck and ears.

The king was entranced, so much so that the delectable Jeanne quickly distracted him from his grief at the death of his queen, which took place on 25 June 1769. Even before the queen died, Louis had bedded his new mistress and next day remarked; 'I am delighted with … Jeanne. She is the only woman in France who has managed to make me forget that I am 60.'

'He is more in love than he has ever been,' commented the Duc de Croy, who had known Louis for many years. 'He seems to be rejuvenated and I have never seen him in better spirits, extremely good-humoured and far more outgoing.'

Jeanne achieved this transformation not only with her beauty, but, more importantly, through her charm and her ability to amuse the king while also giving him warmth and affection. In this, she was much like the late Duchesse de Pompadour, even though she lacked her predecessor's brains and talents. Like de Pompadour, she was at home in the world of the arts. Her *levées*, the gatherings where writers, artists, poets, dramatists and scholars flocked to enjoy her hospitality, became an established part of the intellectual scene. Ministers, financiers and bankers came to her for advice on their various projects. Jewellers regarded du Barry as their patron, for her love of jewels was well known. She was the only lady at court to wear jewels in mixed colours – rubies and emeralds or pink with grey pearls.

A NATION REVOLTS

King Louis was heedlessly extravagant, lavishing a fortune on his mistress at a time when public resentment was growing fast at the fundamental inequalities of French society. As a result, the Comtesse du Barry was in the popular firing line along with the king and the aristocracy. As he aged, Louis became more and more unpopular and was haunted by a fear of death and by guilt over his sexual transgressions. At such times, Louis kept away from du Barry. He paid frequent visits to a convent where his youngest daughter, Louise, had become a Carmelite nun. Louis believed that she had taken her vows in order to save his immortal soul and spent many hours with his daughter, praying for forgiveness.

Although the king always returned to du Barry, time was running out for both of them. In 1774, Louis contracted smallpox and, realizing he was dying, he sent du Barry away to the convent of Pont-au-Dames. Had she remained at Versailles, her 'immoral' presence would have prevented Louis receiving absolution. He died on 10 May.

The attack on the Bastille prison in Paris in 1789 and the release of its prisoners was the signal for the start of the French Revolution. It was, in fact, just a gesture, since there were few prisoners in the Bastille at the time.

THE MAN IN THE IRON MASK

The Man in the Iron Mask was one of Europe's great royal mysteries. First imprisoned in 1687, he was brought to Paris 11 years later and placed under close guard in the Bastille. No one knew who he was – nor were they meant to know. Rumour had it that he was a courtier who had fallen out of favour with Louis XIV, but there seemed to be more to it than mere disgrace. The anonymous man had to wear his mask all the time, and two musketeers stood close by in his prison cell, ready to kill him if he removed it.

He ate, slept and eventually, in 1703, died still wearing his mask. Some 50 years later, the famous French writer Voltaire speculated that the Man in the Iron Mask resembled someone very famous – Louis XIV himself. Among the many rumours surrounding the Man in the Iron Mask, this one gave rise to speculation that he was in fact Louis's twin brother, born a few minutes before him, and being kept confined in order to preserve the king's position.

The mysterious man in the iron mask who was imprisoned for 16 years, sparked off numerous conspiracy theories, a famous novel by Alexandre Dumas, published in 1848, and numerous movies. But his identity was never revealed.

A short while earlier, King Louis apparently remarked: *'Après moi le deluge.'* – 'After me, the deluge.' It was horrifically prescient. Five years after Louis's death, the French Revolution erupted, eventually sweeping away the monarchy and decimating the nobility and clergy. Thousands, including the reigning king and his queen, Louis XVI and Marie Antoinette, died by the guillotine in 1792–3 during the so-called Reign of Terror. One of them was the Comtesse du Barry.

Charged with treason and conspiracy, she was found guilty and condemned to death. On 8 December 1793, du Barry was taken through the streets of Paris in a tumbrel to the Place de la Revolution, where a guillotine was set up, waiting for her. She was panic-stricken and hysterical, screaming at the watching crowds to save her. She struggled with the executioners, but to no avail. They overcame her and she was laid on the scaffold. The knife blade sliced down and cut off her head. With the French Revolution, Louis XIV's famous dictum – *L'état c'est moi* – went into reverse. The king was no longer the state. Instead, the state was king.

In 1774, Louis contracted smallpox and ... sent du Barry away to the convent ... Had she remained at Versailles, her 'immoral' presence would have prevented Louis receiving absolution.

THE KING AND THE VAMP: LUDWIG I OF BAVARIA AND LOLA MONTEZ

Marie Dolores Eliza Rosanna Gilbert, alias Lola Montez (1818–1861), had all the qualifications required to be a femme fatale. She was dark-haired and blue-eyed, with a sensuous mouth and a voluptuous figure. There was also something quite mesmeric about her gaze. With this formidable equipment, Lola bewitched many men, including a king, Ludwig I of Bavaria (1786–1868).

✦

At their first meeting, in Munich in 1846, Lola barged her way into the royal presence and was asked by the king, who knew of her reputation, if her renowned beauty was really the work of Nature. Ludwig, aged 60, may have been deaf, but there was nothing wrong with his vision. He knew what he was looking at when Lola replied by tearing open her

Left: King Ludwig I of Bavaria lost his heart and his throne to the femme fatale Lola Montez.
Above: King Ludwig was not the only man to be bowled over by Marie Dolores Elizabeth Rosanna Gilbert, alias Lola Montez.

bodice to show that, on at least two counts, Nature had done a fine job.

Despite her exotic name, which she devised for her short-lived stage career, Lola Montez was born in Ireland in 1818. Soon afterwards, her father, an English army officer, was transferred to India, and his family went with him. He does not seem to have survived long in India, where climate, epidemics and the excesses of expatriate life decimated Europeans. Her father died when Lola was still very young. Her mother, a very beautiful woman, promptly acquired a second husband, another English army officer.

A COQUETTE IS BORN

In 1836, Lola's mother, having shed her second husband, turned up in England from India escorted by a handsome young subaltern surnamed James. Lola was then a superbly well-equipped 19-year-old. Once Subaltern James set eyes on her, he had no chance. Neither did Lola's mother. James fell hopelessly in love and promptly eloped with Lola. He became the first of her many husbands when he married her in County Meath, Ireland, on 23 July 1837.

The Jameses settled for a while in Dublin, where the stunning Lola swiftly adapted to army social life. She seems to have behaved herself reasonably well, but her animal attraction still fired on all cylinders and the then Lord Lieutenant, Lord Normanby, was entranced as soon as he was introduced to her. Fortunately for Lady Normanby and the other army wives, Lola did not remain in Dublin for long. The city was, in any case, far too unglamorous for a girl brought up in the heady atmosphere of the East. To Lola's delight, her husband was posted back to India after a few months. The couple duly took up residence at Simla, the beautiful hill station that lay in the approaches to the Himalayan mountains.

Life in British India, for all its outward grandeur, could be very tedious and parochial, and Lola arrived in Simla like a firework illuminating a very humdrum scene. At the once-sedate parties, balls and social evenings Lola attended, there was a new and unaccustomed air of excitement. Lola had all the young officers agog in no time. Lola's husband, now Captain James, realized that Lola was too magnetic to other men to be the wife he wanted. He ran off with a less attractive woman who required less surveillance in defence of her reputation and his conjugal rights.

Naturally enough, Lola was mightily affronted, but worse than any ego-bruising she may have suffered was her new social status. As a deserted wife, she completely lost face and, by the brutal laws of expatriate society, became a pariah. The invitations dried up. She was snubbed in company. Lola could hardly stay in India under these circumstances; instead, she headed for Britain.

When Lola reached London, she found her mother had married for a third time and that her stepfather, a Mr Craigie, had decided to take his stepdaughter in hand. Craigie sent a Calvinist, a dour, probably immune character, to accompany Lola north to Perth where, he probably presumed, this wild young hoyden could be tamed. Craigie reckoned without Lola's resolve to do her own thing. She told her Calvinist minder exactly what he could do with dreary old Perth and the domineering Craigie and point blank refused to go. The Calvinist retired hurt, and Lola settled for a time in London, where, inevitably, she went through a string of lovers.

A SOCIAL OUTCAST

Not long afterwards, Captain James divorced Lola, or rather she believed he had done so. Where no other restraint had managed to hold Lola back, this one did. In the 1840s, and for well over a century afterwards, divorce labelled an ex-wife as a 'scarlet woman'. Lola dealt with this inconvenient turn of events in very

> If she was going to be a social outcast, she might as well do the job properly and put herself beyond another social pale of her times by going on the stage.

practical fashion. If she was going to be a social outcast, she might as well do the job properly and put herself beyond another social pale of her times by going on the stage. Actresses were then regarded as little better than prostitutes, and the same went for dancers. Lola loved dancing and decided to specialize in the frankly sensual, unbridled dances performed in Andalusia in southern Spain. She was perfectly suited to the genre, with the dark looks, the curvaceous figure and, after several years of unbuttoned living, the alluring manner.

Marie James, as she was still called, lacked the exotic image required, so she adopted Lola as her first name and added Montez. There were, however, no long stints of 'resting', the frequent fate of newcomers to the world of theatre. Lola's exploits were already well known, not to say notorious, and she was able to attract a ready-made audience. This included the cream of society – Queen Adelaide, widow of King William IV; the Duchess of Kent, mother of the reigning queen, Victoria; and Victoria's uncle, the King of Hanover in Germany. At Her Majesty's Theatre in London, Lola was billed as Donna Lola Montez of the Teatro Real in Seville, but unfortunately one member of the audience, Lord Thomas Ranelagh, knew who she really was. Not long before, Lola had turned down

the lord's advances. In return, he saw to it that her first performance in London was also her last.

The rest of the audience was, at first, entranced by Lola's stage presence and not a little titillated by her suggestive movements. Until, that is, Lord Ranelagh called out: 'Why! It's Betty James!' and proceeded to hoot and boo her. His friends joined in. So did the audience, until Lola, unable to continue, fled the stage. She was so mortified that she left the country the next day.

Lola Montez found it easy to wow a whole crowd of men when she appeared onstage. To see her, it seems, was to fall madly in love with her. As a result, she left behind her a trail of would-be lovers and broken hearts.

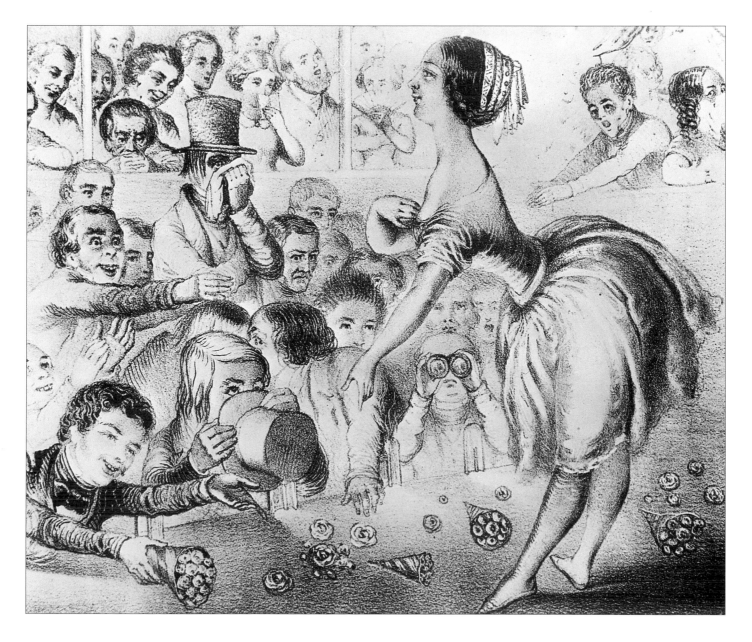

Virtually destitute, Lola wandered Europe until, inevitably, a new lover came to the rescue. He was able to secure a dancing engagement for Lola in Warsaw, and the unsophisticated Poles went mad for her. The critics reached for their most colourful adjectives to describe Lola's performance and Lola herself. According to them, she was Venus, the Roman goddess of love, come to life. There were the shades of 16 different varieties of forget-me-not in her eyes. She upstaged the swan in the elegant whiteness of her neck.

Warsaw's new sensation naturally attracted eminent lovers, the sort who adorned their egos by seeking to possess the latest sex symbol. Lola's own ego was no puny thing by now, and she could afford – or thought

Prince Ivan Paskievich was another famous figure who fell for Lola Montez. This Russian military leader had taken part in the battle of Austerlitz in 1805, and was to command the siege of Silistria (pictured), a precursor to the Crimean War.

> The next thing Lola knew, Paskievich had signed an order for her expulsion and she was unceremoniously dumped over the Polish frontier.

she could afford – to be choosy. This was how the 60-year-old Prince Ivan Paskievich, the Russian Viceroy of Poland, conceived a violent passion for Lola only to find that she was not interested. Paskievich possessed much more power to discredit Lola than Lord Ranelagh could have ever have hoped for. The next thing Lola knew, Paskievich had signed an order for her expulsion and she was unceremoniously dumped over the Polish frontier.

LUDWIG I, A BELOVED RULER

In 1846, when Lola came to Munich, Bavarians were not too concerned about the more oddball Wittelsbachs, as Ludwig I was obviously not one of them. In a reign of more than 20 years, he had unfailingly used his appreciation of the glories of classical Greece and Rome to grace the city of Munich with grand palaces, temples and museums. He made it a city of which every Bavarian could be proud and, despite the massive expense, his subjects loved him for it.

UNGUARDED FAMILY MAN

The man himself, by contrast, was unassuming. Unlike other rulers in Germany, which was then a collection of independent and semi-independent states, King Ludwig did not keep aloof from his subjects or regard non-royals as inferior to himself. Far from it. Ludwig loved to stroll unattended and unguarded along the streets of Munich, chatting to passers-by. He seemed to enjoy not being recognized and so passing for any other man in the street. In much the same vein, Ludwig preferred to live frugally and relished family life, a rare trait where too many other German royals were concerned.

Although King Ludwig I of Bavaria appears here in military dress, he was not personally aggressive, unlike some rulers in nineteenth-century Germany. Bavarians loved him for his kindness, modesty and warm-heartedness.

By the time she presented herself to the director of Munich's Royal Theatre for an audition, the word on the street had already marked her out as undesirable.

Lola set out for Paris, where she made her debut as a dancer in 1845. It was a humiliating failure. The French had far too much taste and artistic discernment to fall for the cavortings of an amateur, and Lola's performance went down in a barrage of hooting, booing and scathing reviews. Lola's next destination was Germany and on from there to Munich, capital of the Kingdom of Bavaria, where she found that tales of her escapades had already made her a celebrity. But reading sensational gossip and allegations of immorality did not mean that Lola was acceptable to the Bavarian powers-that-be. Family life counted for a great deal in Bavaria and, with that, the virtues of fidelity, chastity and, most vital of all, respectability. None of these was in Lola's curriculum. The cornerstone of all this righteousness was the Wittelsbach royal family, a gracious, artistic and, to the Bavarians, lovable crew whose often eccentric behaviour was accepted as part of their charm. At the centre of this family was the king, Ludwig I, revered for his programme of building and his apparent egalitarian attitude.

Lola Montez in a provocative pose, with a supposed 'come hither' look that enslaved virtually every man she met.

The king was not, of course, quite as too-good-to-be-true as his deeds and apparent frugality might suggest. Like other Wittelsbachs, whose family temperament was mercurial where it was not mad, Ludwig was a man of contrasts. He was liberal-minded, but could become very haughty if he thought his royal rights were being infringed. He was wise in many ways, yet gullible. He was an affectionate husband and father, yet he went through his quota of liaisons, and had no defence against a pretty face.

NOT JUST A PRETTY FACE

As many men – and their wives or mistresses – had already discovered, Lola Montez was much, much more than a pretty face. As soon as officialdom learned of the presence in Munich of this outlandish adventuress, the knives were out. Lola was at once seen as a danger to the Bavarian realm and everyone in it. The Church seemed to believe that she was a destabilizing influence. Clerics did not hesitate to pile on the anti-Lola propaganda to this effect; by the time she presented herself to the director of Munich's Royal Theatre for an audition, the word on the street had already marked her out as undesirable.

Whether the rumours affected Herr Direktor's decision is not known. But he watched Lola dance, decided she was not good enough for his theatre and turned her down. The feisty Lola was not to be put off. Her scandal-filled life so far had shorn her of all the restraints that usually keep impudence in check, and her chutzpah was high. Foiled at the Royal Theatre, she decided to petition Ludwig I himself and went to his palace to demand an audience with him. It appears that once she had

> He spent whole afternoons in her boudoir, daily wrote her long, passionate verses and even neglected his once all-consuming interests in art, Italy and the classics.

displayed her magnificent breasts for the king's inspection, he was instantly hooked and soon gave her what she wanted – his permission to dance at the Royal Theatre. Ludwig was there to watch and fall even further under Lola's spell. Later, he told his ministers that he was 'bewitched' and, having seen Ludwig through several liaisons, they were in a good position to realize that this one was different – and dangerous.

Their fears were quickly confirmed. Before long, Ludwig seemed unable to keep away from Lola. He spent whole afternoons in her boudoir, daily wrote her long, passionate verses and even neglected his once all-consuming interests in art, Italy and the classics. Lola and the king always denied that their liaison was sexual and, given his age, some were willing to believe it. Others refused to credit that, if Europe's foremost vamp and the susceptible and amorous old king spent enough time together, nothing would happen.

AN UNHEALTHY OBSESSION

Even more worrying, though, was Ludwig's habit of discussing state affairs with Lola. Lola's liberal views were as well known as her scandalous history, and that marked her out as a potential danger to the state.

Both men and women flocked to the fashionable salons of Europe whenever Lola Montez performed there. The public behaved in the same, wildly enthusiastic, way when she danced at the theatres.

Ludwig's sister, the Dowager Empress of Austria, wrote to Lola offering her a large sum of money to leave Bavaria and leave her brother alone. She refused, and tore up the letter.

Liberals were regarded as perilous to the established political and social order, and most especially to the rights and privileges of the absolute monarchs who dominated the royalty of Europe. Yet this was not all. With her Calvinist – that is, strictly Protestant – background, Lola was staunchly anti-Catholic. The Jesuits, the Catholic activists in Bavaria, were not going to stand for that. Jesuits had long ago proved themselves a fighting breed and, in declaring war on Lola, they did not care that Ludwig I also came into their line of fire. They began a whispering campaign against Lola, which reached the newspapers in the form of savage lampoons. The king, inevitably, was ridiculed at the same time.

The effect, however, was nil. Ludwig, far gone in infatuation, refused to part with Lola or believe any story against her, even if it were true. Mere months after their first meeting, Ludwig gave clear proof of Lola's hold over him by replacing his chief minister Abel with one of her supporters, Baron Schrenk. There was an immediate and vociferous outcry, and rumour began to hint darkly that, through the besotted king,

Right: Demonstrations took place across the German states in 1848, in a series of events known as the March revolution. This romanticized image shows rioters in Berlin, scene of some of the worst troubles, but there was unrest across the region.

Lola Montez would soon be ruling Bavaria. Several officials attempted to prise Ludwig from her grasp, but all failed. The Chief of the Bavarian Police was threatened with imprisonment for his protests about Lola's growing influence. Society ladies who deliberately snubbed her were answered when the king commissioned a portrait of Lola and ordered it to be hung in one of Munich's most important art galleries. Count Arco-Valley was so outraged that he removed the picture of his wife, which hung in the same gallery. Court officials entered the fray, only to be told by Ludwig that, far from setting Lola aside, he intended to make her a countess.

A cardinal threatened the king with excommunication, the direst penalty a Catholic could incur, but Ludwig took no notice. He went on

> Where Ludwig was weak, though, was in his perverse attachment to Lola, which allowed her to exercise controversial influence over him.

spending most of his time with Lola and every afternoon could be seen walking to the magnificent mansion he had given her in Munich. Next, Ludwig's sister, the Dowager Empress of Austria, was persuaded by Jesuits to offer Lola £2000 to leave the country, but Lola was too clever to fall for bribery. She told the king about it. He became incensed and let it be known that the Dowager Empress's letter of offer had ended up on the fire. Ludwig carried out his threat and created Lola Countess of Landsfeld, Baroness Rosenthal and a canoness of the order of St Theresa.

The king was evidently resolved to champion Lola at all costs, but nevertheless had to overcome some hefty resistance before he could raise her to the peerage. First, Lola had to become a Bavarian citizen, but no minister would countersign her letters of naturalization, as required by the constitution. Then, as

Lith Anst v Ed Gust May in Frankfurt a M

one man, the Bavarian Cabinet threatened to resign unless Lola were sent away. Instead, the ministers found themselves sacked and replaced by a new, liberal Cabinet headed by a Protestant, who was only too willing to countersign the letters.

REVOLUTIONARY STIRRINGS

Ironically, Lola's titles came to her at a time when royalty and nobility were starting to lose their grasp on power all over Europe. In 1848, ruling kings, dukes and other nobles were being threatened with riot and revolution if they refused to grant new, liberal constitutions: these enshrined popular rights, equality before the law, free speech and an end to economic deprivation. This was revolution indeed in a world where for centuries, royal rule and Church control had been absolute, and the only response was obedience, unquestioning and total. Many despots caved in and granted the required constitutions, then bided their time for a year or so, until they were able to retrieve their autocratic power.

Bavaria was not quite on the same footing, for its monarchy attracted popular goodwill and its monarch was much admired. Where Ludwig was weak, though, was in his perverse attachment to Lola, which allowed her to exercise controversial influence over him. Bavaria's revolution of 1848, therefore, was an effort to get rid of Lola rather than demote the king. Lola's enemies circulated stories designed to rouse superstitious fears, such as the tale which dubbed Lola a sorceress whose 'familiars' were huge black birds. Rumours that she was a spy gained currency and fired fresh controversy, much of it centred on Munich's university and its radical students.

There, as elsewhere, Lola had her supporters, but she also had vociferous opponents, some of whom got themselves very inebriated at the *bierkeller* and afterwards surrounded her home, booing, shouting and bawling insults. Lola did not frighten easily. Instead of hiding herself indoors, she appeared on the balcony and showered the crowd with Champagne and chocolates. The uproar abated somewhat, more from surprise than anything else, and shortly afterwards

Left: The more mature Lola Montez, pictured holding a cigarette. Cigarettes were invented in 1832, but for a long time afterwards it was considered shocking for a woman to smoke, especially in public. But then, Lola made a career out of shocking people.

Ludwig I arrived. As he let himself in with his key, mounted police dispersed the students.

If Lola and Ludwig learned anything from this incident, it was not discretion. At around this time, a bust of Martin Luther, the original sixteenth-century Protestant, was placed in the Walhalla, one of Ludwig's country mansions. Bavaria's Protestants were delighted at this open concession to Lola's faith, but the Catholic clergy were purple-faced with fury. When Ludwig reshuffled his cabinet to weed out conservatives and replace them with radicals friendly to Lola, liberal-minded Bavarians were delighted. To the more traditional types, the nickname of the new cabinet – Lolaministerium – was an insult.

> Ludwig I stood and watched her go. As the carriage drove off ... the mob rushed the doors of Lola's house and proceeded to rip the place apart for loot.

Fearing that Lola was now in physical danger, a group of her supporters at the University formed a bodyguard, the Alemannia, to protect her. They took to escorting Lola through the streets and guarding her house. Events soon proved that these precautions were very necessary. A band of Alemannia was, fortunately, present on 8 February 1848, when an angry demonstration in front of the University turned violent. Books and other missiles were thrown at Lola, and she was barraged with insults and threats. The uproar could easily have grown out of hand, but Lola went down into the street to answer her enemies face to face. When she threatened to have the University closed, which she presumably had the power to do, the mob made a rush for her. She was saved by the Alemannia, who closed around her.

NARROW ESCAPE

A pitched battle ensued as her enemies tried to break through the protective ring. Lola just managed to get away by running for shelter to a house in a nearby street, the Theatinerstrasse. She chose the wrong sanctuary. The family in the house refused to let her in. With the furious mob howling after her, she fled on to the Theatiner Church, where the doors shut behind her only just in time. Fortunately, a troop of cavalry galloped up as the mob was thundering at the doors, and chased them off.

Ludwig I was naturally appalled at these events, and next day he decreed the University closed. The offending students were ordered out of Munich within 24 hours. Ordinarily, Ludwig would have been obeyed, but with revolutionary fervour increasing all over Europe, the circumstances were not ordinary. The radicals were outraged at the king's decree, and a mob formed around the Residenz, the royal palace,

A nineteenth-century illustration satirizing reactions to Lola's dance routines when she toured the eastern United States from 1851 to 1853. She also toured Australia in 1855.

demanding that Ludwig rescind it, and instead throw Lola out of Bavaria. Barricades went up in the streets, citizens armed themselves, vigilantes grouped and Ludwig I now realized that in these archetypal ways, already perfected by French revolutionaries, Munich was about to rise up against him.

IGNOMINIOUS RETREAT

At long last, through fear and the dread that his throne was tottering, Ludwig saw sense. He summoned his ministers, hoping they had a solution, but they simply confirmed his terror: only the royal signature on an order banishing Lola stood between Ludwig and the Wittelsbachs and disaster. Ludwig signed. The emergency had been so great that the order did not even give Lola decent time to prepare for departure: she had to go within the hour. Lola was stunned. She had been certain that the king would stand by her.

> After he relinquished his throne in 1848, Ludwig fared quite well. He remained in Bavaria and lived at the Wittelsbacher Palace.

Now she had time only to pack her jewels and a few necessities to the tune of curses and threats from a menacing rabble outside her house. Cavalry were sent to protect her as she emerged through her front door and stepped into a carriage. Somewhere in the crowd, incognito, Ludwig I stood and watched her go. As the carriage drove off, surrounded by horsemen, the mob rushed the doors of Lola's house and proceeded to rip the place apart for loot.

The king, already heartbroken, could not bear to see this place of lost happiness destroyed. Shouting out above the uproar, he ordered the pillage to stop. His presence rather than his words seemed to cool the frenzy, for recognizing him despite his disguise, people in the crowd started shouting: *'Heil Unsern Koenig!'* – 'God save the King!' They pressed round him and, in the jostling, Ludwig either lost his balance and fell or was pushed. He managed to regain his feet, but was clearly dazed as he returned, unsteadily, to the Residenz, growing more and more bitter against his subjects for their ingratitude and the sacrifice they had forced on him.

The effect on him was significant. Ludwig neglected his family, lost interest in state affairs and brooded. In this unhealthy solitude, Ludwig's streak of Wittelsbach paranoia, which he possessed despite his basic normality, began to persuade him that maybe the stories about Lola had been true after all. Maybe she was a spy, a revolutionary in skirts, a tool of Giuseppe Mazzini, the Italian liberal republican, or of Lord Palmerston, the Whig foreign minister in Britain. Lola as a Prussian agent or a witch set on destroying the Wittelsbach dynasty were other possibilities that crossed King Ludwig's troubled mind.

CONTRASTING ENDS

After he relinquished his throne in 1848, Ludwig fared quite well. He remained in Bavaria and lived at the

A BITTER ABDICATION

When he sent Lola away, Ludwig had believed he was saving his throne, but the radicals, having tasted one triumph, were hellbent on another. Like revolutionaries all over Europe in 1848, they clamoured for liberal reforms and new popular rights. When Ludwig turned them down, the barricades went up once more and there was rioting near the Residenz. Suddenly, Ludwig realized that he had had enough and, on 21 March, he abdicated his throne in favour of his son, Maximilian. Ludwig's last act as king, the ultimate bitterness, was to sign documents withdrawing the rights of Bavarian citizenship from Lola Montez.

In 1848, King Ludwig was unable to stand the pressure of the Lola Affair and abdicated. Lola left Bavaria and as far as is known, Ludwig was careful to keep his distance from this woman who had ruined his life.

Wittelsbacher Palace. He was regularly seen at the opera and theatre, and had plenty of time for his enduring passion – Italy and its classical past. Now that he had been neutralized, the affection of his former subjects resurfaced and in 1862, when the old

> In her 25-year career,
> Lola contravened almost every rule,
> trampled on all the mores and
> offended most traditions of society
> as her century knew them.

king's statue was erected in Munich, it was unveiled before an admiring crowd. Five years later, the ex-king went to Paris for a grand exhibition and was fêted by the French, for whom his sad, romantic story had great sentimental appeal.

Ludwig died the following year, aged 82, on Leap Year Day 1868, at Nice in the south of France. Munich gave him a splendid funeral. For several days, Ludwig lay in state in the Glyptothek, one of his own neo-classical buildings, as thousands of Bavarians filed by his coffin. Afterwards, he was buried in the basilica of St Boniface, another great structure which his love of ancient architecture had inspired.

By that time, Lola Montez had been dead for seven years. Ludwig arranged for money to be sent to her, but this soon ran out and it seems that at no time between her dramatic departure from Munich and her death, aged 43, in 1861 did the ex-king attempt to make personal contact with her. There were good reasons for his reticence. Having lost face, his reputation, his throne and his family, who abandoned him in 1848, Ludwig may well have decided that the last shreds of his dignity had to be preserved against the woman who had ruined him.

Once her liaison with Ludwig was over, Lola reverted to type and became involved in a parade of scandals, some of which were new even for her. She discovered that Captain James, her first husband, had not divorced her, as she had believed, but just the same she went ahead with more marriages, which were, of course, bigamous. She soon abandoned her 'husbands' and went on to do the same to a long series of lovers, one of whom shot himself. Money ran short. She got into serious debt and her property was distrained after she went on the run from the bailiffs. At times, Lola was so hard up that she returned to the stage, to play herself in dramas about her adventures in Munich. Later, travelling the world as a professional dancer – to mixed success – there were records of fistfights and brawls between Lola and other actresses or dancers in the theatres where she occasionally performed.

SHAMED AND BEMUSED

In this context, it was understandable that Ludwig preferred to distance himself from this outlandish woman. All the more so because, in her 25-year career, Lola contravened almost every rule, trampled on all the mores and offended most

traditions of society as her century knew them. Along the way, she left behind her a mass of wreckage – bemused, exploited or abandoned men, deserted wives and mistresses, outraged officials and clerics, exasperated creditors and, the most prestigious victim of them all, one sad and shamed old fellow who had once been a king.

A portrait of King Ludwig looking older and sadder in his mature years, when his life and reign were wrecked by his obsession with Lola.

CASTLES IN THE AIR: THE TRAGIC STORY OF LUDWIG II OF BAVARIA

Ludwig II of Bavaria (1845–1886) and his physician Dr Bernhard von Gudden had promised to return from their evening walk in the grounds of Castle Berg by eight o'clock on the evening of 13 June 1886. These walks were one of the few pleasurable features of a terrible situation, for Ludwig had inherited the madness that blighted the Wittelsbach royal family to which he belonged.

◆

Three days earlier, he had been declared unfit to rule, and a regent, his uncle Prince Luitpold, was appointed to govern in his place. Ludwig's initial reaction was violent and emotional. Afterwards, though, he calmed down and became quite malleable. When Doctor von Gudden suggested a light meal and bed, Ludwig quietly did as he was told. In fact, he behaved himself remarkably well for the next three

Left: King Ludwig II, grandson of the first King Ludwig, had a taste for fantasy which he expressed not only in his obsession with the operas of Richard Wagner but in the construction of extravagantly romantic castles such as Neuschwanstein.

days, so well that von Gudden was fooled into believing that they could do without the guards who usually went with them on their walks.

Eight o'clock came and went with no sign of the king or von Gudden. Von Gudden's assistant, Doctor Müller, became alarmed and ordered a search of the castle grounds. It revealed nothing. The search was extended, but more than two hours passed before Ludwig and von Gudden were found dead in the nearby Lake Starnburg. Both of them had drowned. Doctor Müller tried artificial respiration, but it was far too late. The king and von Gudden had been dead for nearly six hours.

Although nearly 41 years old when he died, Ludwig looked smooth-faced and young. His good looks were no longer tarnished by madness, as if the moment of death had wiped clean all the years of fearful imaginings known only to those who, like the king, had lost touch with reality. But there was no wiping away the horrifying fact that madness and the fear of madness had again been visited on the Wittelsbach

> There was no wiping away the horrifying fact that madness and the fear of madness had again been visited on the Wittelsbach family.

family. This was an ongoing tragedy for the royal house of Bavaria. Ludwig's cousin Empress Elisabeth of Austria continually embarrassed her husband, the Emperor Franz Josef, with her abnormal behaviour. Her erratic traits emerged again in their son, the

This scene by Lake Starnberg, showing Schloss Berg and the elaborate palace gardens, depicts the last walk of King Ludwig II and his doctor, Bernhard von Gudden, before they were found dead at the lakeside.

King Maximilian II was the son of the ill-fated Ludwig I and succeeded to the throne of Bavaria on his father's abdication in 1848.

morose and suicidal Prince Rudolf. This was not all. Ludwig's younger brother and successor, Prince Otto. was also insane, and came to the throne in confinement, with keepers to monitor him day and night.

DISTURBING EARLY LIFE

Tracking back to Ludwig's early life uncovered several pointers to the particular form his madness took. Born in 1845, Ludwig became Crown prince of Bavaria before he was three, on the abdication of his grandfather, King Ludwig I, in 1848. The position isolated him and planted in his child's mind an obsessive pride and a feeling of superiority. This was reinforced when servants in the royal household were ordered to bow in reverence to the young Ludwig. He

> When chided by his governess ... for stealing a purse from a shop, Ludwig maintained that, as future king, everything in Bavaria belonged to him.

was also styled Royal Highness in a break with the tradition that this title was not accorded princes until they were 18 years of age and, presumably, old enough not to have their heads turned by it.

Ludwig always had to come first, whether it was in games with his brother Otto, who was three years younger, or in the order of precedence when entering a room in company. This extended to anywhere the boys might be. Ludwig once gave Otto a beating when he tried to precede his elder brother into a hothouse in the grounds of the royal palace at Berchtesgaden. After severe punishment from his father, King Maximilian II, Ludwig acquired another obsession: pathological hatred of Berchtesgaden. It was a pattern set for the rest of his disordered life. Any place connected to humiliation or any other unpalatable experience became instant anathema to him.

NO MORAL COMPASS

Even a simple sense of right and wrong seemed to be beyond Ludwig II. When chided by his governess, Fräulein Meilhaus, for stealing a purse from a shop, Ludwig maintained that, as future king, everything in Bavaria belonged to him. Meilhaus was unusual among the tutors and instructors whose task it was to turn Ludwig into a proper German prince. She treated him gently, with explanations rather than strictures, when his introverted temperament led him astray. She

was, in fact, virtually the only person close to him whom Ludwig did not either hate or fear.

Unfortunately, Meilhaus disappeared from Ludwig's life in 1854, when he was aged nine and was considered ready for more rigorous training. The purpose behind the 14-hour day now imposed on Ludwig was meant to forge a brave, self-confident, strong-willed prince worthy to inherit the Bavarian throne. Ludwig was in many ways an apt pupil and made sufficient progress in French and history to please his tutors. He also excelled at the tricky business of Ancient Greek translation and showed a strong talent for mathematics. These accomplishments were, however, a smokescreen covering Ludwig's secret inner life. He realized early on that he dared not reveal the excess of imagination, romanticism and fondness for art that were the mainsprings of his temperament. Surrounded by

A Wittelsbach family portrait. King Maximilian II and his wife, Queen Marie posed for this photograph with their sons, the future King Ludwig II (first on left) and Prince Otto (far right). Otto's insanity was more severe than his brother's.

A scene from *Das Rheingold* (1854), the first of Richard Wagner's four operas in *Der Ring des Nibelungen* (The Ring of the Nibelungs) cycle. Ludwig II was so enthralled by the operas' mythical world that he attempted to recreate it.

tutors intent on stiffening his spine, Ludwig took to active daydreaming to compensate.

What he dreamed of were the ancient Teutonic legends which the German composer Richard Wagner was then using for his mammoth operas. Ludwig revelled in Wagner's world of ancient pagan gods, valiant knights, mythical beasts and ferocious dragons. Wagner's music – huge, imposing, awash with dreamy melody and rich orchestral colour – meant little to Ludwig. It was the fabulous demi-world that Wagner brought to such spectacular life that really fascinated him. While a fantasy world was nothing unusual in early adolescence, for Ludwig, it was never just a stage in growing up that faded with

Below: The young Ludwig on horseback, from a painting by Theodore Dietz.

maturity. To the violent end of his life, Ludwig never relinquished the fantasy.

In order to live undisturbed and undiscovered in this imaginary world, Ludwig assumed a carapace of outward normality. Physically, he had a great deal going for him. He was very handsome and impressively tall, and knew how to make an imposing appearance in public. In 1863, the year he came of age at 18, Ludwig was present when his great-uncle King Wilhelm IV of Prussia visited Munich, the Bavarian capital. Wilhelm's Adjutant-General, Prince Kraft, wrote of Ludwig's 'brilliance, his physical skill and courage,' and recorded admiration for the prince's elegant manner on horseback and knowledge of art and science. Even allowing for the sycophancy usually present in royal officials, Kraft's account glowed with appreciation of a fine, upstanding young prince whose future seemed golden.

FARAWAY MANNER

But Count Otto von Bismarck, the 'Iron Chancellor' of Prussia, was more perceptive. He sat next to Ludwig at dinner and noted the prince's dreaminess, and the faraway manner that made his conversation disjointed and also made it evident that, in thought, he was somewhere else entirely.

It was one thing for Ludwig to put up barriers between himself and men such as Bismarck or Prince Kraft; quite another when he encountered people who, unlike them, knew him as he really was. One of them was Prince Paul of Taxis, his aide-de-camp. Paul was an honest, pleasant young man and for any other prince would have made a friend worthy of trust, but only a friend. Ludwig's approach was much more intense and his attachment to Paul was passionate. He smothered his aide-de-camp with devotion and the need to share his innermost thoughts. Paul found all this overwhelming and kept away from Berchtesgaden

by removing himself to a country estate near Regensburg owned by his family.

Apart from his own experience, Prince Paul had proof of Ludwig's obsessive nature in an encounter with a young woodworker whom they met together while walking in mountain country. Paul saw a strong, healthy, good-looking peasant typical of the farmers and country people of the Watzmann valleys. Ludwig, by contrast, imagined a beautiful, romantic figure,

spoke of him as 'king of the mountains' and daydreamed that one day he might find unspoiled friendship among such peasants, far from the bitchery and conniving of the royal court. But the court was soon to close around him. In 1864, his father Maximilian died and Ludwig, not yet 19 years of age, came to the throne of Bavaria. Almost his first act as

Otto von Bismarck, the so-called Iron Chancellor of Prussia, noticed that Ludwig was strangely dreamy when he met the then 18-year-old in 1863.

WAGNER AND THE KING

Ludwig II's desire for Richard Wagner to be brought to court was a long quest, for Wagner was in hiding from his creditors, a usual state of affairs for him. The composer was eventually located in Zurich, Switzerland, and was invited to Munich by a royal messenger who handed him an effusive fan letter from Ludwig and a gold ring set with a ruby.

When Wagner reached Munich and met King Ludwig, he found himself treated as if he were the Messiah. Ludwig started by embracing him warmly, proclaimed him his 'Great Friend', then ordered a portrait made of Wagner to hang in his study beside those of two of his other heroes, William Shakespeare and Ludwig van Beethoven. Later, the king lavished thousands of florins on Wagner, gave him an annual allowance, bought him a substantial house in Munich, paid his remaining debts and forked out a hefty advance for his next opera – *Der Ring des Nibelungen* (The Ring of the Nibelungs). He even financed the composer's lavish tastes and paid for his large and costly entourage.

ENEMY OF THE PEOPLE

It could not last. The adoring young king was blind to the composer's true nature – grasping, egocentric and exploitative. But Bavarians were quick to see Wagner as a vampire bloodsucking their naive and overheated monarch. Wagner had barely settled into his new home in Munich before a press campaign began with the object of levering him out. The press was helped, unwittingly, by Wagner himself. One of King Ludwig's most pronounced obsessions was his desire to monopolize anyone he loved. Wagner was himself too highly charged and self-absorbed to realize the impact it would make when he sent for his pregnant mistress, Cosima von Bulow.

Wagner's many enemies saw at once what was going to happen. Gleefully, von Linfelder, the Bavarian court archivist, ran to tell Ludwig about Cosima and her unborn child. Instantly, the king cast Cosima as an obstacle between himself and his 'Great Friend' and indicated his displeasure by staying away from

performances of Wagner's *The Flying Dutchman* and *Tannhauser* in 1865. Afterwards, he refused to grant the composer an audience.

Wagner failed to get the message. Instead, he targeted his enemies in the Bavarian government, and intrigued against Prime Minister Ludwig von der Pfordten, little realizing how much the king trusted and needed the politician or how dangerous it was to interfere with the royal dignity and the royal prerogatives. Pride in his royal birth and all it implied had been Ludwig's earliest obsession and proved to be his most enduring. It was unnatural and unhealthy, like so much Ludwig did, but it was also fortunate, for

> The adoring young king was blind to the composer's true nature – grasping, egocentric and exploitative. But Bavarians were quick to see Wagner as a vampire bloodsucking their naive and overheated monarch.

it saved him from the sort of ruin Lola Montez had brought upon his grandfather King Ludwig I.

THREATENED RESIGNATION

Wagner's meddling trod this sensitive ground and Ludwig, for once, failed to rise to his hero's defence when the Prime Minister threatened to resign unless the composer was banished. Ludwig personally informed Wagner of this development and seems to have done so without emotional fireworks. Wagner and Cosima left Munich for Switzerland in December 1865 after some 20 months in the Bavarian capital.

Right: A meeting of musical minds. Richard Wagner (centre) with the composer and pianist Franz Liszt (right) and Liszt's daughter Cosima, also a pianist, who married Wagner.

The king slumped into a depression and in July 1866, after some seven months without Wagner, he threatened to abdicate.

king was to send for his great hero Richard Wagner. The eventual break with Wagner in 1865 (see box) hurt the king deeply. He was not made to withstand emotional shocks and, having been indulged and protected all his life, had no strength to overcome disappointment. He slumped into a depression and in July 1866, after some seven months without Wagner, he threatened to abdicate. Prince Paul of Taxis held him back from a final decision, appealing to Ludwig's ego by telling him that, as king, he was destined for greatness.

WHAT USE IS AN EX-KING?

Paul had more practical reasons for his efforts at keeping Ludwig on the throne. Bavaria was then supporting Prussia in a war against Austria. The departure of the king for personal and emotional reasons would ruin the House of Wittelsbach as well as wreck Paul's own prospects and those of Richard Wagner. Wagner himself had been horrified at the prospect of losing his meal ticket: an ex-king was no use to him at all.

In August 1866, Wagner was working on *Die Meistersinger von Nurnberg* (The Mastersingers of Nuremberg). That month, during a visit to the composer's house at Lucerne, Switzerland, Prince Paul wrote to Ludwig telling him how Wagner longed to complete the work and how totally he relied on Ludwig for the purpose. It was, of course, emotional blackmail and Ludwig fell for it. There was no more talk of abdication, but the king remained severely depressed and was fast becoming subject to delusions.

Left: Richard Wagner by Giuseppe Tivoli. King Ludwig rescued Wagner from his many creditors and admired him inordinately, expecting total devotion in return. But when Wagner brought his then mistress, Cosima, to Bavaria, Ludwig's ardour cooled.

Elsa, seen here, was the heroine of Wagner's opera *Lohengrin*. The opera's first performance took place at Weimar in 1848. Wagner wrote both the music and the libretto.

> Finally, on 7 October,
> Ludwig came clean and wrote
> to Sophie that,
> 'The wedding day was forced
> upon me, just as the day of
> the engagement was.'

Meanwhile, Ludovica, Duchess Maximilian Josef of Bavaria, had picked Ludwig for her young daughter Sophie Charlotte. Sophie, 19 years old, was a delightful girl, and well worth the Crown of Bavaria, which her ambitious mother was resolved she should wear. Ludwig already knew and liked Sophie, which made her unique among his female acquaintances: he usually preferred them to be much older than himself, or at least more mature.

DUTY TO MARRY

Despite his passion for beautiful males, there is no evidence that King Ludwig was homosexual and none that he put up a struggle against his engagement to Sophie. As an unmarried monarch, it was Ludwig's duty to take a wife and secure the succession. So far, he had been let off this commitment because of his youth. At age 21, however, Ludwig's time for marriage had come and the official announcement was made on New Year's Day 1867.

All seemed as it should be. The Bavarians warmly welcomed their future queen. Ludwig professed his love for Sophie and she for him. He even paid her the compliment of calling her Elsa, after the heroine of Wagner's *Lohengrin*. A new state wedding coach was ordered and a boudoir for Sophie was constructed in the royal apartments. The couple exchanged correspondence of the most affectionate kind. 'A thousand inmost greetings from the bottom of my heart' and 'my heart is longing for you' were two of the ways in which Ludwig signed off when writing to his fiancée.

King Ludwig II with his fianceé Princess Sophie Charlotte of Liechtenstein. Ludwig came to regard the prospect of marriage with Sophie as 'the fearful thing', postponed the wedding twice and finally rejected her.

A FIANCÉE SUPPLANTED

Ludwig II had confined his real thoughts about marriage to Sophie Charlotte to his diary. 'Sophie got rid of,' he wrote on 8 October 1867. 'The gloomy picture fades … now I live again after this torturing nightmare.' 'Thanks be to God, the fearful thing was not realized,' ran his diary entry for 28 November, when the twice-postponed wedding would have taken place. But Ludwig had no intention of lacking a love in his life. He had already provided it, unknown to Sophie or to Richard Wagner. In May 1867, the king had noticed Richard Hornig, a young groom at the royal stables. Hornig had all the qualifications for Ludwig's next grand passion. About five years older than the king, he was handsome, graceful, looked marvellous on horseback and, like all great Teutonic heroes, was a blue-eyed blonde.

In July 1867, Ludwig took Hornig off for a jaunt through one of the most beautiful and historic regions in Germany, the Thuringian forest, then proceeded to Paris, where they were entertained by the French Emperor Napoleon III and Empress Eugenie, and visited the Exposition at Versailles. By the time the king and the groom returned home to Bavaria, Hornig was firmly installed as 'Richard, Beloved of my Heart'.

There was, even so, a discordant note. Ludwig was still devoted to Wagner, in spite of everything that had occurred and felt no need to hide it. 'The god of my life, as you know, is Richard Wagner,' he wrote to Sophie in February 1867. Quite probably, Sophie had no reason to believe that this was anything more than the attachment of an artistic young man to a great genius. Nonetheless, by June 1867, two months before the wedding, set for 25 August, Ludwig's twenty-second birthday, Sophie was getting suspicious. For one thing, Ludwig was planning to bring Wagner back to Munich and became abnormally excited as the date for his return drew near. By August, Sophie's forebodings seemed confirmed as Ludwig started to show signs of wriggling out of the marriage. He postponed the August wedding date to October, then again to November. Finally, on 7 October, Ludwig came clean and wrote to Sophie that, 'The wedding day was forced upon me, just as the day of the engagement was.'

For all his emotional excesses, Ludwig was not a cruel man and he tried to let Sophie down lightly in a letter full of assurances of friendship and affection, if not love. He offered, too, to renew their engagement should Sophie fail to find another husband within the year. It was hardly a compliment to Sophie, but it showed generosity. Sophie was too beautiful and charming to remain available for long and, on 28 September 1868, she married a French husband, Ferdinand Philippe Marie, Duc d'Alençon.

At this stage, Ludwig's obsessions were about to scale fresh heights of fantasy. In 1869, he made plans to build the Neuschwangau, a new palace in southwestern Bavaria and one of the fantastic structures that later earned the popular title of 'castles in the air'. Another, the Linderhof Palace, was the only 'castle in the air' completed in Ludwig's lifetime, in 1878. The last, Herrenchiemsee, was meant to 'breathe the magnificence and imposing grandeur of Versailles' where, two centuries earlier, another of Ludwig's great heroes, King Louis XIV of France, had created the most splendid royal complex in Europe.

> In debt to the tune of 14 million marks, Ludwig made plans for more palaces – one Chinese, another Byzantine – before death intervened to stop him.

The Herrenchiemsee featured a replica of the famous Hall of Mirrors at Versailles and cost so much that, by 1886, Ludwig was in debt to the tune of 14 million marks, almost three times his annual income. Undeterred, Ludwig made plans for more palaces – one Chinese, another Byzantine – before death

This painting of Siegfried and the Rhine Maidens by Ferdinand Leeke exemplifies the fantasy world of Richard Wagner's operas, a world which fascinated Ludwig and fed his obsession with Wagner.

intervened to stop him. Wagnerian themes were an inevitable feature of Ludwig's craze for castle building. Paintings of scenes from Wagner's operas covered the walls. The elves and fairies of Wagner's opera world, which Ludwig thought he saw flitting about the palace grounds, provided numerous decorations.

ESCALATING MADNESS

All the while, Ludwig's madness was inexorably progressing. From his secret diaries, it is evident that the king was convinced that he was gradually losing control. He wrote of violent, involuntary physical movements, deteriorating eyesight, nightmares,

Left: Ludwig by Gabriel Schachinger, showing him in a stern martial pose. The impression given of a mighty warrior monarch was contrary to Ludwig's true character which was volatile and emotional.

sleeplessness, persistent headaches and a fearful guilt over some evil he discerned within himself, but could not quite identify.

Ludwig had good reason to fear being taken over by his own insanity. His brother Otto was already subject

---

From his secret diaries,
it is evident that the king was
convinced that he was gradually
losing control.

---

to wild fits of physical violence and had to be guarded by keepers day and night. Otto's crazed mind sometimes persuaded him that disaster would follow if he took off his boots or went to bed. At other times, he made gargoyle faces, barked like a dog or was tormented by hallucinations. He then reverted to normal until the madness started all over again.

Desperately struggling to avert the same horrific fate, Ludwig resorted to cold baths to reduce himself from the dross of his humanity. 'I will never cease [my efforts],' he wrote. 'I will never err.'

QUEST FOR EL DORADO

Meanwhile, Prince Otto was growing worse, and his family was forced to admit he was incurable. Ludwig grew more terrified than ever: he was still seeing how his own symptoms more and more resembled those of his brother, who was officially declared insane in 1878. By 1879, Ludwig was starting to lose his battle to retain control. He decided that he must find El Dorado, the legendary country, or city, of gold tirelessly sought by

Prince Luitpold was the third son of Ludwig I of Bavaria. Like his father and his elder brother, Maximilian II, Luitpold escaped the curse of the Wittelsbach madness but had to serve as Regent for both his insane nephews, Ludwig II and Ludwig's brother Otto I.

excitability. He sought answers in numerology, mysticism and spiritualism. He recorded a solemn oath in his diary to 'refrain from all excitement for three months' or 'abstain from passionate embraces'. Perhaps it helped, if only for a while. Having consigned his most turbulent fantasies to his diary and purged himself through occult dabblings, Ludwig managed to retain an outer shell of normality. Nevertheless, the entries in his diary revealed how remorselessly Ludwig's mind was slipping away. He was increasingly obsessed with the idea of purity and with freeing

Schloss Hohenschwangau in southwestern Bavaria, where Ludwig II grew up, was the official summer residence of the royal family. It was built in 1832–1837 by Ludwig's father, King Maximilian II, on the ruins of a twelfth century fortress.

sixteenth-century Spanish conquistadors in South America, but never found. The king then suddenly lost interest in, and even consciousness of, El Dorado and anything that lay outside his own tortured world. Little by little, Ludwig withdrew into isolation. He dismissed his court officials, refused to see his ministers, sacked his personal staff and finally banished his valets, his dresser and his bedchamber servants. By the end of 1885, Ludwig had become a recluse.

Reluctantly, the Bavarian royal family and government were obliged for a second time to face up to a truth they had always shrunk from making public:

Ludwig was mentally unfit to carry out his duties as king. Too many Wittelsbachs had gone mad, and the lunacy appeared on both sides of the family. The charade had to end. In June 1886, Prince Luitpold, Ludwig's uncle and second in line to the Bavarian throne after Prince Otto, ordered a formal investigation into the mental state of the king. Four doctors conferred on evidence already gathered by Dr von Gudden. Their diagnosis was never in doubt and, on 10 June, a government proclamation was posted in Munich announcing that Ludwig was incapable of ruling and establishing Luitpold as his regent.

Ludwig was not so far gone that he failed to understand what was happening. 'I can bear that they take the government from me,' he said. 'But not that they declare me insane.'

When news reached him at Hohenschwangau that court officials were coming to take him prisoner, he scribbled a hasty plea for aid to his cousin Prince Ludwig Ferdinand and dispatched a servant to deliver it. The servant failed to reach the prince, but in his frenzy to get away Ludwig hatched other plans. Hohenschwangau lay near the border with Austria, and Ludwig contemplated escaping from Bavaria by making a break for it into foreign, and therefore, safer territory. The king also had a counterproclamation drawn up, calling for support from his subjects.

But long before anyone could have made a move to rescue him, the king had been detained and placed under strict supervision in his private apartments. On 12 June, he was locked into the middle carriage of a

King Ludwig's physician, Dr. Bernhard von Gudden, paid with his life when he was fooled by his royal patient into leaving the usual guards behind on their last walk by Lake Starnberg.

Shortly after Ludwig's arrival at the castle, his attendants instantly suspected a suicide bid when the king demanded the key to the 61-metre high main tower.

convoy of three. The inside door handles had been removed, and he was not allowed out until the convoy reached the Castle Berg, some 80 kilometres (50 miles) and eight hours' travel away.

SUSPECTED SUICIDE BID

Shortly after Ludwig's arrival at the castle, his attendants instantly suspected a suicide bid when the king demanded the key to the 61-m (200-ft) high main tower. Ludwig's valet, a man called Mayr, pretended that the key had been mislaid and so fended off his master until Doctor von Gudden and his two assistants arrived. Meanwhile, Ludwig was on his way to the tower, and the doctor decided on an ambush. He placed warders armed with straitjackets along the corridor and staircase leading to the tower and sent Mayr to give Ludwig the key.

When the bodies were examined, it was discovered that von Gudden had been badly beaten up, apparently in a vigorous fight for his life. By contrast, Ludwig was unmarked.

As the king approached, two warders leapt out, pinioned him and forced him into a straitjacket. Von Gudden appeared and suggested that Ludwig return to his apartments. Suddenly, the king calmed down. He went quietly, far too quietly, deceiving von Gudden

MADNESS SUCCEEDS MADNESS

In confinement at Schloss Furstenreid, a royal castle near Munich, Prince Otto became king. He probably never knew that he had ascended the Wittelsbach throne. Certainly, he never truly ruled Bavaria. King Otto died in 1916, four years after the death of Prince Luitpold ended the 26-year regency he served for his nephews. He was succeded as regent by his son, Prince Ludwig Ferdinand.

For the Wittelsbachs, who never knew where the family madness would strike next or what it would do to its future victims, it was a traumatic situation none of them could escape. Eccentricity, 'abnormal' behaviour and even madness itself were one thing, but with Ludwig II, the family legacy, so notoriously unstable, had produced not only these afflictions, but suicide and murder as well. No wonder Prince Luitpold burst into tears and bitterly wept when he heard the news of Ludwig's death and the accession of another lunatic king, in the person of Prince Otto.

Otto I, Ludwig's mad brother who succeeded him in 1886, had already been declared insane 11 years earlier. He spent his entire reign of 27 years in confinement and under medical supervision.

into thinking that he had his royal patient under control. Next, Ludwig became upset after workmen, hired to prepare the castle windows for fitting with iron bars, set up a cacophony of hammering. Ludwig managed to get away from the noise by taking a short morning walk with Doctor von Gudden, but he soon became rattled once again when he saw a policeman walking ahead of him.

At this juncture, except for these two brief bouts of nerves, King Ludwig had been in a calm frame of mind for three days. Von Gudden regarded this as a hopeful sign and decided that, on their next walk, it would be safe for the policemen to stay behind. After dinner on the evening of 13 June 1886, the king and von Gudden set out once more, but this time they never came back, nor were they seen alive again. The unusual calm the mad king had assumed was simply a cover to get von Gudden on his own and kill him before Ludwig killed himself.

Later, it became clear that this had been Ludwig's plan all along. When the bodies were medically examined, it was discovered that von Gudden had been badly beaten up, apparently in a vigorous fight for his life. His right eye was bruised blue; there were deep scratches on his nose and forehead. A nail on one finger of his right hand had been torn off. By contrast, Ludwig was unmarked.

The next night, 14 June, Ludwig's body was taken back to Munich, where he was dressed in sumptuous robes, a sword by his side. He lay in state on a flower-filled bier for three days, the blooms carefully arranged about his head to conceal the work of the surgeons who had performed an autopsy on him. On 17 June, Ludwig was buried with full state honours.

Ludwig's Linderhof Palace took 23 years to build at a cost reckoned to total just over £32.5 millions. Ludwig had long admired the Palace of Versailles and reproduced in the Linderhof its most distinctive feature — the Hall of Mirrors.

THE MAYERLING TRAGEDY

Early on the morning of 30 January 1889, Crown Prince Rudolf of Austria-Hungary was found dead, together with his young mistress, Baroness Maria Vetsera, in the royal hunting lodge at Mayerling, 15km (10 miles) from Vienna. Both had been shot. Maria had apparently died first and lay on the bed in the Crown Prince's bedroom, her body covered with roses. Having killed her, it seems, Rudolph had shot himself through the head, shattering his skull.

✦

Reaction to the Mayerling deaths was cataclysmic. The Crown Prince's father, Emperor Franz Josef, collapsed when he heard the news. His mother, Empress Elisabeth, was inconsolable. Grieving crowds thronging the streets

**Left: Crown Prince Rudolf was a liberal destined to inherit an absolute monarchy that was the antithesis of his beliefs.
Above: Baroness Maria Vetsera was a starry-eyed girl, entranced by a glamorous Crown Prince into a fatal romance.**

of Vienna went so far out of police control that the army had to be called in. One person was killed and several more injured before calm was restored.

What remained after that was a mystery – one that no one seemed able to solve. Why had a handsome, popular prince, heir to one of Europe's most powerful thrones, a man who had charm, intelligence, good looks and talent on his side, unexpectedly taken his own life at 30 years of age in so sombre and furtive a manner?

On the face of it, the handsome, charming Crown Prince Rudolf seemed the ideal prince and a worthy heir to the prestigious Austro-Hungarian throne.

Rudolph, however, was not at all the dazzling Prince Charming he appeared to be. The only son of Franz Josef and Elisabeth, he had inherited too much of his mother's melancholic nature and too little of his father's solidity. Add to those frustrating circumstances a miserable marriage and a sense of isolation and hopelessness, and the tragic Prince had all the makings of a man who to the outside world

The liberal journalist Moritz Szeps saw the maverick Rudolf as a great 'catch' in his efforts to promote radical ideas aimed at transforming the Austro-Hungarian Empire.

appeared to have everything, but in his own mind had nothing.

PROGRESSIVE IDEAS

There was, for a start, no scope in the exalted royal environment for his advanced and progressive ideas. A liberal-minded prince more suited to be a constitutional monarch than a despot, Rudolph had a head full of exciting ideals about improving the lot of ordinary people and ruling by benign example.

Rudolph ... was not at all the dazzling Prince Charming ... The only son of Franz Josef and Elisabeth, he had inherited too much of his mother's melancholic nature and too little of his father's solidity.

His ideas found some expression, though no action, in his friendship with Moritz Szeps, a journalist who edited a radical newspaper, the Vienna *Morgenpost* (Morning Post). Rudolph contributed several articles to the *Morgenpost* anonymously. Szeps, naturally enough, regarded the Crown Prince as a great 'catch' for the liberal cause. So did a maverick within the royal family, Rudolph's cousin Archduke John Salvator of Tuscany. John Salvator's radical opinions went way beyond Rudolph's, to the point where he believed it valid for a man to strip himself of his titles, cast aside his privileges and live a commoner's life with a wife of his own free choice.

Right: The Emperor Franz Josef I of Austria-Hungary had absolute power over his subjects and expected his heir, Rudolf, to continue in the same way.

This, in fact, is precisely what John Salvator did after Rudolph's death. By 1888, he had already found the wife he wanted – a middle-class girl called Milli Stubel, who would never be acceptable to the royal family had he tried to make her an archduchess. John Salvator also proved bold enough to openly criticize the Emperor, his government and the Austrian army, for which Franz Josef had him banned from court. Banishment also served to break up the close friendship between Rudolph and John Salvator, who not surprisingly was considered a disruptive influence on the young prince.

Rudolph nevertheless contrived to see his cousin in secret, and discuss with him the ideas of the major liberal thinkers of the day. These encounters were a kind of sub-life in which Rudolph could give some rein to his deeply held political beliefs. All the same, it saddened him that they had to be clandestine and also that they possessed, of necessity, an element of self-interest. For the archduke, as for Moritz Szeps, the heir to the Austro-Hungarian throne could not be merely a fellow spirit, but a means to their own reforming ends.

IMPOSITION OF CONTROL

John Salvator certainly looked forward to a major role in affairs as and when Rudolph eventually became emperor, and Szeps had no hope of making radicalism reality without the support of a man in high places. Even so, as would-be liberals remaking a world of despots in a democratic image, Rudolph, John Salvator and Szeps all faced a monumental obstacle: the throne which Rudolph stood to inherit was ancient, well founded and extremely powerful. Led by Franz Josef, royal rule in Austria-Hungary was in the hands of men of repressive temperament. Their notion of government was the brutal suppression of all unrest and control by force and fear. To such men, liberals were a cancerous growth eating away at absolute royal authority. The emperor was nevertheless very conscious of how far apart he and Rudolph were, and for the sake of family peace the two of them never discussed politics.

Crown Princess Stephanie of Belgium, daughter of the Belgian King Leopold II, married Crown Prince Rudolf in 1881 after he bowed to family pressure to do his duty and take a wife.

Even so, Franz Josef believed that he could control his recalcitrant heir. He denied Rudolph a part in affairs of state, on the premise that where he had no knowledge, he had no influence. He also sought to shackle Rudolph domestically by finding him a 'suitable' wife, in this case the charmless but respectable Princess Stephanie, daughter of King Leopold II of Belgium. The wedding took place in 1881.

The fact that the marriage soon proved unhappy was not of great concern. A married Crown Prince who dabbled in superficial affairs on the side – as he was almost expected to do – was far less susceptible to outside influences than an unwed heir able to 'play the field'. Without a wife, Rudolph would also have fitted less conveniently into the social requirements of the imperial court, which was stiff with protocol, insistent on strict precedence and marked by that slavish deference so dear to the arrogant hearts of central European monarchs.

Anyone unable to prove a noble genealogy going back at least four generations was not permitted to attend at court, which largely accounted for its stuffy atmosphere. The haughty Princess Stephanie was, in fact, far better suited to such an environment than her husband. Rudolph found it choking, but he performed well enough and when in court circles could not be faulted on manners or protocol. The emperor naturally looked to his son to provide more male heirs to the imperial throne and, although the first child of Rudolph and Stephanie, born in 1883, was a daughter, it was expected that sons would follow and so cement the power of the Hapsburg royal family. In the event, no son was ever born, for it was doubtful that marital relations between the Crown Prince and his wife were very frequent after 1883 – if, that is, they existed at all.

This was hardly surprising when Stephanie was irascible, moody, jealous and disruptive, and pursued her husband with perpetual demands.

Stephanie and Rudolf were incompatible. The haughty, moody and demanding Stephanie could neither understand nor deal with Rudolf's melancholic nature.

> The first child of Rudolph and Stephanie, born in 1883, was a daughter, it was expected that sons would follow and so cement the power of the Hapsburg royal family.

Stephanie grated particularly during Rudolph's periodic moods of depression, which were the fruit of his frustrations and his conviction that he was wasting himself in a hollow world that had no future, and certainly no liberal future. Like his mother, Elisabeth, he was plagued by a deep streak of melancholy and, when the mood was on him, a fearful sense of self-loathing. Stephanie was far too dense and unimaginative to

understand what the problem was, and the rift occasioned by Rudolph's moods and her bad temper soon became permanent.

CRACKS IN THE FAÇADE

The diligent gossips of Vienna quickly realized that the royal pair were chronically ill suited and saw clear evidence of the mismatch in Rudolph's frequent absences from the Austrian capital. They were far more frequent than his ceremonial duties or his obligations as an army officer required, and the rumour mongers were certain that, while Rudolph may not have had a girl in every port, his amours were plentiful in the provinces.

> It was understood that in royal circles, whatever went on behind the scenes, an impeccable front had to be maintained ... Stephanie had shattered that front and revealed a scandal: this made her more culpable than her errant husband.

Unfortunately, Stephanie was just as certain and, unlike many royal wives of the time, did not have the tact to turn a blind eye to her husband's dalliances. She failed to realize, too, how little she had to worry about at this stage, for Rudolph's liaisons were usually short-lived and were more in the nature of brief snatches at oblivion than any quest for a serious relationship. This led her to create ructions at court in the autumn of 1888, when she made a public scene outside the house in Vienna where her husband was visiting the pretty Polish Countess Czewucka. The countess was little more than the latest fashionable flirt – she had scores of admirers – but Stephanie's action spilled a lot of beans. It was understood that in royal circles, whatever went on behind the scenes, an impeccable front had to be maintained. However hypocritical this attitude, Stephanie had shattered that front and revealed a scandal: in the ethos of the time, this made her more culpable than her errant husband.

The infuriated Franz Josef attempted to keep the scandal under wraps, but it soon leapt the bounds of

Right: Maria Vetsera was infatuated with Rudolf long before she even met him and became his mistress. She fantasized about him, seeing him not just as 'Prince Charming' but the epitome of chivalry and all the noble virtues.

court circles and became common talk in Vienna and beyond. A public display of unity was urgently required. This took place shortly afterwards, when Rudolph and Stephanie, both on their very best behaviour, attended a gala ball. The entire aristocracy of Vienna was there to see the royal 'face' restored and the occasion, richly dressed, lavishly victualled, was the sort of dazzling affair the Viennese accepted as a usual part of their social scene.

This was, after all, waltz-time Vienna, a city of legendary gaiety, with the lilting music of the Strauss family providing its theme tunes. When his mood switched away from depression and self-torture, Rudolph was very much part of this pleasure-loving world. His other, sunnier side was gregarious. He greatly enjoyed the theatre, social gatherings, salons, race meetings, concerts or riding in the Prater, the leisure complex of Vienna where the well-heeled paraded for the purpose of seeing and being seen.

A GIRLISH INFATUATION

To catch a glimpse of the Crown Prince or, better still, to be acknowledged by him was the hope of every socially ambitious Viennese. A large number of them went to the Prater for this purpose alone. One of them was the 16-year-old Baroness Maria Vetsera, daughter of a minor Hungarian nobleman. As 16-year-olds will, Maria had developed a strong 'crush' on Rudolph after seeing him at the races in Vienna in April of 1888. Rudolph, for his part, was sufficiently struck by Maria's beauty to stare at her for several seconds.

This was quite enough to send the impressionable young girl into a tizzy of adoration. Maria had numerous admirers and usually created avid male interest, but from that moment on she could think of no one but the Crown Prince. To her, he was a shining knight endowed with all the chivalrous virtues, and an ideal man pluperfect in every possible way.

At this early stage, admiration from afar was all Maria wanted of the prince. Like any ardent 'fan', she quizzed her friends for titbits of news about him, following his movements in the court circular and nagging her mother into taking her to the theatre or

opera driving in the Prater, all in hopes of fuelling her passion with a glimpse of her idol.

Maria knew that she could never entertain hopes of being formally introduced to Rudolph. She could not boast the lustrous ancestry that would have allowed her to be presented at court, although her mother was acquainted with both the emperor and the empress. The 'chance encounter' was a far surer bet and, in time, Maria's persistence paid off. Early in May 1888, a gala performance of William Shakespeare's *Hamlet* took place at Vienna's Burg Theatre, and Maria discovered the Crown Prince was going to be there. Maria persuaded her mother to accompany her – girls of Maria's class were not allowed out without a chaperone – and there, in the first interval of the play, she came face to face with her idol for the first time.

Rudolph's glance was openly admiring, and with it went a smile that made Maria blush furiously. Embarrassed, she fled to a small room nearby. Later

Crown Prince Rudolf (left) riding in an open carriage, covered up against the winter cold by a blanket.

the same evening, Maria caught the prince's eye again. A few days later, while prowling the Prater in her mother's carriage, she saw him once more. As he rode past, he looked at her with evident interest and, on the return journey home, he rode past again and scrutinized her a second time.

Maria was now hopelessly in love with Rudolph, but she had no axe to grind as far as he was concerned. All she wanted was the chance to adore her prince and dream delightful hours away thinking about him. Though he did not yet know it, Rudolph had encountered the one and only person who sought nothing from him but the pleasure of his company. Maria mooned several months away in this ingenuous fashion until, in September 1888, the chance of closer acquaintance came along.

ROMANCE FURTHERED
One morning, Maria's mother returned home from shopping with a friend, Countess Larisch, who was Rudolph's first cousin. The countess, of course, had

Left: Crown Prince Rudolph dressed in military uniform, with decorations. Generally, artists who painted royal personages glorified them, but in this picture Rudolf appeared like his true self — anxious, nervous and unhappy.

known the Crown Prince since childhood, and Maria lost no time pumping the visitor for details about him. Larisch, an astute woman of about 40 years old, did not taken long to realize the depth of Maria's ardour and took an early opportunity to let Rudolph know of his unknowing conquest.

Rudolph, intrigued, wanted to know the name of his admirer and, on being told, at once recalled the delectable teenager with the dark hair and ice-blue eyes who had caught his attention earlier in the season. Maria was almost delirious with joy when the countess afterwards brought her Rudolph's message of regard. Even so, she seems to have entertained no thought as yet of the next step: an actual meeting with the prince. Instead, Maria returned to her previous strategy of the 'chance encounter'.

> Riding in the Prater, he not only noticed her, but also gave her a small but unmistakable bow.

When the encounter occurred, however, Rudolph proved to be more forthcoming than Maria had ever dared hope. Riding in the Prater, he not only noticed her, but also gave her a small but unmistakable bow. A few days later, on 21 October, a letter reached Maria which said all she had ever dreamt of, and more. In it, Rudolph invited her to meet him in the Prater next day. He had admired her for so long, he wrote, that now the time had come to make her acquaintance.

Maria's reply told the Crown Prince a great deal more than it actually said. She could not come to the Prater, she told him, because she had no chaperone. This, to Rudolph, was something quite new. He was accustomed to sophisticated women whose approaches were blatant and who were far less concerned with him than with the status they would gain from knowing him. Yet here was a girl with such a virginal sense of propriety that she would meet the heir to the throne only if she were accompanied. It was refreshing, even startling, and it came at a time when Rudolph badly needed just this sort of distraction.

Recently, the Crown Prince had received some very disturbing news. His cousin John Salvator was not content merely to talk over liberal principles. He was planning nothing less than revolution, and the overthrow of Rudolph's father. John had even enlisted support in the Austrian army for his coup. Rudolph, who counted loyalty to his father's position as his priority, never mind their political differences, was both horrified and saddened. Talk of revolution had lost him his only friend, for John Salvator had been the one person to whom he could talk frankly. Now Rudolf began to doubt the strength of his beliefs. He could not contemplate treason against his father, and if he was content only to talk, not act, his ideals, he felt, must be very shallow.

PRESCRIPTION FOR LOVE

Imperial spies were everywhere, and fear that they might discover John Salvator's plans and that he might be implicated were Rudolph's next depressing thoughts. He was, in any case, beginning to feel the strain of spending most of his time with reactionary oafs at court and dealing with the tedious trivia of the vast bureaucracy that was the Austro-Hungarian Empire. The strain showed. The emperor had grown sufficiently alarmed at his son's pale face and gaunt appearance to have him examined by the imperial physician. He diagnosed what might today be called 'executive stress' and advised Rudolph to relax and rest. Rudolph's commitments made that impossible, but the young, innocent and even childlike Maria Vetsera could prove to be the next best thing.

As soon as he received Maria's reply, Rudolph wrote to Countess Larisch, demanding that she return to Vienna forthwith and introduce him to Maria. Larisch hastened back to the capital and soon performed the task for which she had been summoned. Chaperoned by the countess, Maria Vetsera came to the Hofburg, the imperial palace in Vienna, to come face to face with her hero. Both of them, it seems, found what they wanted in each other.

To Maria's starry-eyed gaze, the prince was more handsome and more courteous than even she had imagined. As for Rudolph, Maria was a beautiful delight and her extreme youth, obvious sincerity and modest charm were a wonder. Best of all, she was quite untarnished either by the sordid political world Rudolph was forced to inhabit or by the tedious social round that had, until now, been his only alternative. Susceptible as he was at the time, the disillusioned, world-weary

> ... the disillusioned, world-weary Rudolph fell madly in love and was soon planning to divorce his sour-tempered wife and marry Maria.

Rudolph fell madly in love and was soon planning to divorce his sour-tempered wife and marry Maria. Rudolph was well aware that he and Maria were being followed by palace agents whenever they met and, although he realized that this meant the liaison would soon reach the emperor's ears, he had become reckless enough not to care. All he cared about was Maria and the fact that he could not live without her.

Rudolph and Maria Vetsera became lovers on 13 January 1889, and the Prince was so wrapped up in this, his first serious affair, that he gave Maria a ring inscribed with the date to commemorate the event. A sharp jolt back to reality was soon forthcoming. By 26 January, the emperor had in his possession a letter from Pope Leo XIII which revealed that Rudolph had written directly to the pontiff, asking him to permit the dissolution of his marriage to Stephanie. Such direct contact was a breach of protocol and told Franz Josef that the liaison with Maria that had prompted the request was going to be a serious problem. A divorce from Stephanie was out of the question, no matter how unhappy the marriage was. The stability of the Austro-Hungarian Empire, which relied on a united royal family, would not permit it.

NO WAY OUT

It was then that Rudolph realized just how much he was in his father's power and how little courage he

The royal hunting lodge at Mayerling, where Rudolf and Maria Vetsera committed suicide, was set in an idyllic environment in the countryside around Vienna.

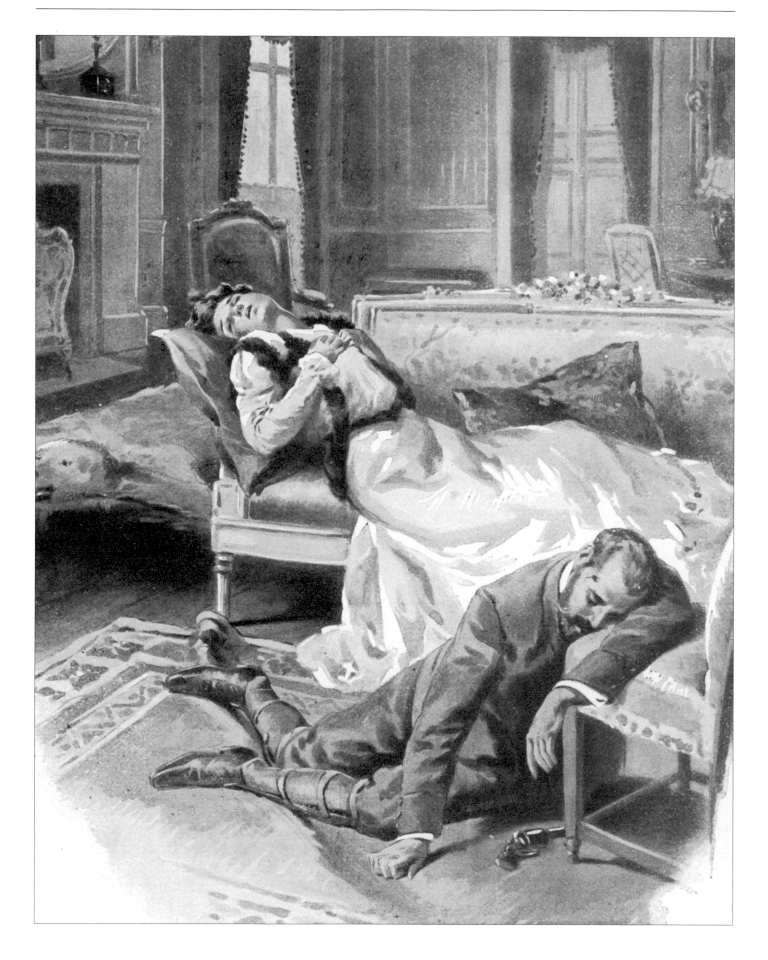

A dramatized illustration of the scene at Mayerling when the bodies of Rudolf and Maria Vetsera were discovered. Rudolf, in fact, was found dead in bed not draped over a chair.

possessed to resist him. Franz Josef summoned his son to appear before him, and demanded a promise that Rudolph would send Maria away. Thoroughly dejected, the Crown Prince complied, asking only that he might see her just once more. Having got what he wanted, the emperor agreed, little realising how shamed and hopeless his son felt as he left his presence.

SUICIDE PACT

Two days later, Crown Prince Rudolph left Vienna for Mayerling, ostensibly for some mid-winter hunting in the surrounding forest. Maria Vetsera was with him. On the afternoon of 29 January, the two of them took a long walk in the forest and there, it seems, Rudolph proposed a suicide pact. To him, it was the only way out of what he saw as his meaningless life.

The besotted Maria agreed. Most likely, she had no realistic concept of death, and doubtless thought only

> It was then that Rudolph realized just how much he was in his father's power and how little courage he possessed to resist him.

of herself and Rudolph mysteriously united in perpetuity beyond the grave. That night, both of them wrote letters to their mothers. Rudolph asked Empress Elisabeth to see that he and Maria were buried together in a small nearby cemetery at Alland. The request was never granted.

That done, Rudolph bolted the door of the bedroom from the inside. Some time around dawn, when Maria was asleep, he fetched his revolver from a drawer and shot her behind the left ear. The range was point-blank.

The body of Crown Prince Rudolph lies in state, partly disguised by a bandage over his head to hide the incisions made during an autopsy.

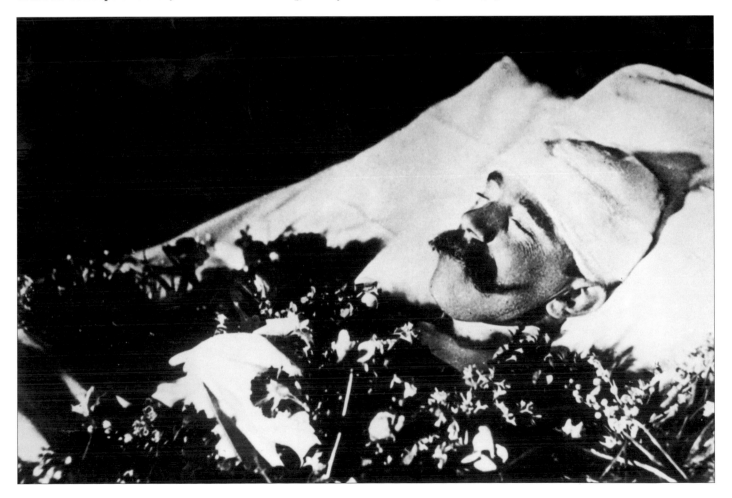

Above: Maria Vetsera was buried in the graveyard at Heiligenkreus in Lower Austria even though Rudolf had requested that they should be interred together.

Suicide was regarded as a sin in the eyes of the Catholic Church. Consequently, a big cover-up was attempted to conceal the circumstances of Rudolf's death.

She died instantly. Rudolph's manservant Loschek heard the noise. He leapt out of bed and rushed along the hallway to his master's room. The second shot rang out as he arrived, too late, outside the door.

VATICAN COVER-UP

In the nineteenth century, suicide was regarded as a sin in the eyes of the Catholic Church. Consequently, a big cover-up was attempted to conceal the circumstances of Rudolf's death. Heart failure was the first official explanation, then a story was disseminated that he had been killed by conservative elements fearful of his liberal influence. Next, the Vatican issued a statement that Rudolph had been mentally unbalanced when he died. No one was really convinced and, eventually, the truth had to be admitted: Crown Prince Rudolf and Maria Vetsera had died in a suicide pact.

This, though, was not allowed to be the end of the story. Conspiracy theories had already sprung up and were proliferating even before the truth about the deaths of Rudolf and Maria Vetsera was reluctantly announced. Conspiracy theories never die and no official announcement, whether cover-up or truth, had the slightest effect on any of the many explanations surrounding the hunting lodge at Mayerling and the tragic events that happened there.

The funeral of Crown Prince Rudolf took place in Vienna, where he was buried in the vaults set aside for the royal family beneath the Capuchin Church.

EMPEROR MAXIMILIAN OF MEXICO

The Archduke Maximilian, younger brother of Emperor Franz Josef of Austria-Hungary (1832–1867), was the 'fall guy' in a scheme hatched in 1863 by the French Emperor Napoleon III. The idea was for Maximilian to retrieve money owed to France by the Mexican government. Napoleon's allies in Mexico, the Catholic Church and a group of wealthy landowners, had also been dispossessed of their land, cash and privileges by the liberal President of Mexico, Benito Juarez. They, too, wanted their money back. With the reluctant assent of Franz Josef, the landowners offered Maximilian the Mexican throne. He accepted. So far, so good – but there was a problem. Maximilian was a naive, starry-eyed idealist with a head full of utopian notions about banishing the poverty, squalor and disease that disfigured life for millions of disadvantaged people in Mexico and around the world.

HIGH-MINDED WIMP

Maximilian arrived in his 'empire' in 1864, accompanied by a substantial force of French troops and his wife Charlotte, daughter of the Belgian King Leopold I. Charlotte, too, had her head in the clouds. To her, Maximilian was an angel, whose destiny it was to serve and uplift humanity. But for his sponsors, Napoleon III and Franz Josef, Maximilian was a high-minded wimp who caused trouble from the start. He refused to restore Church property and privileges on the grounds that the Church belonged to the people. For the same reasons, Maximilian declined to let the landowners take back their lost estates and haciendas.

Next, Maximilian proceeded with utopian schemes such as a national theatre for Mexico and the creation of a world navy. He took to walking through the streets of Mexico City with minimal escort, engaging in friendly conversation with passers-by. He was so

Maximilian, the utopian younger brother of Emperor Franz Josef of Austria-Hungary.

obviously genuine that even Benito Juarez and his supporters found it hard to dislike him.

This did not mean that Juarez approved of Maximilian's assumption of power. Typically, on learning of Juarez's hostility, Maximilian invited him to Mexico City, thinking to offer the Mexican leader a place in his government. Juarez, of course, refused. Mayhem followed. Motley groups of bandits, some of them Juarez partisans, made the night and the roads dangerous. Juarez and his forces were still at large, awaiting their chance to fight and defeat the foreign intruders. The Americans then stepped in with demands that the French leave Mexico and take Maximilian with them. Maximilian refused at first, but as American pressure increased, he began to waver.

Charlotte refused to hear of giving up and sailed for Europe to seek help. She arrived in August 1866, but

soon discovered that nobody wanted to know. Napoleon III was facing fresh pressures from a rampant Germany on France's eastern frontier, and needed his troops at home. He was willing to abandon Maximilian in order to do so. Never very stable, Charlotte's mind gave way as fear, failure and stress finally snapped her sanity. When Maximilian learned of her condition, his first thought was to be with her. His second was to remain in Mexico, where, he believed, deserting his subjects would be cowardly and dishonourable. The same applied to abdication, which his brother urged on him.

HONOURABLE MARTYRDOM

By January 1867, French troops had withdrawn from Mexico and the armies of Benito Juarez were sweeping towards Mexico City. Maximilian still refused to cut and run. The most he would do was leave for Queretaro, northwest of Mexico City. He was still there when the Juarist forces arrived and captured him. Loath to execute him because he was so disconcertingly noble, the Mexicans tried persuading him to escape. Yet again, Maximilian refused. He seemed intent on martyrdom as the only honourable way out. All the Mexicans could do was to oblige.

On 19 June 1867, Maximilian was marched out of Queretaro to the nearby Hill of Bells. A firing squad awaited him. Taking a deep breath of the ice-fresh mountain air, Maximilian declared: 'What a glorious day! I have always wanted to die on such a day.' Seconds later, he was dead.

The news took 10 days to reach Europe. Nine months passed before her family dared tell Charlotte what had happened. She survived her husband by 40 years, which she spent mumbling to herself and gazing at pictures of Maximilian or smashing anything breakable and ripping up carpets, curtains and upholstery in violent fury. She died, still hopelessly insane, in 1927.

The French artist Edouard Manet produced four paintings and one lithograph depicting Maximilian's execution by firing squad which took place on 19 June 1867.

VII

MADNESS IN THE SPANISH ROYAL FAMILY

The madness of Queen Juana I of Castile (1479–1555) took many forms. Sometimes she crouched on the floor of her cell, unmoving. At other times, she backed into a corner, wild-eyed, as if trying to melt through the walls to escape the demons only she could see. She refused to eat if anyone were there to witness it. Instead, her food had to be left outside her door. She then darted out, snatched up the plate and retreated back to her cell. When she had finished, she carefully hid the plate under the bed, or flung it against the wall, laughing madly.

◆

Juana owed her frightening state of mind to her grandmother Isabel of Portugal, who introduced insanity into the Spanish royal family after 1447, when she became the second wife of King John II of Castile in north-central Spain. Her naturally melancholic

Left: Juana succeeded to her mother's throne after the deaths of her brother, Juan, and sister, Isabella.
Above: Queen Juana was the first victim of the madness introduced into the Spanish royal family by her grandmother.

disposition was exacerbated by the birth, in 1451, of her daughter Isabella, the future Queen of Castile. Afterwards, Isabel of Portugal shut herself away, sitting and staring into the distance for hours on end. Later, she progressed to hysterical tantrums and, in 1452, her daughter was taken from her and sent to be cared for by nuns at a convent in Avila. Isabel had already been deteriorating for some time. Her melancholia turned to full-scale insanity and, before long, she was unable to recognize anyone. She did not even know who she was.

In 1520, by the time Isabel's granddaughter Juana reached this same irretrievable depth of insanity, she had long been queen in name only. The real ruler of Spain and its gold- and silver-rich empire was Juana's son, Charles. Born in 1479, Juana was the third child of Queen Isabella I of Castile and King Ferdinand V of Aragon, and became her parents' heir after her elder sister, another Isabella, died in childbirth in 1498. Juana seemed ideal for her exalted position. She was a bright, attractive child, adept at languages. Like all proud parents, Ferdinand and Isabella showed her off

Isabel of Portugal, the melancholy and eventually mad consort of King John II of Castile, blighted several generations of Spanish royals who inherited her insanity.

> Juana ... was a bright, attractive child, adept at languages ... she conversed in fluent Latin with clerics and performed with skill on the clavichord and guitar. But her outward gifts covered mercurial moods and an urge for solitude.

at court, where she conversed in fluent Latin with clerics and performed with skill on the clavichord and guitar. But her outward gifts covered mercurial moods and an urge for solitude. One moment she was calm and dignified; the next, excitable.

AN ARRANGED MARRIAGE

Like most European princesses, Juana was headed for an arranged marriage. The young man picked for her by her parents – Philip, Count of Flanders, Duke of Burgundy and heir to his father, Maximilian of Austria, the Holy Roman Emperor – possessed the most dazzling prospects of any prince in Europe. Later on, Philip proved to be a disastrous choice, but that lay far in the future when the couple were betrothed in 1489: Philip was 11 years old at the time; Juana barely 10. A proxy wedding took place in 1496 and Juana, now aged 16, left for Flanders, accompanied by a magnificent fleet of ships numbering, it was said, up to 130 vessels. After a difficult, stormy journey, Juana disembarked in Flanders suffering from seasickness and a severe cold.

At least, though, the greeting she received was warm-hearted and Juana's entry into Antwerp was a triumph. Clad in shining cloth of gold, she rode through streets decorated with floral arches and reverberating with the greetings and singing of the crowds. A month later, on 19 October 1496,

Right: This illustration from Queen Juana's prayer book shows her (centre) with her parents, King Ferdinand of Aragon (left) and Queen Isabella of Castile (right).

Los altos Reyes don fernado y dona
ysabel y la   Real ifata
doña   Juana

Juana's husband, Philip the Handsome and Philip I of Spain, was a disaster for the Spanish royal family as he manipulated his insane wife for his own purposes.

> Philip ... was 18 years old, golden-haired and marvellously handsome. Juana took in the sturdy physique, the shapely legs and Philip's air of boyish zest and fell in love at once.

Juana and her entourage reached Lierre, now in Belgium, where she met Philip for the first time. The effect they had on each other was electrifying. Juana had never seen him before, but her first sight of Philip confirmed all the exciting stories she had heard about him. He was 18 years old, golden-haired and marvellously handsome. Juana took in the sturdy physique, the shapely legs and Philip's air of boyish zest and fell in love at once. But it was more than just love. It was lust at first sight, and it was mutual.

BLIND INFATUATION

There were tedious official ceremonies to be performed, worthies to be greeted and nobles presented. But as soon as these chores were over, Juana and Philip buttonholed the nearest cleric, the Dean of Jaen, and ordered him to take their proxy marriage one step further and wed them then and there. The hasty ceremony had hardly finished before the couple vanished into one of the hotel rooms, flung off their clothes and made passionate love. Next day, a solemn church wedding officially completed the union that had already been so hotly consummated.

Juana was totally infatuated with Philip, and the spell never wore off. She went through the celebrations in honour of the wedding, which included a full-scale tournament, in a daze of desire for the beautiful creature whom the lottery of royal marriage had so unexpectedly dealt her. Philip appeared, at first, to be caught by the same hunger. What all this concealed, though, was that Philip and Juana were complete opposites. For Philip, the attraction was carnal, little more. Juana, however, wanted total possession – no mistresses, no separate lives, only absolute togetherness. She was too young and too completely consumed by the blaze of her ardour for Philip to realize that he could never give her what she wanted.

Long before he met Juana, Philip of Flanders had become accustomed to igniting nubile young women and already had at least one illegitimate child to prove it. Flemish society was intensely hedonistic and encouraged promiscuity. Almost every pleasure of the flesh was condoned. Extramarital affairs were common, and the registry of births overflowed with bastards. In this environment, not surprisingly, Philip saw no reason why his free-ranging way of life should be interrupted by marriage or why his personal advancement should be curtailed.

RISING AMBITION

In 1498, Philip affronted his Spanish in-laws with an impudent bid for the Crown of Spain. He declared himself next in line to the thrones of Castile and Aragon. The claim had no legal foundation. Ferdinand

A portrait of King Ferdinand II of Aragon, Juana's father, by the painter known as the Master of the Legend of St Madeleine. Like his son-in-law Philip, Ferdinand exploited Juana for his own ends.

Philip the Handsome was the son of the Holy Roman Emperor Maximilian I and Mary of Burgundy.

It was not only Philip's crass claim to the throne that disturbed his parents-in-law. Less than two years after their marriage, Philip's love affairs were tormenting Juana with jealousy and began to corrode her personality as fixation wavered from passion to hate. Juana was so totally obsessed by her husband that she was unaware of important realities. France, for example, was Spain's great rival for supremacy in Europe. Yet Philip, the consort of the future Spanish queen, was a francophile, fed for years by the Flemish Council with pro-French propaganda. Philip, for all his glamour, was

A view of Zaragoza, capital of the Kingdom of Aragon between the twelfth and fifteenth centuries, with the tower of the Church of St Magdalena (foreground) and the four towers of the Cathedral-Basilica del Nuestra Señora del Pilar (background).

and Isabella, appalled at Philip's rampant ambition, sidestepped him in 1499, by persuading the Cortes, the national legislative assembly of Spain, to confirm their grandson Miguel, the late Isabella's five-month-old son, as heir to their thrones. This, of course, superseded both Juana and Philip.

Philip was not thwarted for long. In 1500, little Miguel died and Juana was again named as her parents' heir. Now the law was on Philip's side, for the husband of a Queen Regnant could claim her title as his own, at least in her lifetime. Already, Philip had begun to found a new royal family. Juana gave birth to their first child, Elinor, in 1498, their second, Charles in 1500 and three more by 1505.

> The law was on Philip's side, for the husband of a Queen Regnant could claim her title as his own, at least in her lifetime.

Philip's love affairs were tormenting Juana with jealousy and began to corrode her personality as fixation wavered from passion to hate.

easily manipulated and made the perfect sponge to absorb these damaging political ideas.

As heir to the throne, it was vital that Juana wake up to the truth. The one man who could make her face facts was Juan de Fonseca, Bishop of Cordova, a long-time family friend who majored in tact and diplomacy. When he reached Brussels, Fonseca found Juana deeply depressed, prone to nervous fainting fits, isolated from court life and hedged in by spies. In this state, Juana was susceptible, and by the time Fonseca had finished with her she at last understood the pro-French and anti-Spanish nature of the Flemings and how they had influenced and moulded Philip to their ways.

MELANCHOLY ZARAGOZA

Philip, who left Flanders with Juana for a visit to Spain in 1501, hated his wife's homeland and the melancholy pall that hung over it. He detested the moralistic spartan atmosphere and the

Queen Isabella I of Castile was a reigning monarch in her own right. When she died in 1504, her throne passed to her daughter, Juana, and her husband, Ferdinand of Aragon, ceased to be consort.

sight of religious fanatics crying out for remission of sins while flagellating themselves until the blood ran. The summer heat of Spain blazed like a furnace, raising clouds of shimmering dust that made it difficult to breathe. There was too little green, unlike Flanders – only stern mountains and half-desert terrain. Even the royal court was severe in tone. Philip came gaudily dressed in satin brocade, violet velvet and cloth of gold to meet his parents-in-law, while Ferdinand and Isabella sat like monk and nun in plain dark robes.

The official business of the visit to Spain was to persuade the Cortes of Aragon to recognize Juana and Philip as the official heirs of Ferdinand and Isabella. This proved difficult. Philip lapsed into a foul, sulking mood as the Cortes procrastinated, then made unpalatable conditions. Philip could be Consort only so long as Juana lived and, if her mother died and Ferdinand remarried, any son of this second union would supersede Philip. Philip might just have swallowed that one, but what he could not take was the next subject debated by the Cortes: raising funds for war with his beloved France. At that, Philip wanted nothing more to do with the Cortes or Spain, and told Ferdinand and Isabella that he and Juana, who was pregnant again, were going home to Flanders. His excuse was that he had been too long away from his northern realm.

THE SITUATION WORSENS

Adopting every persuasion they knew, Ferdinand and Isabella tried to make Philip change his mind. Their most cogent reason against Philip's decision was Juana's pregnancy, which would make a long and difficult journey in midwinter potentially dangerous for her and her unborn child. Isabella

> Adopting every persuasion they knew, Ferdinand and Isabella tried to make Philip change his mind.

was gambling on Philip's love and concern for his wife, but she miscalculated. Philip was perfectly prepared to leave Juana behind in Spain and go home alone. Juana became hysterical when she learned of her husband's intentions, but no dramatics, no tears, no wailing, no begging – in fact, nothing – could make Philip set aside his plans. Philip left Spain on 19 December 1503. It took him more than a year to poodle his way through France, Switzerland, Bavaria and Savoy before he finally reached Brussels and home.

King Ferdinand II became king of Aragon in 1469, ten years after he married Isabella of Castile. On their marriage, Ferdinand became his wife's consort in Castile and she became his consort in Aragon.

Meanwhile in Spain, Juana lapsed into brooding silences as she contemplated how Philip had abandoned her. After the birth of her fourth child, Ferdinand, in early 1503, 15 months after Philip departed, she grew more frenzied. She cursed the clerics sent to calm her, flayed the servants with her fury, insulted her mother with language so foul that even the urbane Isabella was shocked. Juan de Fonseca came to the royal castle of La Mota, where Juana was staying, and tried to calm her down. But she threatened him with death or torture for foiling her attempts to leave Spain and return to Philip.

> Philip ... had taken a new mistress. Juana went wild, searched out a pair of scissors and, seizing the woman by the hair, proceeded to scalp her.

Fonseca retreated, horrified, but Juana came after him and he only just escaped before the castle gate closed behind him. Juana flung herself against the iron bars, yelling and screaming until exhaustion overtook her and she slid to the ground. There she remained all the freezing night long, apparently comatose. Eventually, Ferdinand and Isabella realized that Juana's sexual frenzy could be quenched only when she lay with Philip once again. They had to let her go.

EXCHANGE OF INSULTS

Juana returned to Philip in April 1504, but their reunion did nothing to restore her senses. Philip had seen to that. He had taken a new mistress. Juana went wild, searched out a pair of scissors and, seizing the woman by the hair, proceeded to scalp her. The 'mistress' fled, bleeding and almost bald. Philip arrived. After exchanging insults with Juana, he hit her about the face. Even Juana was pulled up short by that. She subsided, retiring to bed for several days.

But she did not remain quiescent for long. Juana's retinue included a number of Moorish slaves, who had accompanied her when she first went to Flanders in 1496. These slaves seemed like devils with their dark, fierce faces scored by ritual marks and their skill with love potions and seductive perfumes. Philip decided to get rid of them. Juana refused to let them leave, but Philip threw them out anyway. A savage argument ensued with Juana's full battery of insults and curses deployed. Philip, who was no slouch with swearwords, fought back in kind. In protest, Juana went on hunger strike. He let her starve and ignored her pleas when she began hammering on the floor of her bedroom, which was situated above his. After a while, Juana graduated to pounding the floor with a rock, then set about it with a knife. The assault lasted all night and next morning, when Philip finally came up to confront her, he found her exhausted but still defiant.

INCREASING ISOLATION

This was war and Juana's mother knew all about it as, herself worn out, she lay near death at the castle of La Mota, Queen Isabella died in late 1504, leaving behind a potentially disastrous situation. Juana was now Queen of Castile but, by her mother's express wish, Ferdinand was to be her regent. He would remain so if Juana turned out to be unable or unwilling to rule. Ferdinand did better than that. He made sure that his daughter would indeed prove unable because of her mental and emotional instability. That, of course, did away with Philip's chance to be king in Spain.

Philip, for his part, also wanted Juana out of the way so that he could claim the throne for himself. Juana's father and husband were, in effect, conspiring against her, each for his own nefarious reasons, and it was just a matter of time before one or other of them triumphed in the race to disinherit her. Philip struck first by forcing Juana, possibly by physical violence, to write a letter informing her father that she was coming to Spain with Philip to assume power in Castile. That done, Philip imprisoned her within the royal palace in Brussels and kept from her anyone who could report her plight to Ferdinand. Twelve soldiers guarded Juana's apartments day and night, and even her chaplain was not allowed to speak with her, except to say mass. Having neutralized Juana, Philip looked round for allies opposed to Ferdinand. He concluded treaties with the French king Louis XII and his own father, Maximilian of Austria, in which

Ferdinand and Isabella met Christopher Columbus (left) in 1486. Columbus visited several royal courts, seeking sponsorship for his transatlantic voyage to America. Ultimately, Isabella agreed to finance Columbus, whose initial voyage took place in 1492.

all three signatories vowed to prevent Ferdinand ruling in Castile.

Ferdinand was outmaneuvered, but there was one recourse left: remarriage, which might provide new sons to challenge Philip. In a move that also undercut Philip's new alliances, Ferdinand went to France, his old enemy, for his second bride and, in October 1505, his proxy wedding to Germaine, the French king's niece, was solemnized. Now it was Philip's turn to be outmaneuvered and this time, to his dismay, Juana refused to play his game. She declined publicly to condemn her father's second marriage, as Philip demanded. Slowly, as Philip and Ferdinand parried for control, the situation was moving towards civil war. It appeared imminent when Philip tired of long-distance sparring. Early in 1506, he embarked an army and, with Juana also on board, set sail for Spain. In response, Ferdinand called out the Aragonese militia and the artillery batteries at Medina del

A portrait of Maximilian I, Queen Juana's father-in-law, who was known as Archduke Maximilian of Austria before his election as Holy Roman Emperor in 1493.

> Juana declined publicly to condemn her father's second marriage, as Philip demanded. Slowly, as Philip and Ferdinand parried for control, the situation was moving towards civil war.

Campo to await what most presumed would be a Flemish invasion.

GUILE AND MACHINATIONS

When Philip's fleet docked at Coruña in the northwestern corner of Spain, Ferdinand realized that his forces were greatly outnumbered and outgunned. He resorted to what he knew best: guile. Before long, news reached Philip that troop movements were under way in Andalucia to the south and Léon in the northwest, and that Ferdinand's army was slowly approaching his own. Any day now, Philip would be encircled. By 19 June 1506, Ferdinand's troops were only 10 kilometres away. The trap seemed about to close around Philip, but there was no fighting. Philip lost his nerve and agreed to negotiate with his father-in-law.

The result of their meeting was a pair of treaties, the first containing an agreement that Ferdinand would withdraw his troops from Castile. The second was a secret arrangement whereby Juana would never be permitted to rule. The ink on his signatures was barely dry before Ferdinand reneged and declared that he had agreed to the treaties under duress and that Juana was the rightful monarch of Castile after all.

Meanwhile, Philip thought he had won. Unaware of the old fox's reputation for cunning, Philip proceeded with plans to park Juana out of the way. But Juana was no longer easy prey. She had come to suspect that anything Philip said or did was in her worst interests and, besides, she very much wanted to be reconciled with her father, whom she adored. To accomplish this, she needed to escape. Her first two attempts failed, but

Juana the Mad was obsessed with her husband, Philip the Handsome, and consummated her marriage to him the first time they met, the day before their wedding took place officially in 1496.

her third bid to foil Philip, using a different tactic, was more successful.

When Philip demanded that the Cortes agree to putting his wife away as a mental incompetent, her cousin Fadrique Enriquez, Admiral of Castile, went to assess the state of her mind for himself. The cousins

> The ink on his signatures was barely dry before Ferdinand reneged and declared that he had agreed to the treaties under duress.

The Convent of Santa Clara at Tordesillas where Juana was confined from 1509 to her death in 1555.

spent 10 hours together; Juana was calm, perfectly in control of herself and the admiral found her conversation both intelligent and astute. No way, he told Philip later, would he connive at any scheme to have Juana pronounced unfit. The admiral defended her so forcefully that the Cortes threw out Philip's proposal. Frustrated and furious, he moved his army on to Burgos in northern Spain. It was here that fate intervened and provided the perfect, if tragic, solution to the problem of Philip the Handsome, scourge of the royal house of Spain.

On 17 September 1506, Philip played a hard game of pelota with one of his men and ended up covered in sweat and ragingly thirsty. He drank a pitcher of water while standing where a cold mountain wind would, he hoped, cool him down. Philip began to feel ill that same night and woke next morning with a temperature. Three days later, he was coughing blood. His throat swelled up and, by 24 September, black and red spots had appeared all over his body. He lapsed into a coma, and died two days later. It was three hours before Juana, who was once again pregnant, would permit his courtiers to dress the corpse and prepare it for burial. After that, she draped herself in black and sat dazed and unresponsive in her apartments.

A MORBID PROCESSION

When, eventually, Juana came out of her trance, she had only one thought in mind: she must take Philip's body south to Granada for burial. A grisly procession set out in the freezing winter fog, with Juana walking behind the hearse. She managed 61 kilometres (38 miles) across hard mountain terrain before exhaustion and the imminent birth of her child forced her to halt at Torquemada in central Spain. There, early in 1507, Juana gave birth to her sixth child, her daughter Catalina.

Every day, a funeral service was performed in front of the altar in the local church, and all day and all night Juana's courtiers stood guard around the catafalque. In April 1507, after plague struck Torquemada, Juana gave orders to leave. The procession took to the road once more and came to its next halt, in a miserable little village called Hornillos. By now, Philip had been dead for seven months, plenty of time for gossip to create lurid tales about Juana's behaviour. It was said that she believed Philip would come back to life after a monk told her of a corpse that had revived after 14 years. Most gruesome were the stories telling how Juana had the coffin opened almost daily and made love with the remains.

The truth was that Juana had the coffin opened four times in all, but she did little more than gaze at what remained of her husband. Philip was still unburied in late August 1507, when Juana set out from Hornillos for her long-awaited reunion with her father. When she saw him at last, she fell to her knees and attempted to kiss his feet. Apparently shocked by his daughter's haggard, ravaged appearance, he burst into tears.

FINAL DESCENT INTO MADNESS

The touching moment of emotion did not mean that Ferdinand was going to play the caring father. At some time during the long conversation that followed, it seems that Ferdinand persuaded Juana to hand over Castile, its government and its revenues. At long last, Ferdinand had everything he wanted. It only remained for him to get Juana out of the way now that he no longer needed her.

A grisly procession set out in the freezing winter fog, with Juana walking behind the hearse.

This truth took a long time to dawn on Juana. All deference was paid to her as Queen of Castile. Even Germaine, her father's second wife, paid homage to her. But then, Juana began to notice that her new courtiers, appointed by Ferdinand, owed allegiance to him rather than to her, and acted more like spies than attendants. In the spring of 1508, Ferdinand showed a glimpse of his hand. He began to press Juana to marry again. The English king Henry VII had asked for her, and it occurred to Juana that Henry's distant realm would conveniently remove her from Spain. Juana refused and Ferdinand finally lost patience.

He was about to set off on an expedition to Cordova in southern Spain to deal with a rebel aristocrat and, he claimed, he wanted Juana to stay somewhere safe in his absence. Ferdinand's idea of somewhere safe was the dank, menacing, prison-like castle of Tordesillas. Juana begged her father not to put her there and, after a tussle, Ferdinand gave in, but took revenge by removing Juana's five-year-old son, another Ferdinand.

PECULIAR BEHAVIOUR

When her father and her son had gone, Juana lapsed into a stupor and her mind, long poised on the edge of madness, began to give way. Her behaviour grew more and more peculiar. She refused to wash or change her clothes. She passed water almost constantly. By early 1509, when Ferdinand returned from Cordova, there

King Charles I of Spain, who bypassed his mad mother, Juana, to succeed to the thrones of Castile and Aragon in 1516. Three years later he succeeded his paternal grandfather Maximilian as the Holy Roman Emperor Charles V.

back in her usual ways – refusing to eat, go to bed, wash or dress – but there is some evidence that she was beaten to make her more tractable. Her father visited her twice – in October 1509 and November 1510. On the second occasion, he brought with him a group of nobles opposed to his takeover of Castile, and took Juana by surprise. The doors to her apartments suddenly opened and, there, the nobles were aghast to see the shrunken, bedraggled Queen of Castile dressed in grubby rags, looking ravaged and smelling worse, in surroundings of utter squalor. Ferdinand never did anything by halves. He had brought the nobles to see the wreckage of his daughter and to see for themselves that Juana was a totally lost cause.

Ferdinand died in 1516, and Juana succeeded him as nominal queen of his realm of Aragon. The new double crown of Castile and Aragon meant

were plenty of witnesses to attest to her descent into madness. Ferdinand ordered that Juana be taken under heavy guard to the castle of Tordesillas. Philip's coffin went with her and so did her daughter Catalina, now two years old.

Locked away in the castle, her final prison, there were few humiliations Juana did not suffer. She fought

> The nobles were aghast to see the shrunken, bedraggled Queen of Castile dressed in grubby rags, looking ravaged and smelling worse, in surroundings of utter squalor.

nothing to her. Her elder son, Charles, proved no less malevolent than his father and grandfather before him. The prize he had to inherit – all of Spain and Spanish America and half of Europe – overcame filial conscience. But Charles would succeed to this vast swathe of territory and its immense riches only if his mother stepped down in his favour. It was not difficult to persuade her. Juana was now so far gone into madness that she gave in meekly and agreed that Charles should rule on her behalf.

Having got what he wanted, Charles kept Juana closely confined and concealed her under an impenetrable pall of secrecy. Juana was not permitted to see anyone from the outside world and, on Charles's orders, was made to keep to her room, preferably in bed. When she heard mass, it was not in the castle chapel, but in the room next to her own.

A PITIFUL FIGURE

Despite her utterly wretched condition, Juana was able to contemplate escape and received her chance after news of her confinement at Tordesillas got out in 1519. Rebels opposed to Charles's heavy taxation marched to the castle and managed to get into the courtyard. This gave Juana the opportunity to break out of her cell and watch the rebels clamouring for her as their rightful queen. But she was too confused to realize what was going on. She stared at her would-be champions with glazed, vacant eyes, then allowed herself to be taken back to the castle and locked up. This time, though, she was put into a pitch-dark, windowless cell. She was let out occasionally, once in 1525, when her daughter Catalina left the castle on her way to marry King John III of Portugal. Juana watched the procession wind away towards the horizon through windows heavily barred to prevent her throwing herself out.

Juana mouldered at the Castle of Tordesillas for another 30 years, falling deeper and deeper into fantasy and the horrible imaginings that fill unhinged minds. She died in 1555, aged 76, after spending two-thirds of her life in confinement. Juana was buried in the royal chapel at Granada next to Philip, whose grotesque odyssey ended in 1525, when he was interred there some 20 years after his death. Juana's parents were similarly paired nearby. As with Philip, their effigies took the customary pose of piety and dignity. Juana's image was different. The sculptor who carved it scored into the marble the lines and hollows that had ravaged her face in real life and, in posthumous consolation, placed in her hands the royal sceptre, the symbol of authority she was never allowed to possess.

The tomb of Philip the Handsome and Juana the Mad in the Royal Chapel, Granada. Juana, who died in 1555, outlived Philip by over fifty years.

VIII

MORE MADNESS IN SPAIN

Madness in the Spanish royal family, which began in the fifteenth century with Isabel of Portugal, spread through subsequent generations, sparing some, but striking others with destructive force. Add to that one further factor – frequent intermarriage, a device for preserving Habsburg family power in Spain – and the stage was set for a sequence of horrors unmatched by any other dynasty in Europe. They appeared most spectacularly in Don Carlos (1545–1568), and, generations later, in King Carlos II of Spain (1661–1700).

✦

Don Carlos was a fearful example of the damage wrought by interbreeding, which disabled him in almost every possible way. His parents were first cousins twice over. Two of his great-grandmothers were sisters: one was Queen Juana, who was still alive,

Left: King Carlos II of Spain was just sane enough to recognize the symptoms of the madness which afflicted him, although he believed the cause was sorcery. His 16th-century ancestor, Don Carlos (above), suffered similarly and died tragically young.

far gone in fantasy and fearful imaginings, in her squalid cell at the castle of Tordesillas, when Don Carlos was born in 1547. The birth was so arduous that his mother, the 18-year-old Princess Maria Manuela, survived for only four days following it.

Physically, the infant Carlos was a monster, a hunchback with his right leg shorter than his left. He was mentally retarded and unable to speak until he was five years of age. Even then, some deformation of his mouth may have prevented him from pronouncing the letters 'l' and 'r', which made it difficult to understand what he was saying. The problem increased when he developed a pronounced stutter. This, in its turn, led to frustrations that fed his violent tendencies. Even as a baby, he was subject to outbursts of sadistic violence which included biting the breasts of his wet nurses so hard that three of them nearly died.

AN UNTENABLE POSITION

Despite his alarming physical and mental state, the fact remained that Don Carlos was his father's only male heir. This position had to be formally acknowledged. But Philip postponed the official ceremony, hoping against hope that his son's condition would improve. There was no improvement. Then, in 1555, Philip's father, Charles, abdicated and Philip succeeded him as King of Spain in the following year. Carlos, for all his manifest disabilities and frightening behaviour, was now one step away from the throne and there could be no more delay. He was officially recognized as Spain's future king and, as he was required to produce his own heirs to the throne, he duly took his place in the royal marriage market.

> A pronounced stutter led to frustrations that fed his violent tendencies. Even as a baby, he was subject to outbursts of sadistic violence which included biting the breasts of his wet nurses so hard that three of them nearly died.

Several potential candidates were suggested, including Queen Elizabeth I of England, who was considerably older than Carlos, by 14 years. Marriage to either of two further candidates, Carlos's aunt Joanna, Princess Dowager of Portugal, and his cousin Archduchess Anna of Austria, would have been

The melancholy, taciturn King Philip II came to the throne of Spain in 1556, after his father, Charles V, abdicated. Philip's severely disabled son, Don Carlos, was the great tragedy in his life.

A PENCHANT FOR TORTURE

On the premise that lack of male company and the absence of what would now be termed suitable 'role models' were having an adverse effect on him, Don Carlos was removed from the exclusively feminine company of nurses and governesses when he was aged seven. This served only to make his propensity for cruelty and violence even worse. By the time he was nine years old, Carlos had taken to torturing little girls and servants. He became worse still after he was aged 13. He maimed the horses in the royal stables so severely that 20 of them had to destroyed. Carlos was also fond of spiking small animals on spits and roasting them alive: his favourites were hares.

One of the characteristics of the mad Don Carlos was extreme sadism. His father, King Philip II, hoped that he would somehow be cured, but it never happened. It was rumoured that Philip engineered Carlos' death in 1568.

This portrait of Don Carlos disguised the truth about him. The hump on Carlos' back is effectively disguised by his cloak and the black background of the painting, but the shapely legs were far from the truth: one of Carlos' legs was shorter than the other.

incestuous. The last thing the Spanish royal family needed was more interbreeding, and it was fortunate that all the unions proposed for Carlos failed to transpire. In the event, Carlos never married. It was just as well, for he spelled enough disaster for his family without reproducing himself.

Carlos's numerous shortfalls included an aversion to learning. His interests stopped at wine, women and the food that lost him his thin boyhood physique and transformed him into an overweight adult. In the forlorn hope that higher education might break through his indifference to learning, Carlos was sent to attend lectures at the University of Alcala de Henares in 1562. Carlos had no interest in lectures, but while at the Alcala he fell madly in love with the daughter of one of the university's servants. Then, one day Carlos was running down insufficiently lit stairs when he stumbled and fell. He was found lying unconscious with a gaping wound in his head. It became infected, and subsequently his head swelled to such an enormous size that he became temporarily blind.

ANXIOUS FATHER

King Philip, meanwhile, was consumed with anxiety and the fear that he was about to lose his one and only male heir. He hurried to the Alcala and prayed for his son's recovery day and night.

> He was found lying unconscious with a gaping wound in his head. It became infected, and subsequently his head swelled to such an enormous size that he became temporarily blind.

Philip threw out the official physicians who had proved useless and turned to 'quacks' who were even worse: their 'cures' were not far removed from those of witch doctors and magicians. Eventually, when Don Carlos was running a high fever and the situation was desperate, Philip called in a group of Franciscan friars who owned a relic, the mummified body of the Blessed Friar Diego, who had died about a century earlier.

The Friars placed the body in Carlos's bed and that night, it appears, the prince dreamed of Friar Diego. From then on, his fever gradually reduced, his pulse became steadier and, after two months, he was able to walk a short distance. But the crisis was not over. The fall and its aftermath had clearly done even more damage to Don Carlos's disordered brain. He would

> Carlos never married. It was just as well, for he spelled enough disaster for his family without reproducing himself.

spend hours sitting in silence, then start talking gibberish. Even more alarming, he became more violent than before.

Without provocation, Carlos assaulted servants and high court officials, and nearly threw one of them out of a palace window. A shoemaker who made a pair of boots Carlos did not like was forced to cut them up and eat them. Carlos was intrigued by weapons of all kinds and once used his sword to threaten the powerful and imposing Fernando Alvarez de Toledo, Third Duke of Alba. The duke was equal to the challenge. He roughly seized Carlos by the arm and removed the weapon from his hand.

WORSENING VIOLENCE

This far, it had been possible to keep Carlos's strange behaviour a secret. But as he sank deeper and deeper into madness, secrecy became impossible. With his rages, his arrogance and his sudden bouts of violence, Carlos was proving too much for his father – or anyone else – to handle. Towards the end of December 1567, Carlos stepped irretrievably too far over the line between what Philip would and would not tolerate when he told his confessor that he 'wanted to kill a

man'. He meant his father. This, of course, was treason. Either the confidentiality of the confessional was broken or Carlos told someone else, but, whatever way the news reached him, Philip soon learned what his son had said. King Philip had been away in the Spanish Netherlands, but on 17 January 1568, when he returned to Spain, he took immediate action.

That night, Carlos was relaxing in his room, surrounded by a mass of weapons, when the door to his room burst open. There, in the doorway, stood three men – King Philip, his adviser and his confessor. Carlos immediately took fright, and apparently fell to his knees in front of his father and begged him to

This portrait of King Philip II, the father of Don Carlos, shows him surrounded by the six coats of arms that symbolized the Spanish territories.

end his life there and then. When the king refused, Carlos tried to throw himself into the fire that was burning in the grate nearby. He was forcibly held back from the flames.

Carlos immediately took fright, and apparently fell to his knees in front of his father and begged him to end his life there and then.

POISONOUS DIAMONDS

Don Carlos was imprisoned in strict confinement in the tower of Arévelo castle, near Madrid. The only light in his tiny cell came from a window set high up in one wall. From then on, King Philip pretended his son

did not exist. No one was allowed to mention his name, enquire as to his whereabouts or say prayers for him in church.

As the months passed, Carlos became more and more crazed. He went on hunger strike and had to be force-fed with soup to keep him alive. Believing that diamonds were poisonous, he swallowed a diamond ring in an attempt at suicide. Finally, on 9 July 1568, Carlos's imprisonment was legalized by charging him with treason for plotting to kill his father. Carlos was not allowed counsel to defend him, and the sentence was pronounced as death. It was a formality. Philip had no intention of executing his son, but he did drop strong hints that if the precautions taken with his diet

Medical knowledge in the seventeenth century was unable to diagnose, let alone treat, the causes of insanity. Exorcism by a priest was all that could be done, although the tragic King Carlos II, shown here, kneeling, failed to benefit from it.

were relaxed, and he was allowed to indulge his natural inclination to stuff food, the eventual result would be excesses leading to his death.

The taciturn Philip shut himself away, to sit brooding for days on end. Meanwhile, in close confinement, his son's condition rapidly worsened. He developed a high fever and vomited incessantly. Ice was poured onto the floor of his cell to cool him down, and Carlos's clothes were stripped off so that he could lie in it. For days on end, Carlos refused to eat anything but fruit. He asked for pastry, but when a huge spiced cake was brought to him, he ate it all, then doused it by drinking more than 10 litres of water. Soon afterwards, he became violently sick. On 24 July 1568, Don Carlos died, aged 23. A cryptic announcement was made that he had 'died of his own excesses', but rumours were soon spreading that the cause of death was slow poison mixed in with Carlos's food.

FAST-FORWARD A CENTURY

King Philip had to wait a further 10 years for another son, the future Philip III, to succeed him. But again he was courting danger, for the mother of the third Philip was Anna of Austria, once a candidate to marry Don Carlos, and King Philip's niece. Worse still, the dangers of interbreeding were compounded even further after Philip IV, son and successor of Philip III, also married his niece, Maria Anna.

> The son of Philip IV and Maria Anna succeeded to the Spanish throne as King Carlos II in 1665 when he was four years of age. He was soon nicknamed *El Hechizaldo*, 'the Bewitched'.

The son of Philip IV and Maria Anna succeeded to the Spanish throne as King Carlos II in 1665 when he was four years of age. He was soon nicknamed *El Hechizaldo*, 'the Bewitched'. His fearful mental and physical state was ascribed to sorcery, and Carlos himself was convinced of it. 'Many people tell me I am bewitched,' he said. 'I well believe it, such are the things I experience and suffer.'

The young King Carlos II of Spain dressed, as children were in the 17th century and afterwards, as a miniature adult.

In an effort to cure him, Carlos was exorcized. The priests involved were ordered to close-question the 'devils' that 'possessed' him, but they refused to make an appearance, and the effort was abandoned.

PHYSICAL DEFORMITIES

Almost everything that could be wrong with the unfortunate Carlos *was* wrong. For a start, he had a

IMPOTENCE AND DEATH

As he grew, however crookedly, to manhood, Carlos II had to face up to a new disability: he was not thought capable of siring a child. Carlos's impotence was said to have been apparent when he was born. Nevertheless, in 1679, he married his first wife, Marie Louise of France, who was, understandably, not best pleased when her uncle King Louis XIV told her of the match that had been made for her. After several years of trying, Marie Louise told the French ambassador to Spain that she was not a virgin any more, but did not believe that she would ever have children. The ambassador somehow got hold of a pair of Carlos's drawers and had them examined for traces of sperm, but the physicians who carried out the tests were unable to agree about their findings.

RAPID DEGENERATION

Marie Louise died, still childless, in 1689, and three months later Carlos remarried. His second wife, Maria Anna, belonged to the fertile Neuburg Line of the Wittelsbach royal family, later to become notorious for its own eccentricities and insanity. Maria Anna's fertility was not in doubt, though, but just to make sure she was exorcised to promote her childbearing chances. Even then, there were to be no children, nor did there seem to be hope of any, for within a few years Carlos was degenerating rapidly. In 1696, at age 35, his hair and teeth had fallen out, and his eyesight was deteriorating. In 1698, he suffered three epileptic fits and became deaf. He was lame and suffered bouts of dizziness. All his physicians could do was place the steaming entrails of animals on his stomach to keep him warm. King Carlos, a wreck of a man if ever there was one, died in 1700, aged 39.

The bizarre-looking Carlos II of Spain dressed in the robes of the Most Illustrious Order of the Golden Fleece, a chivalric order which had been founded in 1430. He was the last Habsburg monarch to wear the robes.

huge, misshapen head. There was also a pre-existing characteristic of his family – an unusually large, jutting jaw known as the 'Habsburg lip'. In Carlos's case, the lip was so exaggerated that the upper and lower rows of his teeth did not meet and he was unable to chew his food. Carlos's tongue was excessively large and protruded from his mouth; this made it difficult for anyone to understand what he said. He drooled continuously. His legs were so weak that he was unable to stand or walk, and frequently fell down in the

Philip V, the first Bourbon King of Spain. Though not as severely afflicted by the family madness as some of his relations, Philip was eccentric and suffered from melancholia and hallucinations.

Congenital syphilis was another ingredient of Carlos's disastrous genetic cocktail, the probable result of the visits his father paid to brothels in Madrid.

attempt. His overprotective family would not allow him to walk unaided until he was almost full grown. Similarly, Carlos did not feed himself until he was aged five or six: instead, he was fed by wet nurses. He was

considered so frail that he was not required to keep clean or even have his hair combed.

As if all this were not enough, the inherited hormonal disease acromegaly may have been added to Carlos's numerous afflictions. Caused by excessive amounts of hormones, particularly growth hormones, this rare but severe disease produced overlarge hands and feet, and weak muscles, among other symptoms. Congenital syphilis was another ingredient of Carlos's disastrous genetic cocktail, the probable result of the visits his father, King Philip IV, paid to brothels in Madrid.

> To compound these already fearful genetic prospects, Philip V's mother, Maria Anna of Bavaria was a Wittelsbach and hence from a family whose instability had been passed down to her over several centuries.

Carlos was also mentally retarded, though not so severely that he was unaware of his disabilities. He was deeply superstitious. His apparent lack of intellect seems to have been due less to a defective brain and more to his lack of an education. The royal family, it appears, feared to put him under undue strain and preferred to leave him barely able to read or write. Little wonder that Carlos II was unable to comprehend the world in which he lived. What knowledge he possessed derived from superstition, which exercised a strong hold over him.

A NEW LINE, BUT NO RESPITE

Carlos II was the last of the Spanish Habsburgs. His death in 1700 without a son to succeed him was the signal for an outbreak of faction fighting and, in 1701, a full-scale war. The War of the Spanish Succession, the struggle to decide who would be the next King of Spain, came to an end in 1713, with victory for another powerful European family, the Bourbons of France. Tragically, though, Philip V, the first Bourbon king of Spain, brought another disastrous legacy to his new throne, for interbreeding was endemic in his

> ... for Philip's Wittelsbach melancholia came so close to madness that he was unable to rule effectively or, indeed, rule at all.

family background, too. Philip V was a grandson of King Louis XIV and his Spanish Habsburg wife, Maria Theresa, who were double first cousins. Maria Theresa was also a daughter of Philip IV and so a direct descendant six generations on from the mad Queen Juana of Spain. To compound these already fearful genetic prospects, Philip V's mother, Maria Anna of Bavaria was a Wittelsbach and hence from a family whose instability had been passed down to her over several centuries.

Fortunately, Philip V remained stable enough for long enough to hold the Spanish throne for all but seven months of 46 years. The seven months occurred in 1724, four years after Philip, who was a deeply devout man, had made a solemn vow to renounce the world and his throne with it. 'Thank God I am no longer king,' he declared after he abdicated on 14 January 1724. 'The remainder of my days I shall apply myself to the service of God and to solitude.'

The expectation was premature. Philip's son Luis I succeeded him, but the following August he died of smallpox and his father was, with difficulty, persuaded to resume his reign.

ECCENTRICITY AND INSANITY

Despite the length of that reign, a distinct achievement for such a crazy mixed-up family, Philip V's tenure of the Spanish throne was punctuated by lapses marked, at best, by eccentricity and, at worst, by full-blown insanity. Sometimes, it came to the worst, for Philip's Wittelsbach melancholia came so close to madness that he was unable to rule effectively or, indeed, rule at all. He himself doubted that he was fit to be a king. At such times, Philip retreated into prolonged periods of

Philip V of Spain (first from left) with his second wife, Elizabeth Farnese (third from left) and their son and heir the future Ferdinand VI (fourth from left).

solitude and displayed most, if not all, the symptoms of a recluse. Company was anathema to him. He was suspicious and trusted no one. He had little self-confidence or self-esteem. His ancestor King Philip II had possessed many of these same characteristics two centuries before him.

A RAVAGED RULER

Philip V suffered his first really serious attack in 1717, when he was all but overcome by deep melancholia that verged on hysteria and provoked horrible imaginings. Philip said he felt as if a raging fire was consuming his innards like a shaft of sunlight piercing him through and through. He was convinced, too, that he was dying in mortal sin and shut himself away in his apartments. The only visitor allowed in from the outside was his confessor. The confessor had his work cut out, for Philip was sure that he was being made to suffer by divine punishment for his personal inadequacies. A more scientific explanation was that these delusions were typical of manic depression.

> Philip's moods ranged rapidly from lethargic to madly excited and back again. He was delusional and believed that he could not walk because his feet were of different sizes.

Although he was sufficiently recovered to return to his public duties by 1718, Philip's sufferings had exacted their toll. Although he was only 35 years old, he looked as if he was well advanced into extreme old age. He was bent over with a shrunken body and, according to the French writer Louis de Rouvroi, Duc de Saint-Simon, he walked in a strange way with 'his knees more than one foot apart'. Saint-Simon went on: '… his words were so drawled, his expression so vacuous, that I was quite unnerved.'

Ten years later, when he suffered another attack of manic depression, Philip's moods ranged rapidly from

King Ferdinand VI was neurotic, melancholic and went around in constant fear of sudden death. He was also subject to violent rages.

lethargic to madly excited and back again. He physically attacked his doctors and his second wife, Queen Elizabeth of Parma, leaving her black and blue with bruising. Philip was delusional and believed that he could not walk because his feet were of different sizes. He refused to be shaved or have his toenails cut. Eight months passed before his son and heir, Ferdinand, managed to persuade him to let his barber shave him.

SPAIN GRINDS TO A HALT

In 1732, Philip retired to bed, and declined to get up. He ate his meals in bed, but refused to change his clothes or shave. He also refused to speak to anyone except Queen Elizabeth and Ferdinand because, he let it be known, he was dead. Neither would Philip agree to see his ministers or sign documents. With this, government in Spain virtually ground to a halt. Fortunately, Philip recovered in 1733, after some seven months.

Six more years went by before Philip succumbed yet again. This time, it manifested itself in fearful howlings that echoed through the apartments and corridors of his palace. His ministers and courtiers had to work hard to prevent the news getting out that the King of Spain had once more lost his mind.

There was, though, another side to Philip V, and a paradoxical one. His Bourbon ancestry had given him a voracious appetite for sex. At the same time, his scrupulous morality prevented him from doing as other monarchs did and take a mistress. He continually moved between the confessional and his queen's bedroom, and his demands on his first wife, Marie Louise of Savoy, were excessive. In 1714, she died, worn out, at the age of 26, and a near-hysterical Philip had to be forcibly removed from her deathbed.

Philip retired distraught to his palace of Medina Coeli in Andalucia. He wept loud, long and copiously, for he needed sex to live as much as he needed air to breathe. After eight months, Philip married again, and had seven children by his second wife, Elizabeth of Parma, to add to the four borne him by the unfortunate Marie Louise. Eventually, though, the hurly-burly of Philip's life caught up with him. On 9 July 1746, he suffered a stroke and died. He was 63 years of age.

Unfortunately, Philip's third surviving son and successor, Ferdinand VI, was fully equipped for yet

another round of royal madness. Ferdinand was born in 1713 and succeeded to the Spanish throne at age 33. Initially, the future seemed brighter for the Bourbons, who had suffered so much anguish and embarrassment over Philip V. At first, Ferdinand ruled as a benign monarch, eager to care for his subjects and improve their lives. He gave vast sums to charity and in 1750 withdrew taxes due when Andalusia was stricken with drought.

GRANDEUR AND SHOW

Ferdinand was a keen patron of the arts and sciences, founding the San Fernando academy of fine arts in Madrid and building three royal astronomical observatories. His favourite relaxation was the opera with his wife, Maria Teresa Barbara, and he delighted in sailing downriver in a luxurious barge equipped with a plush red velvet pavilion trimmed with silver. The fleet of boats accompanying the royal barge was made in the shapes of peacocks or deer. Luxury all the way was the watchword, for Barbara loved grandeur and outward show. She, too, loved music and opera, and was a talented harpsichordist. During a river voyage, she accompanied songs sung by the great castrato counter-tenor Farinelli, who was a great favourite at the Spanish court.

> Like Ferdinand, the queen came from a mentally unstable background and shared with him a deep fear of sudden death and a neurotic, melancholic nature.

Ferdinand's public face made him deservedly popular with his subjects, and the splendour of his public appearances assured them of his high status among the great monarchs of Europe. Yet beneath all the glitz and grandeur, and the royal *bonhomie*, there was a dark underside to the Spanish Bourbons. Like Ferdinand, the queen, who belonged to the Braganza family of Portugal, came from a mentally unstable

Both Ferdinand VI and his wife Barbara loved lavish royal show. In this 1756 painting, they are shown with members of their court in the gardens of the palace of Aranjuez, near Madrid.

AN END TO THE MADNESS

With King Ferdinand VI, the long and tragic tale of royal insanity, melancholia and instability came to an end. There had, though, been a chance that the sequence might have continued. Ferdinand was succeeded by his half-brother, King Carlos III, who escaped the curse of royal insanity, but after him the family problem resurfaced. The heir to Carlos III's throne by birth was his elder son Don Felipe, who was mentally retarded or, as some physicians classed him, an imbecile. He was also epileptic. This was enough for the direct line of royal descent to be diverted to a more suitable heir. Felipe was passed over in favour of his younger brother, who succeeded to their father's throne as King Carlos IV in 1788. It had taken almost 300 years, and too many lives had been ruined along the way, but the Spaniards had learned a vital lesson at last: absolute monarchs, like the kings of Spain, might be chosen by God, but earthly realities must sometimes supervene.

King Carlos III, an enlightened despot who succeeded his half brother Ferdinand VI in 1758, escaped the legacy of madness that had blighted the Habsburg and Bourbon royal families.

background and shared with him a deep fear of sudden death and a neurotic, melancholic nature.

> He asked for poison,
> which was, of course, refused,
> then tried to stab himself
> with scissors or make a rope to
> hang himself out of knotted napkins
> and curtains.

Barbara could be outgoing and vivacious, but Ferdinand, whose mental problems were more intense, turned out to be another Philip V – only worse. He was neurotic and suspicious by nature and was subject to sudden violent rages. He went about in the daily fear that he would fall victim to sudden death. Without warning, he would be consumed by violent fits of rage. Longing for solitude, Ferdinand would withdraw to a monastery where his ministers could not reach him. Like his father, he signed no documents and refused to speak. As time went on, his rages, which drove him to bang his head against the wall, grew increasingly violent. Afterwards, Ferdinand collapsed to the floor and for several hours lay motionless where he fell. He was convinced that, if he lay down, he would die, but then changed his mind and refused to leave his bed for days on end.

Between these episodes, the king could be quite lucid and pleasant, but he finally sank into irretrievable insanity in 1758, when Queen Barbara, whom he adored, died. If anyone

Like her husband, Barbara, Ferdinand VI's queen came from a mentally deranged family, the Braganzas of Portugal. Her death in 1758 pushed Ferdinand over the edge into total insanity.

suggested to him that he remarry, he flew into a frenzy. He refused to wash, shave or dress. He went without sleep for 10 nights at a stretch. He attacked members of his entourage without warning: his most frequent weapon was his own excrement. Ferdinand refused to eat anything but soup, but then refused all food. He suffered such severe weight loss that he shrank to little more than a skeleton covered in skin. Several times he attempted suicide. He asked for poison, which was, of course, refused, then tried to stab himself with scissors or make a rope to hang himself out of knotted napkins and curtains. Before long, Ferdinand was suffering from convulsions, and it was in one of these fits that he died on 10 August 1759, aged 46.

QUEEN CHRISTINA OF SWEDEN: A QUESTION OF GENDER

The gender of Queen Christina of Sweden (1626–1689) was in doubt after she was born at Stockholm castle, the fourth and only surviving child of King Gustavus Adolphus II and his wife, Queen Maria Eleonora. At birth she was greeted as male, but it was afterwards realized that a mistake had been made. How that mistake came about was – and still is – a mystery.

◆

It is possible that Christina was born with some malformation of the genitals that made her appear to be male. Whatever the reason, Christina's sex remained ambiguous throughout her life and later led

Left and above: Queen Christina of Sweden, heir to the hero-King Gustavus Adolphus II Vasa, was brought up as the prince her father had wanted. She hated being feminine, disliked women and made a point of dressing, gesturing and swearing like men.

to claims that she was a hermaphrodite, part-male/part-female, a bisexual or a full-blown lesbian. She was certainly masculine in appearance and manner, sitting, riding, walking, talking, gesturing and swearing as men did. She was also a misogynist.

DESPISED HER OWN SEX

'As a young girl,' Christina later wrote, 'I had an overwhelming aversion to everything that women do and say. I couldn't bear their tight-fitting, fussy clothes. I took no care of my complexion or my figure or the rest of my appearance…. I despised everything belonging to my sex.'

In distancing herself from the 'feminine' side of life, Christina did not content herself with being a tomboy. As a young child, she studied for 12 hours a day, six days a week. She claimed that she needed no more than four hours of sleep before getting up at four in the morning to start her day's work. By age 15, Christina could speak and write five languages – French, German, Italian, Spanish and Latin, the lingua franca of her time. She read intensively and took as her heroes the great men of ancient history, such as Alexander the Great and Julius Caesar. Any time left over from study

Christina's father, Gustavus Adolphus, was a much admired warrior-king and was known as the Lion of the North.

was spent in vigorous exercise and Christina's favourite sports, riding and hunting bears.

A DETERMINED NATURE

Her father had specifically ordered that Christina receive this rigorous and far-reaching education, even though it was usually confined to princes. Christina took to it with zest. With her formidable intellect and abundant physical energy, she relished the challenge.

> Her father had specifically ordered that Christina receive this rigorous and far-reaching education, even though it was usually confined to princes. Christina took to it with zest.

She cared nothing for the idea that she was 'abnormal' for her interest in 'non-feminine' subjects such as literature, politics and statecraft, philosophy, history and, for her the most intriguing, the ancient world.

Gustavus Adolphus was killed aged 38 while leading a cavalry charge at the battle of Lutzen during the Thirty Years' War.

It was just as well that she was so determined to go her own, natural way, for the circumstances of her early life demanded that Christina mature quickly and cope with the responsibility of succeeding to the Swedish throne at a very early age. In 1632, her father, King Gustavus, was killed in battle during the Thirty Years' War and, with this, Christina, aged five, became Queen of Sweden. Her mother, Maria Eleonora, who tended to be hysterical, went into paroxysms of mourning at her husband's untimely death. She clung obsessively to Christina and forced her to share a life given over to grief and the manifestations of that grief.

The royal apartments were dark with black curtains and hangings; the windows were covered over so that no daylight could filter in. Priests intoned prayers and sermons all day and all night. Maria Eleonora insisted that her daughter sleep in her bedchamber, where a casket containing her dead father's heart was kept.

Christina never forgot this macabre experience, which held her in thrall to her unstable mother for three years. Later, it helped to create in Christina a disenchantment with Lutheranism, the official religion of Sweden, which, to her, was steeped in gloom and an obsession with sin. Already, at age nine, she was not only questioning the credentials of Lutheranism, but also, as she wrote later, thinking for herself and making her own decisions. While still a child, she proved capable of handling royal duties with a self-assurance that was well beyond her years. She also acquired a regal personality and a grand manner that inspired respect among her courtiers and ministers.

Although King Gustavus Adolphus had appointed five regents to handle the day-to-day business of government, Christina was already attending council meetings at age 13, and acquainting herself with the

In her portraits, Queen Christina was often shown in feminine dress wearing a female hairstyle. In reality, she preferred male dress, complete with a sword by her side and a short haircut.

royal role in government. More than that, she was firmly convinced that she had been appointed by God to rule Sweden and to do so not as a reigning queen, but as a king. Christina even dreamed of leading her troops into battle, as her father had done.

THE EXPECTED PATH

Although Christina was so precocious and clearly averse to everything labelled 'feminine', she was still expected to marry and produce heirs, while her husband would either rule alongside her or instead of her. Plans for Christina's marriage were already in place in 1630, when she was only four years old. Her proposed husband – her first cousin Friedrich Wilhelm – was aged 11. The match fell through and, two years later, so did the next, with Archduke Ulrich, son of King Christian IV of Denmark, who was some 15 years older than Christina. As she later revealed, however, Christina was not all that keen on marrying anyone, and she refused to contemplate sharing her royal rights with a husband.

> Christina was not all that keen on marrying anyone, and she refused to contemplate sharing her royal rights with a husband.

Nevertheless, when she was 16 years old, she developed a powerful 'crush' on her splendidly handsome, dark-eyed cousin Karl Gustav, son of Johann Kasimir, Count Palatine of Zweibrücken-Kleeburg. Karl Gustav and Christine had been close childhood friends, but when friendship turned to romance it was, for her, more of a sentimental adventure than a love affair. Christina, it seems, enjoyed the secret meetings, the passionate notes written in code and the declarations of 'eternal love' and 'faithfulness unto death', but she took care not to get too seriously involved and she made no promises.

Consequently, in 1644, when she turned 18, the age of majority, and her Regency Council was disbanded, there were no signs of an impending royal marriage. Karl Gustav lived in hopes for another five years, but the prize offered him in 1649 was not the queen's hand, but an extraordinary advancement: Christina

Karl Gustav on horseback in a military pose greatly favoured by seventeenth century painters. Charles was Christina's cousin and succeeded her as king after she abdicated the throne in 1654.

announced that she was making Karl Gustav the official heir to her throne.. The connotations were, of course, unmistakable. After making her announcement to a shocked Rikstag, Christina rammed home the lesson in strong terms.

'I am telling you now,' she told the Swedish parliament, 'it is impossible for me to marry. I am absolutely certain about it.… My character is simply not suited to marriage. I have prayed God fervently that my inclination might change, but I simply cannot marry.'

UNSUITABLE LIAISONS

Playing the field, however, was still an option for Christina, who from time to time created scandals with her outlandish conduct. In 1645, for example, she began keeping company with colourful adventurers and even fell in love with one of them, Count Magnus Gabriel de la Gardie. Part French, part Swedish,

---

'I am telling you now,' she told the Swedish parliament, 'it is impossible for me to marry. I am absolutely certain about it.'

Magnus was a handsome charmer whose father had once been a favourite of King Gustav Adolph. He was, nevertheless, a man on the make, and the rumours that the queen was madly in love with him increased his attraction. Magnus became Colonel of the Queen's Guard and Ambassador Extraordinary to France. He

departed for Paris in a special gold and silver carriage, accompanied by a 300-strong retinue and a lavish expense account that helped to make him rich in only a couple of years. Gardie, however, matched his royal mistress for headlong extravagance, and the queen had to go on rescuing him from debt until their relationship ended in 1651.

Meanwhile, Christina seems to have moved on and into another, highly controversial liaison. She formed a close attachment to one of her ladies-in-waiting, the pretty Ebba Sparre, whom the Queen called 'Belle'. Belle was Christina's opposite – timid where the Queen was outspoken, with no intellectual interests, and the diffident, 'feminine' ways which Christina disliked, but accepted in a relationship where she was evidently the stronger partner. Christina and Belle frequently slept in the same bed. The queen embarrassed the strait-laced English ambassador Bulstrode Whitelocke when she told him that Belle's 'inside' was ' as beautiful as her outside'. The ambassador was so shocked that his ears turned red.

Although controversial, indulging favourites and taking up sexually deviant practices were not usually serious enough to imperil thrones or monarchs. Nor were some of Christina's other activities, such as selling noble titles to solve a financial crisis or maintaining an extravagant lifestyle. What was not so easily accommodated was Christina's long-standing attraction for Roman Catholicism, which was illegal in Lutheran Sweden. Nevertheless, by 1651, she was already planning to convert, knowing full well that as a Catholic she could not remain Queen of Sweden. Instead, she would have to abdicate. The Rikstag went into uproar when Christina announced her decision, but no amount of nagging, begging or pleading succeeded in making her change her mind.

Once across the border and into Denmark following her abdication, Christina took on the identity of one of her companions – Count Christophe von Donha, who

was about 27 years old, the same age as the ex-queen. She exchanged her skirts for trousers and, in this male disguise, headed west, making for Rome. She rarely wore female dress after that, but often appeared with her hair cut short and a sword at her side.

A NEW LIFE IN COSTUME

At the end of 1654, after passing through Germany and into the Spanish Netherlands, Christina was

A QUEEN ABDICATES

The abdication ceremony took place on 6 June 1654 in the grand hall of Uppsala Castle; however, when Christina commanded that the crown be removed from her head, no one came forward to perform the task. At length, though, two of her courtiers took the crown and laid it on a velvet cushion. After that, her ceremonial robes were removed and set aside, until all she wore was a simple white dress. Christina's appointed heir was crowned King Karl X Gustav the same morning. A few days later, Christina was gone, racing towards the Danish border on horseback, with no official farewells, no ceremony and no regrets. She was accompanied by only four attendants. Ebba 'Belle' Sparre, the only person Christina was sorry to leave behind, was not one of them.

received into the Catholic Church at a private ceremony in Brussels. Her new Catholic status was subsequently confirmed at Innsbruck, in Austria, where she was formally accepted into the Catholic communion. After that, Christina took the second name of Alexandra, probably as a compliment to the pope, Alexander VII.

Christina formed a close attachment to one of her ladies-in-waiting, the pretty Ebba Sparre, and frequently slept in the same bed.

The one-time Queen of Sweden was a splendid 'catch' for the Roman Catholic Church, which was still struggling to reassert itself after the schism caused by the Protestant breakaway more than a century before.

The building of Uppsala Castle, north of Stockholm, began in 1549 and was later the scene of several important royal events. One of these was the announcement in 1654 that Queen Christina intended to abdicate the throne of Sweden.

Celebrations for the event were high-profile, including bells ringing and cannon firing, which greatly pleased the ex-queen, who was extremely vain and thrived on veneration. Afterwards, her journey to Rome resembled the Triumphs of the ancient Roman emperors. On the way, Christina's love of luxury and extravagant show was continuously satisfied. A gilded barge was provided to take her across the River Po near Ferrari. Once within the territory of the Papal States, she travelled in a new carriage specially sent by Pope Alexander. Alexander also provided two beds, with canopies and matching armchairs, a splendid set of table silver and a top chef, Luigi Fedele, who was famous for his imaginative use of spices.

> At the end of 1654, after passing through Germany and into the Spanish Netherlands, Christina was received into the Catholic Church at a private ceremony in Brussels.

On 10 December, Christina arrived in Rome and was received by the Pope in private audience. It was unusual for a woman to be allowed to spend the night in the precincts of the Vatican, but the Pope conferred a singular honour on the former queen by having prepared a suite of beautiful rooms at the top of the Tower of the Winds. The rooms, which afforded a magnificent view of the city, were decorated in satin, brocade, lace and embroidery. Frescoes were painted on all the walls.

RENAISSANCE HOME
After a few days in the Vatican, Christina moved to a more permanent place, the Palazzo Farnese, one of the loveliest palaces in Rome, partly designed by Michelangelo and a gorgeous example of Renaissance architecture. The rooms were furnished with magnificent paintings, sculptures and tapestries, and there was a painted gallery built in imitation of the Sistine Chapel, as decorated by Michelangelo.

Christina achieved her long-held wish to convert to Roman Catholicism in 1655 and is seen here, being blessed by the pope, Alexander VII.

Unfortunately, with her often coarse manners, Christina could be an embarrassing guest. For example, at the Palazzo Farnese, she revealed parts of the body usually kept hidden for reasons of modesty: this was done by removing strategically placed fig leaves and carefully arranged draperies from some of the paintings. When taxed about it, Christina declared that she was not going to be confined by 'rules made for priests'.

A STEP TOO FAR
With irreverent attitudes such as this, Christina was soon the subject of gossip, which thrived on her activities and her power to shock. As a woman, she was supposed to be modest, diffident and pure. Christina was frequently rude, pushy and ambitious. As a Catholic, Christina was expected to be submissive to God and His Church, and spurn the carnal and other ribald temptations of the devil. Instead, Christina frequented the theatre and its often bawdy entertainments, and relished the forbidden pleasures of the flesh, which she enjoyed with a parade of lovers.

One of them, allegedly, was her Master of Horse, the Marchese Gian-Rinaldo Monaldeschi, a minor Italian nobleman, who was the sort of rough-mannered rogue Christina appreciated. But he was untrustworthy and the ex-queen suspected – and accused – him of betraying to the Pope plans which she made in 1656 to seize the Kingdom of Naples

> She revealed parts of the body usually kept hidden for reasons of modesty... When taxed about it, Christina declared that she was not going to be confined by 'rules made for priests'.

with military backing from France. Naples, which was then a Spanish possession, had a dual purpose for Christina. The kingdom could have served as a replacement for the royal power she had relinquished in Sweden, which she now sorely missed. Naples could also help to solve her perennial financial problems. The Swedish treasury paid her an allowance, but Christina often found it difficult to extract the monies due. The real problem, though, was that the payments could never keep up with the former queen's luxurious lifestyle. Consequently, Christina had to live on loans and gifts, or was forced to pawn the silver plate, jewellery and other valuables she had brought with her from Sweden.

Mondaleschi's betrayal ruined her chances in Naples, but Christina waited to extract her revenge until she was in France, where she went to confer with her French allies about their joint Neapolitan adventure. The former queen was staying at Fontainebleau, near Paris, on 10 February 1657 when,

This painting by the artist Niclas Lafrensen (1737–1807) portrays a seated Christina of Sweden joking with 'Belle' as they visit the sick French scholar Claude Saumaise.

Christina gives the order for Monaldeschi to be murdered in this painting by Eugène Delacroix (1798–1863). The case fascinated artists and playwrights in the ensuing centuries.

on her orders, Monaldeschi was done to death by members of her entourage. He took more than 15 minutes to die, from sword thrusts to his stomach, head and throat.

The French were profoundly shocked by the gruesome murder and even more by Christina's heartless behaviour. She justified the killing as a punishment an absolute monarch, which she still believed herself to be, had the right to impose on a member of her retinue. No one was impressed. The ex-queen was soon shunned by Paris high society, the royal court and the Church, and Pope Alexander made it clear that he did not want her back in Rome. Christina went back anyway. She arrived in mid-May 1658, only to find herself as ostracized there, as she had been in Paris. Pope Alexander, alarmed at her

The former queen was staying at Fontainebleau, near Paris, on 10 February 1657 when, on her orders, Monaldeschi was done to death by members of her entourage.

return, sent Christina a message to leave forthwith, though in time he relented. All the same, the relationship between them was always wary.

A FINAL BID FOR ROYAL POWER

Christina was not yet done with outrageous adventures. She made one last bid to retrieve royal power in 1668, when she attempted to acquire the crown of Lithuania-Poland, then the most extensive

country in Europe. The Polish monarchy was elective and Christina had a good case, for the Swedish House of Vasa, to which she belonged, had already provided several monarchs for Poland. Realistically, though, she had little chance of success. She was a woman, when the Poles wanted to be ruled by a man. In 1668, she was 42 years old, unmarried and likely to remain so, with no heirs of her own, and a murky reputation that included the Monaldeschi scandal. The successful candidate, Michael Korybut Wisniowiecki, who became King of Lithuania-Poland in 1669, had better credentials and he was, most importantly, Polish by descent from the Jagiello dynasty, which had ruled Lithuania-Poland between 1386 and 1572.

After this last tilt at royal power, Christina returned to her intellectual interests. She studied astronomy, had an observatory built in the Palazzo Riario and staffed it with two live-in astronomers. She sponsored archaeological 'digs' and, in 1670–1, began writing a book of maxims. She also went into the theatre business, employed a company of actors and staged several successful plays which became renowned for their bawdy content. This was followed by the Tordinona, one of the first public

Pope Innocent XI, the prudish pope, who after 1676 closed down the bawdy theatres which Christina liked to attend.

opera houses in Rome, and academies of literature and philosophy. Before long, the Palazzo Riario became a focus of cultural and intellectual activity in Rome. But not everyone approved. Some of the more conservative popes seemed to believe that theatres and sin were synonymous. Christina's and other theatres, bawdy and otherwise, were closed down after 1676, when a new, more prudish pope, Innocent XI, was elected.

Left: Christina (centre) meets René Descartes, (pointing at document), the French philosopher and mathematician who was one of the greatest minds of the seventeenth century.

PEACE IN DEATH

Christina had another brush with Innocent after she became attracted to Quietism, a contemplative form of Christian mysticism. In 1687, this became a dangerous interest when it was banned by the Catholic Church after its chief proponent, Miguel de Molinos, was convicted of heresy.

The passive, retiring nature of Quietism seemed an odd match for the turbulence of Christina's life and the furious energy and egotism that typified her nature. Yet, after she died of a fever in Rome on 19 April 1689, Quietist influence was evident in the instructions she left for her funeral: it was to be 'a private affair, without undue ceremony' and 'no pomp or exhibiting of the body or other vanity'. A further request was

A TRUE FRIEND

Fortunately, Christina made a much truer friend than some of those in her past in Cardinal Decio Azzolino, her priest, whom she first met in 1656. Azzolino, who had a passionate but platonic relationship with the former queen, remained loyal to her through all her tribulations and was responsible for much of the improvement in her public relations. It was Azzolino who found her a charming Renaissance-style villa, the

Palazzo Riario, when most aristocratic landlords in Rome wanted nothing to do with her. He went on to regularize Christina's everyday life, ejecting the ruffianly hangers-on and other sycophants who had accumulated around her. Instead, Azzolini hired reliable servants and staff, many of them his own relatives who, with his keen eye always on them, were less likely to take undue advantage of the former queen.

more like the imperious Christina, the queen with an overwhelming sense of her own greatness: she asked for three new chaplains to be specially appointed at St Peter's in Rome, with the task of saying 20,000 masses for the repose of her soul.

The heartbroken Cardinal Azzolino, who was himself dying, had kept vigil at Christina's bedside during her last night. But though well aware that she wanted no fuss at her funeral, he could not bring himself to let her go quietly. Instead, Azzolino proposed a public event, one that would see Christina into the next world in a grand manner befitting her royal status. The Pope gave his permission, and Christina's embalmed corpse lay in state at the Palazzo Riario, dressed in a white satin gown embroidered with flowers and an ermine-trimmed purple cloak decorated with gold coins. On her head, she wore a small silver crown, and she held a silver sceptre in her hand. A silver mask covered her face. She looked magnificent, just as the grieving Azzolino had intended.

This 18th century engraving inaccurately portrays Christina in the fashions of a century after her death, but it does illustrate her interest in science and passion for intellectual activity.

REVERENT MONKS

Carmelite monks stood on guard as the local populace moved past Christina's coffin in silent awe and reverence. After four days, she was taken to the Church of Santa Maria in Vallicella, near Rome. There, by the light of 300 torches, a requiem was said for her, in the presence of hundreds of monks and other churchmen, together with the entire College of Cardinals. Only Azzolino, who was too weak to attend, was absent.

Afterwards, watched by cardinals, diplomats, scholars and artists, Christina was buried in the great Basilica of St Peter's, a rare honour for a woman and unique for a woman who had once been a reigning queen. Azzolino, who died seven weeks after her, had understood very well what Christina's love of grandeur and reverence needed. This was why the show he put on for her was a perfect fit for her requirements and a fitting farewell.

KING ERIK XIV VASA OF SWEDEN (1533–1577)

King Erik XIV Vasa married his mistress Karin Mansdotter, the commoner daughter of a jailer in 1567. The following year Karin was made a member of the aristocracy and was crowned queen.

Erik XIV Vasa, who became King of Sweden in 1560, was educated as a true Renaissance prince, the ideal polymath of his times. Erik studied geography, history and political thought. He played the lute, wrote his own music and spoke several languages. Erik also possessed a trait, however, that was the exact opposite of scholarship – his barbaric streak. His father, King Gustav I Vasa, was on a similarly out-of-control-wavelength: he was subject to violent, manic rages. This mixture of sophistication and wildness produced a curious mentality: Erik was determined to make Sweden the dominant power in the Baltic region of northeast Europe, yet he felt disadvantaged by his descent from a family of the minor Swedish nobility.

This gave him an inferiority complex and planted in him the fear that another, similar, noble family would supplant his own. As a result, Erik became paranoid and suspected every noble at his court of plotting against him. Erik had bizarre ideas of what constituted plotting. Anyone fell under suspicion if he cleared his throat, whispered or coughed. In addition, Erik patrolled the corridors of his palace, sword in hand, looking for any smartly dressed courtier, pageboy or servant who, to his disordered mind, was intent on seducing the ladies of his court.

ECCENTRIC FANTASIST

By 1567, Erik was becoming more and more eccentric and unable to sort fantasy from reality. He suddenly ordered the arrest of several aristocrats and condemned them to death. He imprisoned Svante Sture and his son Nils, who belonged to a family that had once ruled Norway, and stabbed Nils to death in his cell at Uppsala Castle. Later, after Nils's father died, Erik was overcome with remorse and arranged for both the Stures to be given magnificent funerals.

Eventually, in 1569, Erik was deposed and put on trial for his crimes. He was found guilty, and imprisoned with his wife, Karin, and their children, while his half-brother, John, took his place as king. While in prison, Erik was in constant fear of assassination and ultimately, in 1577, his fears came true. He was murdered by poison mixed in with a dish of pea soup – although a public announcement made it known that he died 'after a long illness'.

HAEMOPHILIA: THE ROYAL DISEASE

When haemophilia made its first appearance in the British royal family,
it was as if the tenth biblical plague had struck the House of Hanover.
If anything, haemophilia was worse than the killing of the first born visited by
Jehovah on the Ancient Egyptians, for this deadly condition, in which the blood
fails to clot normally, could strike younger sons as well, and lie hidden in
the genes of daughters, ready to be passed on to their children.

✦

Haemophilia lay low for some time in the family of Queen Victoria and her husband, Prince Albert of Saxe-Coburg-Gotha, and advanced to be recognized only in their fourth and last son, Leopold, who was born in 1853. Leopold was

Left: Tsar Nicholas II of Russia with his haemophiliac son, the Tsarevich Alexis. Above: The British Queen Victoria (seated, centre) with her family. Many of Victoria's descendants were affected by haemophilia.

diagnosed with haemophilia three years later. His brothers Edward, Prince of Wales (born 1841), Prince Alfred (born 1844) and Prince Arthur (born 1850) had all escaped the affliction. Unknown to anyone until after they married, however, three of Victoria's five daughters – Vicky, Alice and Beatrice – were carriers of the disease. All three married European princes, with the result that haemophilia was carried into several European royal houses and many of their children and grandchildren suffered cruelly because of it.

Prince Leopold, the fourth and youngest son of Queen Victoria and Prince Albert, believed that his haemophilia had ruined his life.

A DEVASTATING LEGACY

Leopold's haemophilia was all the more worrying because its origin was unknown. There was no history of the disease in Victoria's family, nor in Prince Albert's, and the medical knowledge of the time was insufficient to explain the mystery. It was possible, though, that the problem arose spontaneously. Queen Victoria may have inherited the defective gene for haemophilia from one of her parents, probably her father, Edward, Duke of Kent, the fourth son of King George III. Later research revealed that the gene and its mutation in the X chromosome occurred more frequently in older fathers: the Duke was 51 when the future Queen Victoria was born in 1819.

The fearful legacy of haemophilia soon became apparent, for it could make an otherwise mild

Leopold was intellectually brilliant, with an active, questing mind that made his frail health a great frustration to him. In order to lead the normal life he craved, Leopold had to take risks.

childhood illness fatal. This is what nearly happened in 1861 when Prince Leopold caught measles. So did Prince Arthur and Princess Beatrice, but, whereas they fought off the infection and were not so badly affected, Leopold nearly died. The eight-year-old prince managed to survive through his own powers of recovery which, this time, proved equal to the task.

MASSIVE HAEMORRHAGE

But it was not always so. Prince Leopold had several narrow escapes before he was finally carried off by a massive haemorrhage in 1884, 10 days before his thirty-first birthday. What killed him was a second injury to his knee, which occurred within a few weeks. His end came swiftly, in 24 hours. Anyone else might have had a bruised knee and a limp for a while, but would have thought nothing of it. Leopold, on the other hand, had to be constantly aware of the danger in which he stood and considered that haemophilia had ruined his life.

Had he been a dullard, without much zest for life, his problems might have been less. But like his father Prince Albert, Leopold was intellectually brilliant, with an active, questing mind that made his frail health a great frustration to him. In order to lead the normal life he craved, Leopold had to take risks. He also needed to defy his strong-minded mother. Despite Victoria's repeated attempts to smother him in overprotection, Leopold managed to escape to university, took part in public life and married and had children. Victoria was gratified, but surprised, for she had imagined that haemophilia would make it impossible for Leopold to father a family.

Right: The melancholy and depressive Tsarina Alexandra of Russia, seen here with her son the Tsarevich Alexis, made herself ill with guilt because she had 'given' him haemophilia.

Even royal families ... were not
immune, so that Vicky and Alice,
mourning their young sons,
could view haemophilia
as yet another threat to survival
among many others.

For a haemophiliac, Leopold's achievements were a
significant success. All the same, he was always aware
of the reality that overshadowed them. He even told his
sister Alice, Grand Duchess of Hesse-Darmstadt, that
the death in 1873 of her three-year-old son in an
accident was a blessing in disguise: the child, Frederick
William, was another haemophiliac. Leopold told Alice
that his death after falling out of a window had spared
him a life of suffering and misery.

Seven years earlier, in 1866, Alice's elder sister
Vicky, Crown Princess of Prussia, had also lost a son,
Sigismund, when he was under two years old. Another
son, Waldemar, Vicky's youngest, died aged 11 in 1879.
Both these deaths were caused by infections –
meningitis and diphtheria – but the fact that both boys
were suspected haemophiliacs could well have
hastened their demise.

Not that death in infancy or childhood was unusual
at this time. It was one of the grimmer realities of
nineteenth-century life that one or more children in
large families would die prematurely – from accident,
disease (especially infectious disease) or as a result of
unsanitary living conditions. This was accepted as a
sorrowful fact of everyday life. Even royal families, who
presumably lived in the best conditions, were not
immune, so that Vicky and Alice, mourning their
young sons, could view haemophilia as yet another
threat to survival among many others. For royal
families, however, haemophilia was no ordinary
disease, for its intrusion into their bloodlines could
mean dynastic disaster.

A CONTINUING CURSE

The wider implications of this disaster did not become
clear until after Alice, Vicky and Queen Victoria were
dead, and the next generation of royal daughters had
children of their own. Haemophilia cursed the royal

houses of Hohenzollern (through Vicky) and of Hesse-
Darmstadt (through Alice). Next, it appeared with
destructive force in the Bourbon dynasty of Spain and
the Romanov ruling house in Russia, after one of
Queen Victoria's granddaughters married the Russian
Tsar Nicholas II and another wed the youthful King
Alfonso XIII of Spain.

Nicholas's wife was Princess Alexandra of Hesse-
Darmstadt, the fourth daughter of Princess Alice.
Nicholas and Alexandra married in 1894, just over
three weeks after Nicholas became Tsar of all the
Russias. Both were aware that Alice had been a carrier
for haemophilia and that Alexandra's sister Irene had
given birth to a haemophiliac son, Prince Waldemar, in
1889. Remarkably, Waldemar lived into his fifties,
dying in 1945. But another of Irene's three sons, the
haemophiliac Heinrich, was not so lucky. He died aged
four in 1904, after he fell and struck his head.

The fact that Alexis suffered
from haemophilia became
apparent six weeks after his birth,
when he began to bleed from his
navel: the bleeding went on for
three days before it stopped.

Ten years of marriage passed before Nicholas and
Alexandra were themselves confronted with the
terrible legacy ill fortune had planted in her family.
Their first four children were daughters, but the fifth
was their only son, the Tsarevich Alexis, born in 1904.
The fact that Alexis suffered from haemophilia became
apparent six weeks after his birth, when he began to
bleed from his navel: the bleeding went on for three
days before it stopped. Later on, Alexis suffered
unusual bruising whenever he fell or tripped because
of bleeding beneath the skin, as well as the appalling
agonies of internal bleeding or bleeding in the joints
from casual injuries.

Nicholas and Alexandra were distraught. This,
though, was not only a family tragedy. A diseased royal
heir was the worst thing that could have happened in
Russia, for Nicholas's hold on his throne was tenuous
as popular unrest and demands for a Duma, or
Parliament, and more representative government

Alexandra became spellbound by Rasputin and was soon dependent on him for her son's life, which he subsequently 'saved' more than once.

steadily undermined his autocratic rule. Alexandra, who tended to be morose and pessimistic, took to praying desperately for hours on end. She was wracked with guilt, knowing that she had transmitted the disease to her son. She began to suffer heart problems and developed sciatica, together with a whole range of symptoms which today might be termed 'psychosomatic'.

In her state of extreme, even obsessive, anxiety, Alexandra became overprotective. Two sailors were employed to follow the Tsarevich everywhere and prevent him from hurting himself, and his haemophilia was kept a dread family secret. Doctors, servants, members of the imperial household and anyone else who might know or guess what was wrong were all forbidden to talk. Just the same, there were rumours, for it proved impossible to keep the secret when Alexis nearly died from a nosebleed or a minor fall required him to stay in bed for weeks on end.

RASPUTIN AND THE ROMANOVS

Then, in 1905, a holy man, or *starets*, from Siberia named Grigori Rasputin arrived at the royal court in St Petersburg. A *starets* was supposed to have extraordinary healing powers, achieving cures by prayer, and it was not unusual for aristocratic families to keep one of these peasant mystics in their household for use as and when their skills were required. For Alexandra, Rasputin was the answer to her prayers, for he seemed to have the ability to cure the Tsarevich, even when his haemophilia threatened to kill him and his doctors had given up. In 1905, the Tsarevich Alexis was

The *starets* or holy man Grigori Rasputin who achieved extraordinary power over the Tsarina Alexandra after he apparently enabled Alexis to recover from bouts of bleeding.

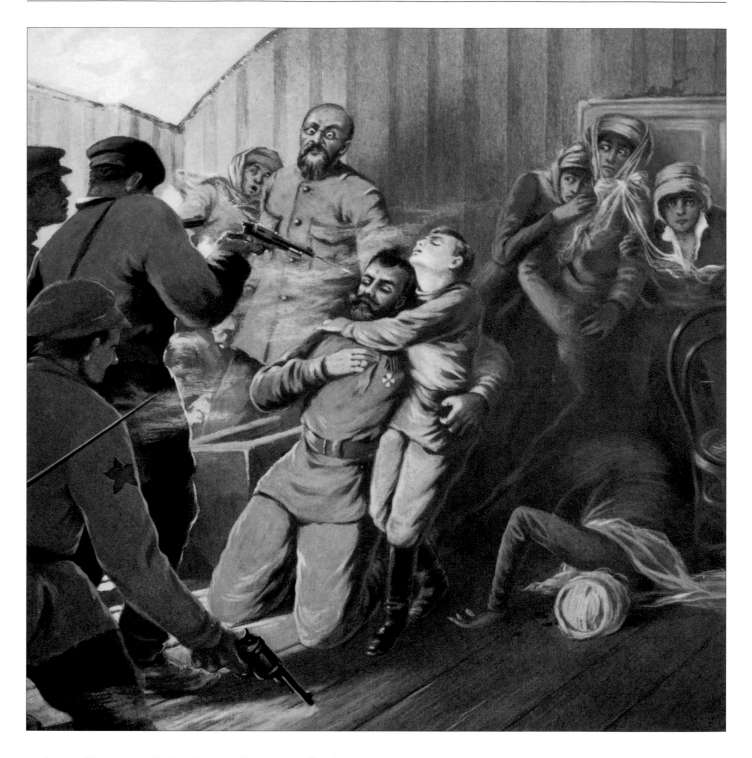

The Tsar and Tsarina and their children, their servants and even their little dog were killed at Ekaterinburg in Siberia on 17 July 1918.

seriously ill and wracked with pain from a swollen leg. Overnight, Rasputin restored the boy to full health, although no one saw or could even guess how he had achieved this 'miracle'.

RASPUTIN IN CHARGE

From then on, Nicholas and Alexandra were Rasputin's devoted disciples and, where the imperial household was obliged to address the Tsar and Tsarina with excessive reverence, they allowed him unprecedented freedom of speech and conduct in their presence. Alexandra became spellbound by Rasputin and was soon dependent on him for her son's life, which he subsequently 'saved' more than once. From there, Rasputin moved easily into a position where he was exercising political influence at court and handing out plum positions to his cronies. After Russia entered World War I in 1914, Nicholas departed for the front, leaving Alexandra in charge. Or so he thought. Before long, Rasputin was dominating the Tsarina to the point where he was virtually running the country.

This was too much for some younger members of the Romanov imperial family whose influence Rasputin had supplanted. In 1916, a group led by the Romanov Prince Felix Yousoupoff poisoned, shot, clubbed and finally drowned Rasputin in the River Neva at St Petersburg. Nicholas and Alexandra were horrified. Alexandra now believed that, with Rasputin dead, her link with God had been severed and her son had been abandoned. Russia, she was sure, was now doomed – and the Romanov family with it.

This was not one of Alexandra's morbid fantasies. On 15 March 1917, less than three months after Rasputin's death, Tsar Nicholas was forced to abdicate when Russian troops mutinied, hunger riots broke out and a new provisional government under Alexander Kerensky took power in St Petersburg. Seven months after that, Kerensky was overthrown by the Communist Bolsheviks under Vladimir Lenin and, with that, the fate of the Romanovs was sealed. Imprisoned in the grimly named House of Special Purpose at Ekaterinburg in Siberia, the entire family was shot dead by a Bolshevik firing squad on 17 July 1918. Ironically, the last to die was the Tsarevich Alexis.

HAEMOPHILIA IN SPAIN

Around the time the ill-fated Alexis was born, the scenario of haemophilia was becoming better understood. There was still no cure, of course, nor any certain treatment, but the hereditary pattern was now recognized. Consequently, in 1905, when the nineteen-year-old King Alfonso XIII of Spain arrived in England seeking a bride, he was warned that several eligible English princesses might carry the curse of the bleeding disease.

Alfonso's fancy ranged over Princess Patricia, daughter of Prince Arthur; Beatrice of Saxe-Coburg, Prince Alfred's daughter; and Princess Victoria Eugenie, daughter of Queen Victoria's last child, Princess Beatrice of Battenberg. Beatrice of Saxe-Coburg and Patricia were almost certainly not carriers of the haemophelia gene, as their fathers were free of

the disease. Unfortunately for Alfonso, he chose Victoria-Eugenie, known as Ena, who had received the carrier characteristics from her mother. There was certain evidence that Ena's mother, Beatrice, was a carrier; her son, another Leopold, suffered from haemophilia and later died of it, aged 33, in 1922.

IRRESPONSIBLE ALFONSO

With this evidence before him, Alfonso knew perfectly well the chance he was taking in marrying Ena. He was warned by his own Foreign Minister, by his family, by Ena's mother, by King Edward VII, Ena's uncle, and by Ena herself. He listened to all of them, but failed to hear. Alfonso possessed the hot blood of the Bourbons and the arrogant insouciance of youth, and he wanted the curvaceous Ena with a fierce passion. He reckoned, quite irresponsibly, that if they had a sufficient number of children some of them at least would escape the bleeding disease.

> ... the scenario of haemophilia was becoming better understood. There was still no cure, of course, nor any certain treatment, but the hereditary pattern was now recognized.

Alfonso was able to deceive himself for only a short time. He rapidly changed his attitude and his marriage to Ena, which took place in Madrid in 1906, headed for disaster when their first son, Alfonsito, was born in 1907. When the time came for the infant prince to be circumcised – a practice long ago introduced into the Spanish court by Jewish doctors – the surgeons found to their dismay that the child bled profusely for several hours. There was no doubt that it was haemophilia, and Alfonso descended into an abyss of depression and despair. He blamed Ena, he blamed his mother-in-law, Beatrice, but he also blamed himself for being led on by his foolhardy lust for his English bride.

This, though, did not prevent the king from trying again. In 1908, Ena gave birth to another son, Jaime, who was perfectly healthy. At this, Alfonso rallied somewhat and persuaded himself that Alfonsito would somehow recover from his illness, just as

A MARRIAGE DESTROYED

After eight years of marriage, in which Ena had borne seven children, the royal Bourbon house of Spain had only one fully healthy heir, Don Juan, who was born in 1913 and eventually became the father of the present Spanish king, Juan Carlos. Of the others, three had been haemophiliacs and Don Jaime became deaf and dumb after an attack of mastoiditis in 1911, when he was three years of age. This appalling family experience ruined the relationship between the King and Ena. He turned to his mistresses and the healthy children they bore him; she to good works and charity. In 1931, after King Alfonso was forced to abdicate in the face of demands for more democratic rule in Spain, he lost no time in obtaining a judicial separation.

The marriage of Alfonso and Ena went down in the flames of mutual recrimination and charges of adultery that, on Alfonso's side, were certainly true. Curiously, Ena kept up hopes of a reconciliation for some years, but it never transpired, even though the deaths of their two surviving haemophiliac sons gave them opportunities.

Princess Victoria Eugenie of Battenberg, known as Ena, was a grand daughter of Queen Victoria. She received the gene for haemophilia from her mother, Princess Beatrice, and like Beatrice, was herself a carrier of the disease.

Alfonso XIII, who was born as King of Spain, refused to listen when Beatrice, Victoria Eugenie and several others warned him about the dangers of haemophilia.

Prince Albert had once hoped would happen with Prince Leopold.

Like Leopold, Alfonsito, Prince of Asturias, was bright and intelligent, and his father, full of hope, enrolled him in the First Royal Regiment of the Spanish army and made plans for his training as the future King of Spain. But however much Alfonso fooled himself over his eldest son and heir, the shock of haemophilia in his family had drastically altered his attitude to his wife. Hatred, bitterness and fury consumed Alfonso when his mood, always mercurial, swung towards the morbid thought that the Prince of Asturias would not live to inherit his crown. The birth of his next son, after a daughter was born in 1909, confirmed Alfonso's darkest imaginings. The boy, who arrived in 1910, was stillborn, but he was also another haemophiliac. So was the last child of Alfonso and Ena, Gonzalo, who was born in 1914, a year after another daughter, Maria Christina.

AN ATTEMPT AT NORMALCY

Like their erstwhile great-uncle, the English Prince Leopold, Alfonsito and Gonzalo insisted on leading active lives and, once their father's abdication released them from royal restraint, both went their own way. Gonzalo, who appeared to suffer from a less virulent form of haemophilia than his older brother, entered the University of Louvain in 1934 to study engineering. Then, one day in August 1934, while Gonzalo was out driving with his sister Beatrice, their car swerved to avoid an oncoming cyclist and crashed into a wall. Brother and sister suffered only slight injuries, but soon afterwards Gonzalo began to bleed. He died two days later, aged only 20.

Alfonsito, meanwhile, had been sent to a clinic in Switzerland once the family was exiled from Spain. It proved impossible to keep him there, despite the risks he would run in trying to lead a normal life. In 1933, Alfonsito, then 26 years old, fell in love with a fellow patient at the clinic and, despite his father's disapproval, insisted on marrying her. Ten days before the wedding in June 1933, Alfonsito was forced to renounce his rights to the Spanish throne. Alfonsito's wife, a grandly named Cuban girl called Edelmira

Left: Alfonsito, Prince of Asturias, the first child of King Alfonso XIII and Queen Ena, as Victoria Eugenie was known in Spain, was the first victim of haemophilia in the Spanish royal family.

Sampedro-Ocejo y Robato, was not considered to be a fitting consort for a young prince whose father still had hopes of retrieving his Crown.

The newlyweds left for the United States, where Alfonsito planned to indulge his lifelong interest in farming. Instead, he indulged the full Spanish royal taste for promiscuity and, by 1937, his marriage had perished. The same year, Alfonsito married another Cuban, but the union ended after only six months.

In August 1934, while Gonzalo was out driving with his sister Beatrice, their car crashed into a wall. Gonzalo began to bleed. He died two days later, aged only 20.

With all the desperation of a young man cramming life with experience before his time ran out, Alfonsito embarked on a series of passionate love affairs which finally led to a liaison with Mildred Gaydon, a Miami nightclub hostess. Once again, Alfonsito's thoughts turned to marriage; however, one night in September 1938, he was driving Mildred home when he crashed his car. After being rushed to hospital, Alfonsito took several days to bleed to death. He was 31 years old.

A GLIMMER OF HOPE

The chronicle of ruined lives and hopes in the Spanish royal family which haemophilia had authored could never have had a happy ending. But at least its tentacles did not reach as far as King Alfonso feared. For years, he felt duty bound to warn would-be suitors with an eye on his daughters Beatrice and Maria Christina that they might be transmitters of the deadly disease. Many, not surprisingly, were put off by the warning because the story of the girls' haemophiliac brothers was now common knowledge.

Beatrice and Maria Christina, both attractive, with a fine sense of fashion and deservedly popular on the European social circuit, were made to feel like pariahs, condemned through no fault of their own to the wastage of spinsterhood. In time, though, King Alfonso relented and, rather late in the day for princesses, the sisters were allowed to marry. In 1935, when she was

26, Beatrice married Prince Alexander Torlonioa of Civitella-Cesi. Maria Christina, 27, wed Enrico Marone-Cinzano, a member of the famous vermouth company. For her sake, he was created Count Marone, and the Spanish princess became his second wife and first Countess Marone in 1940. Both girls had children, but none inherited haemophilia. Nor did the other grandchildren of King Alfonso and Queen Ena.

Haemophilia had nevertheless clocked up a fearsome record of depredation. It affected, in all, some 16 of Queen Victoria's descendants in three generations, ruined two royal families, shortened several lives, made miserable many more and, perhaps most insidious of all, created a climate of fear pervading royal families who did not, and could never, know where the dread disease was going to strike next.

> Beatrice and Maria Christina, both attractive, with a fine sense of fashion and deservedly popular on the European social circuit, were made to feel like pariahs, condemned through no fault of their own to the wastage of spinsterhood.

Queen Ena (centre) with her daughters Beatrice (left) and Maria Christina (third from left). After their long-delayed marriages, however, neither Beatrice nor Maria Christina passed on haemophilia to their children.

A BRIEF HISTORY OF HAEMOPHILIA

Haemophilia, a condition confined to males, was first scientifically observed and described in 1803 by an American physician, John Conrad Otto, of Philadelphia. The disease had been known since biblical times as a mysterious malady which caused profuse bleeding from even the most trivial cause. Cases had been recorded of boys bleeding uncontrollably if their gums were rubbed too roughly. A minor cut could kill. A boy could die from grazing his knee in the rough and tumble of childhood games. A bruise to the knee, joint or elbow might set off serious internal bleeding.

CRIPPLING DISEASE

Early death was very likely, but even if a haemophiliac survived he would endure agonies of pain before the blood at last coagulated and the bleeding ceased. The process might take a minimum of 30 minutes, or could last several hours. In a normal male, the blood would clot in wounds after five minutes or, in more serious cases, in up to 15. But severe bleeding was only part of the horror of haemophilia. The condition so damaged the body's systems that few haemophiliacs escaped crippling joint disease, such as arthritis, or

another danger, anaemia: both laid them open to infections that, but for their weakened state, they might have been able to resist.

Morphine could be used to mitigate the pain, but it was addictive, and virtually the only other relief was for the sufferer to pass out when the agony became too much to bear. What was missing was a scientific therapy, but that was out of reach until the mid-twentieth century. In the 1930s, egg white, peanut flour and snake venom were suggested as potential treatments for haemophilia, but the real, successful breakthrough had to wait until the cause of haemophilia was discovered some 20 years later.

In haemophiliacs, it was found, there was a mutation in one of the X chromosomes of their genetic make-up; this caused a deficiency of the clotting agent Factor VIII, which was also known as anti-haemophilic globulin. Although haemophilia was, and still remains, incurable, this discovery made it possible, after 1955, to control the disease with intravenous Factor VIII.

The coffin of Prince Leopold, Duke of Albany, the haemophiliac son of Queen Victoria, lying in a room at the Villa Nevada, Cannes in France festooned with wreaths.

XI

KINGS AND COMMUNISTS: CAROL II OF ROMANIA

His cousin, the British King George V, called King Carol II (1893–1953) 'an unmitigated cad'. He was twice thrown out of his kingdom, made lurid headlines in the newspapers with his scandalous escapades and married three times – twice morganatically – and yet he ended up largely forgotten and in exile, with only two members of his family in attendance at his funeral.

◆

From the start, though, there was little chance that King Carol II of Romania would turn out to be ordinary. Carol was too much like his mother, Marie, a granddaughter of the English Queen Victoria and a passionate creature much given to dramatic gestures. The strong-minded Marie never

Left and above: King Carol II of Romania was a nasty piece of work but extremely attractive to women. His escapades made lurid newspaper headlines across Europe.

hesitated to shock and, only five years after Carol was born in 1893, she embarked on a series of affairs and romances that lasted to the end of her life.

Carol's father, Crown Prince Ferdinand of Romania, could not have been more different. Shy, self-effacing and malleable, he lived under the thumb of his uncle King Carol I. Unlike Marie, who was not afraid to clash with the formidable king, Ferdinand allowed his uncle to order his life from waking to bedtime. He followed to the letter King Carol's decreed regime of study, performed to order on state occasions and never agitated for the social life that his uncle denied him.

Carol's mother, Queen Marie, was a granddaughter of Queen Victoria and, like her son, revelled in outrageous behaviour. Her lovers were legion.

It was hard, even cruel, but the received wisdom at the court of King Carol I was that 'Der Onkel', as he was usually called in awed tones, always knew best. In fact, what Der Onkel knew best was the relentless creed of discipline, obedience to authority and devotion to duty he brought with him from his native Germany when he was elected King of Romania in 1866. As king, the former Karl Eitel, Prince of Hohenzollern-Sigmaringen, took it as his right to impose his iron grip not only on Ferdinand, but also Ferdinand's son. It started in the nursery, where the king chose for the younger Carol an English nanny, Mary Green, who was a formidable example of that draconian breed, and went on to the martinet tutors in charge of steering young Carol through a punishing schedule of study.

MERCURIAL AND SECRETIVE

Carol soon soaked up the many frictions of his home environment – the weakness of his father, Marie's restlessness, his domineering great-uncle, the atmosphere of tension and intrigue in a household packed with the king's spies and suppressed fury at his mother's many lovers. As a result, the 'extremely amiable' outgoing boy Queen Marie had called Carol as a small child became wilful, mercurial, secretive and much given to depressions.

Fortunately, in 1913, Carol was able to enjoy some relief from this poisonous atmosphere after his mother suggested, and the king agreed, that he should attend the military academy in Potsdam. Carol took readily to military training and even seemed to enjoy the strict Prussian-style routine that prevailed there. He became liable to army service after World War I began in 1914. Two months later, in October 1914, old King Carol died, so that in 1916, when Romania entered the war against Germany, Carol's father, now King Ferdinand, made the decision.

SECRET MARRIAGE

As Crown prince and heir to the throne, Carol was kept well away from the fighting – in Bucharest, the Romanian capital, where he fell in love with Iona Lambrino, known as Zizi, a Romanian aristocrat whose family were frequent visitors at court. He wanted to

Right: Carol with his first wife Iona Lambrino, known as Zizi. The marriage was morganatic: when Carol became king, Zizi would not be queen. But the union did not last that long, anyway.

marry her, but his way was barred by law: after Carol I had been elected king in 1881, it was forbidden for members of the royal family to marry Romanians.

Carol, however, played cunning. He took Zizi across the Russian border and married her in secret. The clandestine wedding took place at an Orthodox Church near Odessa on 31 August 1918. That done, he sent his father a telegram announcing the marriage. In Bucharest, there was consternation. King Ferdinand wept and pleaded with his ministers for time to see Carol and maybe prise him away from Zizi. Ferdinand began by sentencing his son to 75 days' imprisonment at Horaitza, a monastery in the mountains near Bicaz. To save royal face, no mention was made of the marriage. Instead, it was announced that the punishment was for leaving his army command and crossing the Russian border without permission.

> Carol took Zizi across the Russian border and married her in secret. The clandestine wedding took place near Odessa on 31 August 1918. That done, he sent his father a telegram announcing the marriage.

But before his prison sentence could be anything more than an empty gesture, Carol had to be persuaded or pressurized into returning to Romania. With Zizi, Carol was tempted on board a train at the Russian border and was soon back in Bucharest. From that moment on, Carol was barraged with demands to give up his wife. At first, he resisted, but in the end Carol became sufficiently worn down to cave in. On 20 September 1918, three weeks after the marriage, he finally agreed to an annulment. The situation seemed resolved, but the time for sighs of relief was short.

RENEWED CONTROVERSY

The controversy quickly burst back to life when Zizi announced that she was pregnant. The news propelled Carol out of his complaisance and he burned with a new zeal, this time to stand by Zizi, even at the cost of giving up his right to the throne. Carol also underlined his resolve by making two attempts to disable himself – once by throwing himself under his horse; once by shooting himself in the leg. This, though, was not the time for heroics.

In 1919, Romania was being threatened by its neighbours Czechoslovakia, Hungary, Poland and Yugoslavia. An heir apparent who, like Carol, was prepared to desert his dynasty and his country put both at risk at a potentially perilous time. Romania's political problems succeeded, however, where his father had failed. Neighbouring Hungary fell under the power of communist revolutionaries and the Romanians, highly agitated at this development, invaded Hungary to keep the communists away from their frontier. Carol, still an army officer, was obliged to leave Zizi and join his regiment.

Carol's parents exploited this opportunity to the full. They made sure that military orders kept their son well away from Bucharest and his wife. For the next six months, Carol was confined to one army camp after another, while pressure was again exerted to make him come to heel.

CAPITULATION AND REMARRIAGE

Gradually, Carol's resistance crumbled until at last, at Christmas 1919, he sent Zizi what she called a 'letter of rupture and abandonment'. The letter reached her two weeks before her child, a son named Carol Mircea, was born on 8 January 1920. Carol made no attempt to see his son. It was evident that he was putting his illegal and therefore nonexistent marriage to Zizi out of his mind when he agreed to an arranged marriage with Princess Helen of Greece. The impulsive Carol asked Helen to marry him only a week after first meeting her in Switzerland. His mother, Queen Marie, was overjoyed. She looked on Helen as Carol's saviour, fondly believing that a good, properly royal marriage meant lifelong rehabilitation.

The marriage of Carol and Helen, which took place in Athens on 10 March 1921, proved to be nothing of the sort. The couple had little in common, and the premature birth of their only child, Michael, the following 25 October, exhausted Helen before any relationship had time to form. Helen soon became homesick for Greece and, in early 1922, took young Michael on a visit to Athens. She stayed away for four months.

Carol married a more acceptable wife, Helen of Greece, in 1921. Their only child, Michael (right) was born seven months later. Michael was to be the last king of Romania.

While she was there, her father, King Constantine, was driven into exile, and the rest of her family were being hounded by the Greek revolutionaries. When, finally, Helen returned to Romania, she brought her mother and her youngest sisters with her as royal refugees. Before long, it was not lost on Carol that his wife had grown some distance away from him. Carol had been unfaithful more than once, even while 'married' to Zizi Lambrino, and this time the most likely reason for Helen's coolness was the gossip that Carol's latest liaison, with Eleana Lupescu, was no passing fancy.

Discretion had never been one of Carol's virtues, and he did not hesitate to flaunt his new infatuation.

As a result, Lupescu's character, ancestry and personal history were soon to become common gossip and newspaper sensation. The coverage was, of course, salacious and hostile.

MAGNETIC PERSONALITY
 Red-haired and green-eyed, Eleana Lupescu, later known as Magda, was born in 1899, the daughter of a Jewish pharmacist in Jassy. When Carol met her, she was still the wife of a Romanian army officer, Lieutenant Ion Tampeanu. Tampeanu later divorced Lupescu for adultery. Lupescu was a familiar peril for

Eleana Lupescu, known as Magda, was the great love of Carol's life. They met in 1923 and remained together for 30 years, until Carol died in 1953.

those beleaguered wives who had to struggle to keep hold of straying husbands. She was neither beautiful nor charming, yet possessed powerful sexual attraction and a magnetic personality that could easily overwhelm susceptible males. Carol, of course, was extremely susceptible. He was inevitably hooked and, before long, Lupescu was being vilified as his 'Jewish whore'. With this, Carol's enemies were handed the perfect opportunity to topple him.

Carol's indiscretions had not only been sexual, but political as well. He alienated the Liberal Party, which came to power in Romania in 1922, by threatening that, when he became king, he would outlaw the party and exile the Liberal Prime Minister, Ion Bratianu. And not only Bratianu, but also his brother-in-law and supporter, Barbu Stirbey, Queen Marie's most enduring lover and reportedly the father of her last child, Mircea.

AN OPPORTUNITY GRASPED

It was an unwise move for Carol to lay his cards so openly on the table before a cunning politician such as Bratianu, who hit back in more subtle and more invidious fashion. Jews were greatly hated in Romania and, probably engineered by Bratianu, there was an upsurge of anti-Semitic feeling against Magda Lupescu and, through her, against Carol. Carol also found himself excluded from the Regency Council when his parents went abroad on a goodwill tour in 1924. Usually, he would have headed the council. Next, Bratianu accused his Air Minister of taking bribes over the acquisition of new machines for the Romanian Air Force. This directly implicated Carol, who was Inspector-General of the Air Force. Even though a subsequent inquiry exonerated the hapless minister and his associates, there was no antidote for the poison, once it was sown.

Within a short time, the entire Romanian establishment, orchestrated by Bratianu, was opposed to Carol. The end came in November 1925, when Carol was sent to England to represent Romania at the funeral of his great-aunt, Queen Alexandra, the widow of King Edward VII. He had no intention of leaving Lupescu behind and so risk losing her. Instead, he arranged for Lupescu to leave Romania for Paris. Instead of returning home after the funeral, he headed for the French capital, picked up Lupescu and moved on to Italy.

This was disturbing enough, but the real bombshell burst later in December, when Carol wrote to his father from Venice, shedding his army commission, his status as Crown prince and his membership of the Romanian royal family. He even asked King Ferdinand to give him a new name.

A NEW LIFE AND A NEW HEIR

Pressure to return, reconsider and recant descended on Carol in full force, but, for once, with Lupescu's support, he was well placed to resist all blandishments. At last, it dawned on all concerned that Carol was not going to be persuaded. Not long afterwards, on 20 July 1927, King Ferdinand died and his demise was widely ascribed to a 'broken heart'. Carol's five-year-old son Michael succeeded him, with his uncle Prince Nicolas as regent. Carol, meanwhile, was living in Paris, having taken a new name, Caraiman. He was happy with Lupescu and with the freedom he now enjoyed to indulge his interests in philately, music and fast cars. Nevertheless, Carol hankered after Romania and remained alert for any sign that might give him a chance to return home.

Lupescu was neither beautiful nor charming, yet possessed powerful sexual attraction and a magnetic personality that could easily overwhelm susceptible males.

The chance came after Ion Bratianu died in 1927 and the Liberal Party lost its motive power. The following year, on 10 November, Bratianu's successor, Juliu Maniu, leader of the National Peasant Party, which was sympathetic to Carol, took office as Prime Minister. But before Carol could return, Maniu needed to make sure that his power base was sufficiently secure. This was why another 18 months passed before Carol could board an aircraft in Munich and land at Bucharest's Bancasa airport on 6 June 1930, to be greeted by intense rejoicing throughout Romania. At last feeling secure in his support, Carol made it clear that he had not returned, as Maniu had

Ion Bratianu, who became Liberal Prime Minister in Romania in 1922, was daggers drawn with Carol who threatened that when he became king, he would exile Bratianu.

hypocrisy, Carol punished Nicolas for a 'crime' which he himself had already committed: Jeanne was a Romanian, like Zizi Lambrino, but Carol told his brother that he could not recognize his marriage, stripped him of his title and threw him out.

> Carol wrote to his father from Venice, shedding his army commission, his status as Crown prince and his membership of the Romanian royal family.

supposed, to be co-opted onto the Regency Council. Carol meant to be king with full royal rights and that meant autocratic rights.

EXACTING REVENGE

For the first time in his life, Carol, now 36, was free to do as he chose and what he chose to do first was exact revenge for past wrongs. His principal victim was his mother, Queen Marie. He had never forgiven Marie for her part in destroying his first marriage. Now, he placed spies in her household. Her income was cut and she was banned from attending state functions.

Eventually, to escape Carol's depredations, Marie went travelling outside Romania until, in 1938, she returned home to die. She almost failed to make it. Marie was in a Dresden sanitarium after years of ill health when she realized that her end was nigh. But Carol refused to send an aircraft for her, and Marie had to make the journey by train. She survived to reach Bucharest and the Pelisor Palace on 18 July, but died there the same evening.

Carol was not finished yet. His vengeance also took in his brother Nicolas, whom he exiled with his Romanian wife, Jeanne, in April 1937. With stunning

Magda Lupescu returned to Romania soon after Carol, probably by August 1930, and was installed in a splendid house in Bucharest's most fashionable suburb. Carol spent a fortune on his mistress, decking her out in the finest jewels, specially made for her in Antwerp and elsewhere. He visited Lupescu every evening, but had the grace not to give offence on official occasions, which he did not allow her to attend. Lupescu, however, was not made for a back-seat existence. In time, she gathered her own informal court about her, entertaining industrialists – especially arms manufacturers – and, curiously, mixing together her Jewish friends with fascists. Carol doted on his mistress, who was indeed extraordinary in taming a man who, until then, had womanized as naturally as he breathed.

AN ACTIVE RULER

As sovereign, though, Carol proved to be much more than a king of dalliance and self-indulgence. To keep vital foreign investment continuing, Romania had to be perceived as a country under strong rule. Carol was perfectly capable of exercising firm but not too despotic control, and among his initiatives were the revival of the Romanian oilfields, a rapid increase in the manufacturing industry, the promotion of scientific studies and the nationwide airlines and the fostering of Romanian music, literature and art.

Only a few years after Carol's return, his country was culturally and industrially in better shape than it had ever been. But this was the 1930s, the decade of dictators in Germany, Italy, Portugal and Spain, and Romania was not going to be left alone to enjoy its revival for long. Germany under the Nazis was already spreading tentacles across Europe, soon after Adolf Hitler seized absolute power in Germany in 1934. Hitler's plans for Romania were to make it increasingly dependent on Germany through trade links, particularly the trade in oil. The Nazis also fostered ideological ties with Romania in the form of the Iron Guard, an extreme right-wing element that the Nazis financed.

> He had never forgiven Marie for her part in destroying his first marriage. Now, he placed spies in her household. Her income was cut and she was banned from attending state functions.

Like Hitler, the Iron Guard and its leader Ion Antonescu were dedicated to wiping out Jewish influence and, with it, all Romanian Jews: Magda Lupescu was top of the list. The Iron Guard's links with the Nazis remained clandestine for some time, and King Carol did not become aware of them until late 1937. To counter the Iron Guard and its Nazi backers, Carol and his Prime Minister Nicolas Titulescu sought new trade links with Britain and France, and friendlier relations with states such as Czechoslovakia, which could act as geographical buffers between Romania and Germany.

Carol also took steps to weaken the Iron Guard by decimating its leadership. Corneliu Codrianu, who founded the Iron Guard in 1927, together with his associates, was put on trial for treason and imprisoned. In 1938, they were shot dead while trying to escape, or so

Carol's mother, Queen Marie, was a seemingly ageless, fashionable woman. This 1926 picture shows her with the bobbed hairstyle adopted by women in the 1920s.

it was given out. In reality, Codrianu and his followers were strangled by their guards.

A NEW FIGURE RISES TO POWER

Eventually, inside a rapidly shrinking Romania, there emerged the inevitable 'strong man' who claimed to have the power to save the country. He was General Ion Antonescu, who had Nazi sympathies but wanted a fascist Romania independent of German control. When he proposed to provide just that, but wanted absolute power to do it, the embattled Carol was, unfortunately, tempted. In accepting Antonescu's terms, he turned himself into a figurehead, and a figurehead Antonescu lost no time in throwing overboard.

A scene of splendour at the inauguration of the new Romanian government under Prime Minister Armand Calinescu in 1939, nine years after Carol's return from exile.

Carol was perfectly capable of exercising firm control, and among his initiatives were the revival of the Romanian oilfields, a rapid increase in the manufacturing industry, the promotion of scientific studies and the nationwide airlines and the fostering of Romanian music, literature and art.

THE FOLLY OF APPEASEMENT

Unfortunately, French and British reaction to the Nazi threat was far less muscular than Romania's. They turned instead to appeasement, a craven policy that ultimately led to the outbreak of World War II in Europe on 3 September 1939. The shock waves soon reached Romania. On 21 September, Carol's trusty Prime Minister Armand Calinescu was ambushed and murdered, together with his bodyguards. The culprits were, of course, members of the Iron Guard. Six months later, in May/June 1940, the war brought the major part of continental Europe under Nazi occupation. At that, Russia seized Romanian Bessarabia and Germany, together with Bulgaria and Hungary, poached even more territory.

Antonescu is shown making a speech, surrounded by his Nazi-backed Iron Guard, an extreme right-wing, paramilitary force originally founded in 1927.

> The Nazis also fostered ideological ties with Romania in the form of the Iron Guard, an extreme right-wing element that the Nazis financed.

The strong man assumed power on 4 September 1940 and at once, Carol was faced with anti-royalist demonstrations and popular demands to abdicate. Completely outmaneuvered, Carol stepped down on 5 September; the following day, his son, 16-year-old Michael, who had been demoted when his father returned to claim the Crown in 1930, became king for a second time. On 8 September, with Magda

Lupescu and a small entourage, Carol was bundled out of Romania on a train that did not stop until it crossed the border with Yugoslavia. On the way, members of the Iron Guard attempted an ambush and several shots were fired at the carriages, but no one was hurt.

LIFE IN EXILE

Carol and Lupescu became nomads, moving from Yugoslavia to Switzerland, on to France, Spain and Portugal, then across the Atlantic to Mexico and Brazil. In Latin America, Carol felt more assured that

December 1941: Michael I, the youthful King of Romania, with General Antonescu as they study the progress of Romanian troops in the Soviet Union. Nazi Germany had invaded the USSR six months earlier.

his 'Jewish' mistress was safe than would have been the case in Nazi-dominated Europe. At the same time, a base across the Atlantic was handy for keeping in touch with influential war leaders. This, Carol believed, was vital to prevent him sinking into oblivion, after his ignominious exit from Romania. The ex-king set up a court in exile with former officials

Magda Lupescu (left) and ex-King Carol (second from left) in a carriage driving through Hamilton, Bermuda in 1941 with Carol's Royal Chamberlain Ernest Urdarianu (third from left).

who had remained loyal to him and never let a chance go by of keeping the world in mind of his existence. He kept contact with the United States ambassadors in Havana and Mexico City, wrote to US President Franklin Roosevelt and to his cousin King George VI in England, outlining his plan for a National Council for Free Romania.

But, to Carol's dismay, the British, who were already hosting other royal and government exiles from occupied Albania, Czechoslovakia, France, the Netherlands, Norway and Poland, declined to add

Romania to the list. The letter that reached the ex-king from Buckingham Palace was couched in terms of exemplary politeness. But the answer was still no. The US State Department reacted in the same way.

HOPES FOR RETURN DASHED

Despite being spurned, Carol never lost hope that the British and Americans would win the war and allow him to return to Romania. In 1944, the ex-king had the satisfaction of seeing his son Michael gather enough support to arrest Antonescu for war crimes. Found guilty, Antonescu was executed in 1946. This, though, did not bring salvation for Carol. Even before the war ended in 1945, King Michael was faced with an even greater challenge – a takeover masterminded by Communist Russia. A communist government was imposed on him, and the Romanian Democratic Popular Republic was declared. By 1947, Michael, too, was an ex-king and went into exile early in 1948.

Now, Carol had little or nothing to hope for and, by mid-1947, it seemed that what little he had managed to retain was about to be

Carol and Magda pictured just after their wedding on 5 July 1947. Although she looks well, Magda was desperately ill with anaemia. It was a surprise to many that she ever recovered.

Carol and Lupescu became nomads, moving from Yugoslavia to Switzerland, on to France, Spain and Portugal, then across the Atlantic to Mexico and Brazil.

taken from him. Magda Lupescu, it appeared, was dying. In what Carol saw as a last loving gesture, he married her on 5 July and gave her the title of Her Royal Highness Princess Eleana of Romania. But although the new princess seemed far gone in anaemia and depression at the time, she recovered with the help of blood transfusions and ultimately outlived Carol by 24 years.

KING PETER II OF YUGOSLAVIA

King Peter II of Yugoslavia (1923–1970) was another royal exile, forced out of his kingdom after his country was invaded by the forces of Nazi Germany in 1941. Only 17 years of age at the time, Peter had exercised full royal powers for only 10 days before he went on the run and eventually arrived in England as a refugee. But while other royals retired sadly but gracefully into exile, Peter never accepted the situation. Instead, he became obsessed with the forlorn hope of regaining his throne, regaling anyone and everyone with the tragedies of his life and the

beauties of Yugoslavia. His wife, Princess Alexandra of Greece, whose family had long experience as royals in exile, attempted to persuade him that retrieving his throne was a lost cause. Eventually, the issue came decisively between them and the marriage broke up.

DRINK AND DOOMED PLOTS

Afterwards, in 1965, Peter moved to the United States, where he tried but always failed to make a new life for himself, first as a consultant, then as a

King Peter II of Yugoslavia reigned for only 10 days before he was forced out by a Nazi invasion in 1941. Here is the 17-year-old ex-King (left) with US President Franklin Delano Roosevelt (right).

financier. He sought solace in drink and attempts to gather together a band of royalist Yugoslavs to back his efforts to retrieve his Crown. They soon dwindled away. Frustration and resentment ate away at him. He never forgave wartime British Prime Minister Winston Churchill for backing Marshal Tito, his Communist rival in Yugoslavia, rather than himself. Believing that the British had cynically betrayed him, the ex-king hatched plots against Tito, who took over in Yugoslavia after World War II. But all of them were doomed.

By his mid-forties, Peter was an old, tired man, bloated by drink, worn down by self-pity and broken by failure. In 1970, he died of liver failure, aged only 47 and an all-but-forgotten figure. Peter's lack of standing among the monarchs and ex-monarchs of Europe was poignantly illustrated when press interest, such as it was, centred on the fact that Peter was the only monarch ever to die in the United States.

> By his mid-forties, Peter was an old, tired man, bloated by drink, worn down by self-pity and broken by failure. In 1970, he died of liver failure, aged only 47 and an all-but-forgotten figure.

Other royals in exile after World War II adjusted to their fate because they were able to adapt to alternative ways of life. But Peter II was never meant to be a businessman, an executive or a consultant. As he himself confessed, he was suited only to be a king and, with a mere 10 days in 1941 as the only time he held real royal power, he had scant experience even of that.

When she was strong enough, the newlyweds left Rio de Janeiro in Brazil and settled in Estoril, the fashionable coastal resort near Lisbon in Portugal. There, in 1949, to scotch rumours that they were about to divorce, Carol and Lupescu went through a religious wedding ceremony at which she appeared a dazzling bride. Carol, by contrast, looked pale and drawn, and far from well. Four years later, he began to suffer chest pains and, after a particularly bad attack on 3 April 1953, a doctor was called. By the time the doctor arrived, Carol seemed better; however, when the doctor turned to leave, another, swifter heart attack suddenly killed Carol. He was 59.

> The news of Carol's death made only modest copy in the press that had once gorged itself on his headline-making escapades. The one-time king was past history, and the world had no more use for his high-profile type of monarch.

ALMOST IGNORED IN DEATH

Through his paternal grandmother, Carol was related to the erstwhile royal family of Portugal, who had lost their throne in 1910. Consequently, he was given full royal honours at his funeral and was buried in the Pantheon reserved for the Portuguese kings. His widow was there, shrouded in black from head to foot. She wept throughout the ceremony. Of Carol's immediate family, only his nephew Prince Alexander of Yugoslavia, yet another royal exile, and Carol's estranged brother, Prince Nicolas, attended the funeral. Everyone else, including Michael, found reasons for staying away.

The news of Carol's death made only modest copy in the press that had once gorged itself on his headline-making escapades. The one-time king was past history, and the world had no more use for his high-profile type of monarch. For a man such as Carol, who had lived on controversy and its attendant publicity, that was a fate much more ignominious than the death in exile which, at the end, was all he could expect.

THE NETHERLANDS: A ROYAL FAMILY IN TROUBLE

The Dutch have experienced problems with their monarchy ever since Queen Wilhelmina of the Netherlands married Prince Hendrick of Mecklenburg-Shwerin in 1901. Since then, the ruling dynasty, the Royal House of Orange-Nassau, has thrown up a long series of difficulties, stemming from one or other of two main sources.

✦

One was the tendency of Dutch monarchs to abdicate when the going got rough. The other derived from the marriages of three successive reigning queens – Wilhelmina, her daughter Juliana

Left: Queen Wilhelmina of the Netherlands taking the oath of the constitution at the new church in Amsterdam on 1 August 1898.
Above: Princess Juliana, who became Queen in 1948, seen before her accession with her controversial husband Prince Bernhardt.

and Juliana's daughter Beatrix, to Germans whose nationality alone provoked alarm and enmity among their subjects.

The abdicating habit began with the first Dutch monarch, Willem I, who declared himself king in 1815 only to find, in time, that his royal powers were limited by a liberal constitution. Unable to live with the popular rights, free speech and democracy which liberal rule required, Willem, a natural autocrat, abdicated in 1840. His grandson, Willem III, who became king nine years later, was a chip off the same royal block and struggled hard against the same restraints. He was constantly trying to escape liberal controls, and threatened abdication several times. But Willem III never got away: he was talked out of it by his strong-minded Russian mother, Queen Anna Pavlovna, and ended up reigning in the Netherlands for 50 years.

UNEASY ALLIANCES

Wilhelmina, his 10-year-old daughter and only surviving heir, succeeded him as queen regnant on his death in 1890. This introduced new trouble: the discontented male consort. Wilhelmina's husband,

Prince Bernhardt, pictured here in military uniform, was a daredevil risk-taker and womaniser but did a great deal of work for the Netherlands.

Prince Hendrik, disliked being a royal consort, hated having to walk one step behind his wife and was, as he put it, thoroughly bored with being a mere decoration. Hendrik had no real power in the Netherlands, and it did their marriage little good when Wilhelmina saw to it that it stayed that way.

> Wilhelmina's husband, Prince Hendrik, disliked being a royal consort, hated having to walk one step behind his wife and was, as he put it, thoroughly bored with being a mere decoration.

Still, the policy of keeping Hendrick on a leash may well have commended itself to Wilhelmina's subjects. Hendrick's homeland, Germany, was the rising power in Europe, and the neighbouring Netherlands was, at best, wary of its ambitious and expansionist neighbour. This long-lasting perception turned to real fear after 1933, when the Nazis and their leader Adolf Hitler seized power and turned Germany into a racist totalitarian state ruled by terror and repression that soon became a threat to the peace of Europe and the world.

Dutch fear of Germany and Germans was strong enough by 1937 to provoke serious objections to the prospect of Juliana, Wilhelmina's heir, marrying a German husband, Prince Bernhardt of the Lippe-Biesterfeld. Despite the objections, the marriage took place in The Hague on 7 January 1937.

A PLAYBOY AND A HERO

Bernhardt had his attractions, as a dashing 'man about town' with an exciting though often dangerous lifestyle. He was a reckless driver who crashed several cars in his time, and he often injured himself quite seriously. He loved big-game hunting, boating and flying, and was almost killed in high-speed accidents. A prince as reckless as this had a certain daredevil glamour which was augmented by the loyalty to the Netherlands which he displayed during World War II. Bernhardt helped to organize Dutch resistance to the

Nazi occupation, saw action with the British Royal Air Force, carried out reconnaissance missions over Europe and, in 1945, took part in arranging the German surrender in the Netherlands.

After the war, the initial enmity the Dutch had shown Bernhardt had turned to admiration, and he was now regarded as a hero. But rather unfairly, he still carried his playboy label and regularly made the gossip columns in the newspapers with his jet-setting lifestyle, his extramarital affairs, his lavish partying and his shady friends who included Juan Péron, the Argentine President and his wife, Eva.

ATTENTION DIVERTED

Bernhardt never entirely shed this fly-by-night reputation, but in 1947 he moved out of the scandal spotlight for a time. Attention was beamed instead on Juliana and her unorthodox methods of trying to cure the eye problems of her youngest daughter, Princess Marina Christina, usually known as Marijke. Marikje, born in 1947, was the fourth daughter of Juliana and Bernhardt, after Beatrix (1938), Irene (1939) and Margriet (1943). At birth, Marijke had cataracts over both eyes, after her mother caught German measles during pregnancy. World-class physicians and surgeons were called in, but the most they could do was restore blurred vision to one eye.

> At birth, Marijke had cataracts over both eyes, after her mother caught German measles during pregnancy.

Juliana and Bernhardt were distraught, but hope of a full cure was restored after the couple encountered Greet Hofmans, a faith healer who claimed to be a representative of God. Hofmans told Juliana that, with sufficient prayer and belief, God would give little Marijke her sight. Juliana, who believed in miracles and astrology, and had a penchant for the supernatural, became convinced of the faith healer's powers. When the child was brought in to meet Hofmans, the healer fell to her knees and prayed long and fervently. Afterwards, she told Juliana: 'God will give the child sight in two years, if we pray hard enough.'

Princess Marikje, the youngest daughter of Queen Juliana, who was born with severe eye problems.

Juliana and even Bernhardt, who had reservations about Hofmans, were impressed. The faith healer moved into the Soestdijk Palace near Amsterdam. Every day, the entire royal family attended prayer sessions at the palace. But, before long, Bernhardt began to suspect that his wife was becoming unduly dependent on the faith healer. He realized that Hofmans would always promise a dazzling future. 'You will be the greatest queen (the country) has ever had,' she told Juliana. But this future would transpire only as long as Juliana prayed fervently enough and listened to God, which, of course, meant listening to Greet Hofmans. After that, Bernhardt resolved to get rid of the faith healer. Juliana, of course, would not hear of it.

Queen Wilhelmina (foreground, left) at the bombed out ruins of the Dutch church at Austin Friars in London on 10 May 1941, the first anniversary of the Nazi German invasion of the Netherlands. She was accompanied by her son-in-law, Prince Bernhardt (saluting).

MISPLACED FAITH

The situation became even more serious in 1948, when Wilhelmina abdicated and Juliana became queen. Now Juliana possessed the powers of a sovereign and, though they were limited by law, a measure of political muscle as well. To the worried Bernhardt, this gave much more room for Greet Hofmans to influence his impressionable wife.

Bernhardt's fears soon came true as Hofmans extended her activities to giving the new queen political advice. This was too much for Bernhardt. In 1950, he ordered Hofmans's belongings removed from the Soestdijk Palace, where she had been living for the past nine years.

But this was by no means the end of Hofmans' royal connection. The faith healer went on to hold

Wilhelmina abdicated the Dutch throne after a reign of 58 years. This photograph, taken on 2 September 1948, four days before the formal abdication, shows crowds in front of the royal palace in Amsterdam to cheer Wilhelmina as she appeared on the balcony.

meetings where she propounded the virtues of pacifism and mysticism, and the need to make contact with creatures from outer space. Juliana and her mother, ex-queen Wilhelmina, attended several of these meetings and were strongly influenced by them. This became clear when several of Juliana's fellow 'believers', such as Baron von Heeckeren van Molecatan, who became the Queen's private secretary, were given important positions at court.

To add another layer of unease, this was the Cold War era. This made the Hofmans affair even more alarming when Juliana's public speeches began to reflect the faith healer's pacifist ideas: Juliana advocated Dutch disarmament and the disbanding of the Dutch armed forces. Alarm bells rang in Washington and other Western capitals at the prospect of the Netherlands, tiny though it was, providing a hole in the defences the United States

and the West were striving to maintain against the spread of communism.

By this time, Bernhardt and Juliana were on opposite sides over the Hofmans affair, and their disagreement was so serious that it was starting to affect their marriage. This placed Bernhardt in a dangerous position. He owed everything – his public posts, his titles, his business connections and much more – to remaining married to the Queen of the Netherlands.

Usually, protocol demanded that no story of this kind reached the Dutch media. But in 1956, in a desperate move, the prince leaked news about the Hofmans affair to the German magazine *Der Spiegel*. The story spread from there to the world's press. The respectful Dutch media sat on the revelations for a while, but eventually could keep silent no longer. Now, Juliana's subjects, too, learned about the weird goings-on behind the royal scenes.

> Juliana advocated Dutch disarmament and the disbanding of the Dutch armed forces. Alarm bells rang in Washington and other Western capitals

The publicity unleashed by *Der Spiegel* had been so embarrassing that powerful political and business figures, who had a lot to lose unless the Hofmans affair was solved, exerted heavy pressure on Juliana to send the faith healer away or abdicate or face being forced to resign. This was stern stuff, but thankfully it made the queen pause and think again. So did the fact that Hofmans had failed to cure Marikje's eye troubles. Juliana agreed that the faith healer's contacts with the court and the royal family should be severed, and purged her household of Hofmans supporters. After that, Greet Hofmans faded away and died in obscurity in 1968. By then, new medical treatments had vastly improved Marijke's sight until she was able to lead a normal life.

FURTHER RUCTIONS

Meanwhile, Juliana and Bernhardt had been through another serious problem with another of their daughters, Princess Irene. In 1963, news broke that Irene had secretly converted to Catholicism and was engaged to Prince Carlos Hugo of Bourbon Parma, heir to Xavier, Duke of Parma, a pretender to the Spanish throne.

The new Queen Juliana with Prince Bernhardt on their way to her inauguration ceremony after her mother's abdication, 6 September 1948.

Princess Irene, second daughter of Queen Juliana, with Prince Carlos Hugo of Bourbon-Parma. Juliana strongly opposed their marriage which nevertheless took place on 29 April 1964.

For the fiercely Protestant Dutch and their queen, Irene's conversion was bad enough, but there was more. Prince Carlos Hugo was a supporter of General Francisco Franco, the fascist dictator who had ruled Spain since the end of its Civil War in 1939. Franco, in his turn, was detested by the Dutch for supporting Nazi Germany during World War II.

> For the fiercely Protestant Dutch and their queen, Irene's conversion was bad enough. Queen Juliana became desperate to prevent Carlos Hugo's marriage to her daughter.

Against this background, Carlos Hugo meant big trouble for Queen Juliana, who became desperate to prevent his marriage to her daughter. Irene, however, proved to be extremely stubborn and also had no qualms about deceiving her mother. Juliana sent one of her secretaries to Madrid to see the princess and to Juliana's relief reported that the engagement was off and that Irene was returning to the Netherlands. Juliana's relief was short-lived. When the aircraft supposedly flying her daughter home arrived, Irene was not among the passengers. Juliana and Bernhardt resolved to go to Madrid themselves and make their daughter see sense, but Dutch hatred of all things Spanish was so great that the government vowed to resign to a man if the queen were to set foot in Spain. Juliana returned home deeply distressed and in tears. Meanwhile, in Madrid, Irene went into hiding, first at a convent, then afterwards in rooms near Carlos Hugo's apartment. Both suspected that they were under some sort of covert surveillance, which included tapping their telephones. They resorted to standing at windows exchanging hand signals. Back in the Netherlands, resistance to the marriage remained as fierce as ever, but early in 1964 a breakthrough appeared imminent when Irene indicated that she was ready to come home.

NO COMPROMISE

Hopes rose that the impasse would be resolved, but they were false hopes. When Prince Bernhardt flew to Madrid and brought Irene and Carlos Hugo back to the Netherlands, it was soon plain that the young couple was in no mood to compromise. If anything, their impudence knew no bounds. In a heated six-hour exchange at the Soestdijk Palace, they made it plain that they expected a lavish Roman Catholic wedding in the Protestant Nieuwe Kerk in Amsterdam, with all members of Europe's royal families invited. Juliana, utterly taken aback, told the couple in no uncertain terms that she would never sanction the wedding and that, if one did take place, it could mean the end of the royal House of Orange-Nassau.

> Juliana, utterly taken aback, told the couple in no uncertain terms that she would never sanction the wedding and that, if one did take place, it could mean the end of the royal House of Orange-Nassau.

Juliana was by no means overstating the case, for a full-blown constitutional crisis was certainly in prospect unless a way out was found. Until now, Irene, who was second in line to the Dutch throne after her elder sister, Beatrix, had been anxious to preserve her rights of succession. Only if she renounced those rights, Irene was told, would she be

> Irene's reaction was defiant. With Carlos Hugo, she went to Rome where the couple had an audience with Pope Paul VI.

able to marry Carlos Hugo and at the same time preserve the monarchy.

Irene's reaction was defiant. With Carlos Hugo, she went to Rome where the couple had an audience with Pope Paul VI. As a public statement of her intransigence, this was hard to beat. All the same, Irene managed it. Soon after returning from Rome, she was scheduled to make an official visit to Mexico with her mother, but she failed to turn up at Schiphol Airport. The departure was delayed, but still no Irene. Juliana, badly shaken by this public humiliation at her daughter's hands, had no option but to fly to Mexico alone.

Irene was not finished yet. She publicly supported the claim of Carlos Hugo and his father to the Spanish throne and was photographed attending a rally staged by the Falangist party of General Franco. Irene had attracted some sympathy in the Netherlands as a young woman being thwarted in love, but the sentimental Romeo-and-Juliet image faded away after she openly sided with the fascist Franco and his right-wing rule in Spain.

YET ANOTHER CONTROVERSIAL MARRIAGE

Back in the early 1960s, the Dutch had little respite from controversy before another royal marriage caused another uproar. In July 1966, Queen Juliana broadcast on television and radio the news that Princess Beatrix, the heir to the throne, was engaged to the diplomat Claus-Georg von Amsberg.

'I assure you,' Juliana told her people. 'It is a good thing.'

As far as Juliana's subjects were concerned, it was very far from being a 'good thing'. Claus von Amsberg, an aristocrat who had met Beatrix on a Swiss skiing holiday, would be the third German in succession to marry into the Dutch royal family. More than that, he

MARRIAGE AT A PRICE

Irene and Carlos Hugo were married in Rome on 29 April 1964. No member of her family was present at the ceremony, and all important members of European royalty stayed away. As the marriage had not been sanctioned by the Netherlands Estates-General, or Parliament, as required by law, Irene automatically lost her rights of succession to the throne. She had already agreed to live with her husband outside the Netherlands, which many Dutch people agreed, sadly, was just as well.

Ultimately, this painful experience proved to be all for nothing. Irene and Carlos Hugo divorced in 1981, and Irene returned to the Netherlands with their four children. The dramatic events of 1964 were not forgotten, however, and, when Irene's book *Dialogue with Nature* was published in 1995, the Dutch media could not resist a 'dig' at its author by publicizing those passages that revealed her conversations with trees and dolphins.

Princess Irene and Carlos Hugo were married at the Basilica of Santa Maria Maggiore in Rome. The Dutch royal family was not present. They are pictured here in their car shortly after the controversial ceremony.

Crown Princess Beatrice, heir to the Dutch throne, and the West German diplomat Claus von Amsberg, at their wedding on 10 March 1966. Like her sister Irene, though for different reasons, Beatrix's marriage was controversial.

had been a member of the Hitler Youth and the Wehrmacht, the German Army.

Inevitably, it was not long before demonstrations and protests against the marriage erupted onto the streets. There were anti-Claus marches and rallies. Furious crowds chanted, '*Claus raus! Claus raus!*' ('Claus out! Claus out!') Orange-coloured swastikas appeared on buildings and billboards, and were chalked on pavements and walls, and even on the walls of the royal palace in Amsterdam, daubed there by an audacious protester who managed to get through the security cordon. More worrying still, cries of 'Up the Republic!' were heard in some places, indicating that a vociferous section of the public, albeit a probable minority, was tiring of monarchy.

There was little real danger of a republic, but, according to a public opinion poll taken soon after the engagement was announced, support for the monarchy dropped from 86 to 74 per cent. The

A LESS-THAN-SERENE WEDDING DAY

In spite of all the problems and protests, the marriage of Princess Beatrix and Claus von Amsberg took place in Amsterdam on 10 March 1966. But it turned out to be one of the most disorderly weddings in royal history. Most European royals and nobles, apprised in advance of serious trouble, stayed away, and their caution proved justified. The wedding day started with a protest march on the royal palace, followed by street fighting between protesters and police, and several arrests. It continued with a smoke bomb that was rolled underneath the wedding carriage and exploded. The carriage was also struck by a dead chicken with a

There were boycotts and anti-German demonstrations in Amsterdam on Beatrix's wedding day. Smoke bombs were thrown, one of them into the path of the golden coach carrying the newlyweds.

Nazi swastika painted on its body. Stink bombs and more smoke bombs were flung at the procession until a column of acrid smoke rose some 50 feet (15 metres) into the air.

Rabbis, remembering the sufferings of Dutch Jews during World War II – thousands were sent to die in the Nazi concentration camps – boycotted the event. So, too, did the members of Amsterdam city council and several government employees. The police who were supposedly charged with keeping the peace beat several protesters to the ground, in a display so savage that the Burgomaster of Amsterdam and the Chief of Police were afterwards dismissed from their posts. But much, if not quite all, was forgiven a year later, in 1967, when Beatrix gave birth to the first of her three sons, Willem-Alexander, who became the first surviving male heir to the Dutch throne in 116 years.

newspaper *Nieuwe Courant*, published in Rotterdam, commented: 'Can a German put flowers at our memorials for heroes he fought against?' A group of six prominent Resistance fighters who had fought the German invaders during World War II publicly denounced the marriage of Beatrix and Claus as 'unbearable'. A monthly magazine *De Gide* suggested that, like her sister Irene, Beatrix should abdicate her rights to the throne.

AVERTING ANOTHER SUCCESSION CRISIS

Beatrix, who was ambitious and not a little impatient for her mother to abdicate so that she could become queen, would never have agreed to that. But Juliana, who was not as keen on the marriage as she gave out, had her own plan to avoid such a situation, by preventing the marriage taking place at all. Juliana made contact with the West German foreign minister, Claus's superior in the diplomatic service, and asked him to have Claus transferred to somewhere outside

> The newspaper *Nieuwe Courant*, published in Rotterdam, commented: 'Can a German put flowers at our memorials for heroes he fought against?'

Europe. Juliana's plan failed after the strong-minded Beatrix heard of it and went on a three-day hunger strike that so alarmed her mother that she gave up.

Instead, in a complete turnaround, Juliana decided to commend Claus von Amsberg to her subjects by arranging for him to appear at a televised press

In March 1954, Prince Bernhardt visited Maxwell Air Base in Alabama, USA, where he met Dean C. Strother, Deputy Commander of the Air University. Bernhardt had an interest in buying aircraft for the Dutch air force.

conference with Beatrix. This was a significant concession by the House of Orange-Nassau, which had hitherto shrunk from exposing themselves to media scrutiny. But 38-year-old Claus had not been a diplomat for nothing, and his 'stage presence' was perfect. Slim, handsome and elegant, he appeared on screen as a modest man, very much in love with Beatrix, regretful about the Nazi past of his youth, and aiming above all to win the acceptance of the Dutch people.

> Claus's personal wartime record in Soviet Russia and East Germany was checked and nothing incriminating was found.

This last was easier said than done. Claus won over many viewers and others who believed he should have a fair chance to prove himself. But there were still many who could not be mollified – not even when Claus's personal wartime record in Soviet Russia and East Germany was checked and nothing incriminating was found. All the same, the protesters made their point quite forcefully. Anti-royal pamphlets were thrown onto the deck of a ship taking Beatrix and Claus on a tour of Amsterdam's canals. Despite a nationwide appeal, less than US$20,000 (£9790) was raised for a wedding present from a populace that soon afterwards contributed almost 18 times that much for the relief of famine in India. Even Claus's mother, Julie, Baroness von dem Bussche-Haddenhausen, was targeted, and received letters signed 'with hate'.

A SCANDAL TOO FAR
While the drama of Beatrix's marriage grabbed national and world headlines, yet another controversy for the House of Orange-Nassau was brewing in the background. Serious though the others were, this one eclipsed them all and proved to be one scandal too far for Juliana and Bernhardt.

Although he was in his mid-sixties by the time Beatrix married, Prince Bernhardt was still essentially the fast-living, jet-setting man about town he had been since his youth. He was no gadabout wastrel, though: Bernhardt worked long and hard to promote the Netherlands

economy and did it so successfully that he rarely returned home from abroad without obtaining overseas contracts for Dutch companies and corporations.

SAILING CLOSE TO THE WIND
Nevertheless, Bernhardt sometimes sailed too close to the wind. His travels around the world on official, charity or private business afforded him a wide-ranging social life which included ties with disreputable entrepreneurs and other wheeler-dealers Foreign travel also gave Bernhardt opportunities for extramarital affairs. Queen Juliana was not a strong-minded, outspoken woman like her mother, Wilhelmina, or her daughters, Beatrix and Irene. She was more comfortable in the dreamy world of mystic religion and was not the sort to deal effectively with an errant husband. This, though, did not mean that Juliana was

Prince Bernhardt photographed on 2 July 1979, when he was already in trouble over his suspect deals with the Lockheed Corporation.

Juliana (centre) with Prince Bernhardt on her left, makes a speech on 30 April 1980, the day her daughter (left) became Queen.

unaware of what Bernhardt was up to. For one thing, she knew all about his liaison with Helène Grinda, known as the 'Paris Poupette', who gave birth to Bernhardt's daughter Alexia in 1967, 13 years after he fathered another girl, Alicia, on another mistress.

One of the Prince's biggest business contacts was the American Lockheed Corporation, the military aircraft of which he had been urging the Netherlands government to buy since the early 1950s. But somewhere along the line, proper business relations

> Proper business relations strayed into malpractice … In return, Bernhardt would 'improve the climate' in the Netherlands on Lockheed's behalf.

strayed into malpractice and, in around 1959, through a Swiss lawyer, Lockheed proposed to pay the prince one million US dollars (£490,770), spread over the following three years. In return, Bernhardt would 'improve the climate' in the Netherlands on Lockheed's behalf.

JULIANA STANDS BY HER MAN

The arrangement remained confidential for some 16 years, until rumours about what was, effectively, a very large bribe began to circulate at the end of 1975. Bernhardt at once denied any wrongdoing, claiming that a man in his exalted position was 'above such things'. The time was long past, however, when royalty could place itself above the law and get away with it. If found guilty of taking bribes, Bernhardt faced prison, prince or no prince. He was fortunate, though, that Juliana saw it as her duty to stand by him. She threatened to abdicate if Bernhardt were not exonerated.

THE ACCUSATIONS DEEPEN

Neither government nor people wanted Juliana to go; however, despite denials, the accusations against Bernhardt kept on coming from Lockheed operatives and others who had known the prince over the years. Another bribe allegedly received by the prince from Lockheed, in 1968, was for US$100,000 (£49,077), which was paid to a certain 'Victor Baarn'. Lockheed claimed that Victor Baarn was Prince Bernhardt under an assumed name. Among further allegations, Bernhardt was said to have given the Argentine dictator Juan Péron US$1,000,000 (£490,770) as part of a deal in which Argentina ordered Dutch railway equipment.

> Juliana had ... been queen for almost 30 years and was approaching 70 years of age. These facts meant that she could abdicate with honour instead of in a blaze of adverse publicity.

All these stories were given headline coverage by the European media, together with revelations about Bernhardt's affairs. One of these alleged that Bernhardt had mistresses in such outlandish places as Tanzania and the Ivory Coast in Africa, as well as in Mexico. It was alleged, too, that he had bought an expensive apartment in Paris for Helène Grinda and threw lavish parties for his friends where Champagne, caviar and oysters were on the menu. So were the attentions of 'beautiful women' – or, in more candid parlance, call girls.

Bernhardt's personal and business lives were unravelling fast. Ultimately, he was saved by a special government commission, which published its findings on 26 August 1976. The commission concluded that Prince Bernhardt, acting in the belief that his position was unassailable, had been careless when he entered into 'transactions which were bound to create the impression that he was susceptible to favours'.

Bernhardt's position was boosted by a vote in the States-General of 149 to 2 in favour of not prosecuting him and also by the fact that Juliana did not, in the event, abdicate in the wake of the Lockheed scandal. But Bernhardt's escape from prosecution had its price. He was obliged to resign from all his official, military, charitable and business posts, give up wearing his many uniforms – a lifelong pleasure of his – and, effectively, retire from national and international life.

A NEW QUEEN

Although Juliana had chosen not to give up the throne in 1976, by then she had been queen for almost 30 years and was approaching 70 years of age. These facts meant that she could abdicate with honour instead of in a blaze of adverse publicity. Juliana signed the Act of Abdication on 30 April 1980, the day she turned 71 years of age. Afterwards, she reverted to her original title of princess.

Beatrix succeeded her mother, so realizing her own long-awaited ambition. Prince Claus was now the queen's consort. But, like Prince Hendrik, the consort of Queen Wilhelmina, Claus eventually became discontented with his secondary position. He particularly resented the fact that it placed him behind his own sons in the royal order of precedence. Claus began to suffer from depression, which continued for many years before his death in 2002.

Juliana and Bernhardt, who both died two years later, spent their remaining years in charity work, which doubtless afforded them a much-needed time of quiet after the many storms of their 67-year marriage. For Bernhardt, the contrast was total. In the Netherlands, as in other European monarchies, there was no traditional role on offer for the consorts of reigning queens. Instead, they had to make their own way. Bernhardt's way had taken him to impressive heights – politically, militarily, financially, internationally. In his time, he was arguably the mightiest of male consorts. But Bernhardt's way had a fatal flaw ...

'He thought he was a ninetheenth-century prince,' one Dutch politician commented. 'That he could do whatever he wanted, that he was above the law.'

Queen Beatrix attending the Queen's Day celebrations on 30 April 2002, the anniversary of her accession and also her official birthday.

KING LEOPOLD II
AND THE BELGIAN CONGO

In the late nineteenth century, Africa, the 'Dark Continent', was one of the great unknowns of world geography. Unknown, that is, to Europeans who suspected, rightly, that its as yet unexplored interior was a treasure house of untapped mineral and other commercial wealth. In particular, for the major imperial powers – Britain, France, the Netherlands, Spain and Portugal – Africa meant more trade, more wealth and more territory to add to their already extensive empires.

✦

The so-called Scramble for Africa that resulted saw the rival empires carve up the greater part of the continent between them. But virtually unknown for more than 20 years, the Scramble also saw the greatest humanitarian crisis – one that verged on genocide – ever to come out of nineteenth-century

Left: King Leopold II of Belgium. Leopold was the major villain of the European Scramble for Africa.
Above: A much earlier photograph of Leopold, the second king of Belgium, a newcomer nation created in 1830.

Africa. The culprit was not a major player, but a king: Leopold II of Belgium, who ruled one of the smallest countries in Europe.

VISIONS OF EMPIRE

Belgium was a newcomer nation that became independent only in 1830. Nevertheless, King Leopold was not content to let his realm, with an area of only around 30,500km² (11,800 sq miles), remain among the small fry of Europe. He wanted to match the big imperial powers with a colony of his own.

At the personal level, Leopold was well equipped to bulldoze his way through all obstacles to his ambition. He was tenacious and stubborn, and never took no for an answer. He cared little for personal popularity. Admittedly, Leopold had a surface charm, but beneath it he was vindictive and cunning. Above all, he was dangerous when let loose to work out his ambitions unrestrained, guided by nothing more than his autocratic will to succeed.

When Leopold became king in 1865, there were still many blank spaces on the map of Africa, and the French and Germans were busy filling them – in the Sahara, along the border with Nigeria and at the mouth of the Congo (Zaire) River. Non-Europeans were getting in on the act, too: the Sultan of Zanzibar and the Khedive of Egypt were together planning to carve out a huge Muslim empire in central Africa. Leopold followed these developments very closely

and promoted his own colonizing schemes in 1875, with plans to send Belgian settlers to Mozambique in east Africa, the island of Borneo in the Malay Archipelago and the Philippine islands. All these ventures failed, however, not least because the territories in question were already occupied by the Portuguese, the Dutch and the Spaniards, respectively. None of them was keen to have Belgians or anyone else poaching their preserves.

The chief focus of Leopold's interest was the Congo, a vast area of central Africa more than 75 times the size of Belgium. Sited in a huge depression of the African plateau, the potential wealth of the Congo was immense. Among the prizes there for the taking were rubber, industrial diamonds, gold, silver, copper and other valuable metals. Large areas of this enormous treasure house were still unclaimed in 1876, when Leopold revealed his plan for establishing a Belgian foothold in Africa. The king summoned Baron Auguste Lambermont, a civil servant at the Ministry of Foreign Affairs, to his palace and told him: 'I would like to do something in Africa. You know exactly what the explorers have done there and together we shall see what we can make of it with a peaceful humanitarian objective – my only concern and aim.'

> Among the prizes there
> for the taking were rubber,
> industrial diamonds, gold, silver,
> copper and other valuable metals.

A SHARE OF THE CAKE

Leopold's real objective was very different. Peaceful humanitarianism was the last thing on his mind. In 1876, when he convened a Geographical Conference in Brussels, ostensibly for the purpose of exploring and 'civilizing' Africa, he deliberately concealed his true intentions from the delegates.

'Needless to say,' Leopold told them, ' in bringing you to Brussels, I was in no way motivated by selfish designs. No, gentlemen, if Belgium is small, she is also happy and contented with her lot.'

Except for the British, who saw through him at once, the delegates   representatives of foreign governments, explorers, philanthropists, business entrepreneurs – became convinced of Leopold's altruism and hailed him as the leader of Europe's humanitarian mission in Africa. But far from lacking colonial ambition, as he pretended, the king was a

The Belgian Congo was a phenomenally rich territory. This photograph was taken in around 1905 showing a dredge sampling the waters of the Congo River for gold.

brutal opportunist who wrote: 'I do not want to miss the [chance] of our obtaining a share in this magnificent African cake.'

The slicing of the cake took place at the Conference convened in Berlin on 15 November 1884, but not without controversy. So much self-interest was in play that, inevitably, proceedings were marked by rival claims to the most advantageous areas of Africa. One thing soon became clear, though: none of the major colonial powers wanted any of the others to claim an area large enough to give them a dominant interest. The greatest of these areas was the Congo, where Leopold had created for himself an exemplary image as the champion of law, order and civilization – to make sure

The African continent was carved up between several Europe countries aiming to create or enlarge their empires. This is a scene from Nigeria, showing representatives of local tribes meeting with British officials after Britain appropriated the region In 1885.

Leopold took the name King-Sovereign of the Congo Free State and began by taking the initiatives expected of an enlightened nineteenth-century ruler. By 1889, he had a railway built to create a modern system of communications through what was effectively near-impenetrable mountain and jungle. In

> As ever the humanitarian overtones were deceptive. Leopold's real purpose was to promote profits.

1889–90, he hosted an anti-slavery conference in Brussels designed to destroy the slave trade. The conference was attended by Britain, France, Germany and other imperialist powers, and Leopold proposed that all of them construct a series of forts in their various territories. These would put a stop to raids by 'Arab' slavers and serve as bases for pursuing caravans carrying slaves into the interior.

LEOPOLD CLAIMS HIS PRIZE

It looked good, as Leopold meant it to look, but as ever the humanitarian overtones were deceptive. Leopold's real purpose was to promote profits. For example, decrees issued by Leopold in 1891 and 1892 effectively turned the ivory and rubber trades into a state monopoly. This, in turn, dispossessed the Congolese living in and around the forests in the Ubangi-Uele river basins where they hunted elephants for ivory and tapped the rubber trees. This was now forbidden, unless they handed over their produce to the Belgian authorities. At the same time, all trading was banned in the Uele valley, damaging if not destroying the livelihood of the native Congolese.

ABUSE AND EXPLOITATION

While the native inhabitants struggled to survive, exports of rubber from the Congo Free State rose from less than 250 metric tons in 1893 to 6000 metric tons by 1901. Economically, the Free State seemed to be thriving. But socially it was a disaster. Behind these

that the prize would be his when the time came. The time came on 25 February 1885, when the Berlin Act was signed and the Congo was allocated to Leopold, as the only 'neutral' involved in the Conference. When he was mentioned by name, the delegates rose to their feet and cheered in an outburst of approval. It was an emotional moment. Leopold's triumph was complete.

Two Congolese rubber workers weigh their loads as Belgian officials watch. Native workers could be severely punished if they failed to reach set targets.

soaring trade figures, shocking tales of abuse and savage exploitation were coming out of the Congo. After 1891, numerous letters and reports reached the British Colonial Office in London recounting how Belgian authorities were cruelly misusing Africans. Witnesses spoke of floggings, torture, forced labour, hostage-taking, imprisonment in chains, and several deaths in consequence. There were, too, fearful tales of other inhumane treatment and even the massacre of entire Congolese villages.

This, though, was by no means the end of it. Missionaries in the Congo weighed in with their own evidence of cruelty towards the natives, and the looting by State soldiers of their homes and property. These stories were emblazoned across newspaper headlines and received particular attention in *The Times*, Britain's most renowned and respected newspaper.

Henry Morton Stanley warned King Leopold of the deleterious effect the horror stories were having in Britain. 'The [British] are such believers in what they see in print,' he told the king. King Leopold appeared to take the lesson to heart.

'If there are abuses in the Congo, we must stop them,' he wrote to Baron Edmond van Eetvelde, the

Right: Henry Morton Stanley was a journalist-turned-explorer who helped King Leopold develop the Congo. Here he is shown dressed for his most famous exploit: finding explorer Dr David Livingstone.

KING LEOPOLD THE HYPOCHONDRIAC

King Leopold II was something of a hypochondriac and went to extreme lengths to preserve his health: his self-protection went so far that he had a waterproof cover made for his beard so that, if it got wet in the rain, he would not catch a cold. If anyone sneezed near him, he almost panicked at the prospect of catching something. Some of Leopold's aides-de-camp soon learned how to play on his fear of illness to their advantage, securing a day or two off duty by pretending to have a cold: Leopold forbade them to come near him or his court until they had recovered.

The elderly King Leopold was a health and fitness fanatic. For his aides, the way to get a holiday from his service was to pretend to be ill, preferably with something catching.

> ## Leopold set up a Commission for the Protection of Natives, the task of which was to advise of any malpractices that came to their attention.

Secretary of State in the Congo. 'If they are perpetuated, they will bring about the collapse of the State.'

A CYNICAL SMOKESCREEN

Leopold set up a Commission for the Protection of Natives, the task of which was to advise of any malpractices that came to their attention. This, though, seemed to be yet another of Leopold's smokescreens, for the new Commission was organized in a way that virtually guaranteed it could not work. Its members, all missionaries, were sited hundreds of kilometres apart so that contact between them, never easy in the best of times, was greatly compromised. In addition, the Commission's powers were limited: it had no right to demand information, even though it was dealing with

the very officials who had every reason to conceal it. Unsurprisingly, the Commission achieved little, if anything, of note, and the abuses continued.

Some of the worst examples of maltreatment came about because of the quota system applied to rubber production, the most vital component of the Congolese economy. If the native inhabitants did not produce as much rubber as they should, vicious punishments – floggings, beatings, mutilation, even the murder of family members – were applied to make them do better.

One missionary, the Reverend John Harris, wrote a truly harrowing account in 1905, describing how brutally underproduction was punished. He wrote:

'The people from Esanga [south of the Congo River] told how, on one occasion, because 49 instead of 50 baskets of rubber were brought in, some [of them] were imprisoned and sentries were sent to punish the people.... all had harrowing stories to tell of the brutal murder of near relatives. Some they had seen shot before their eyes; in other cases, they had fled into the

In 1865, when Leopold became king of Belgium there were many blanks in the map of Africa. By 1884 large areas had been filled in by European colonization.

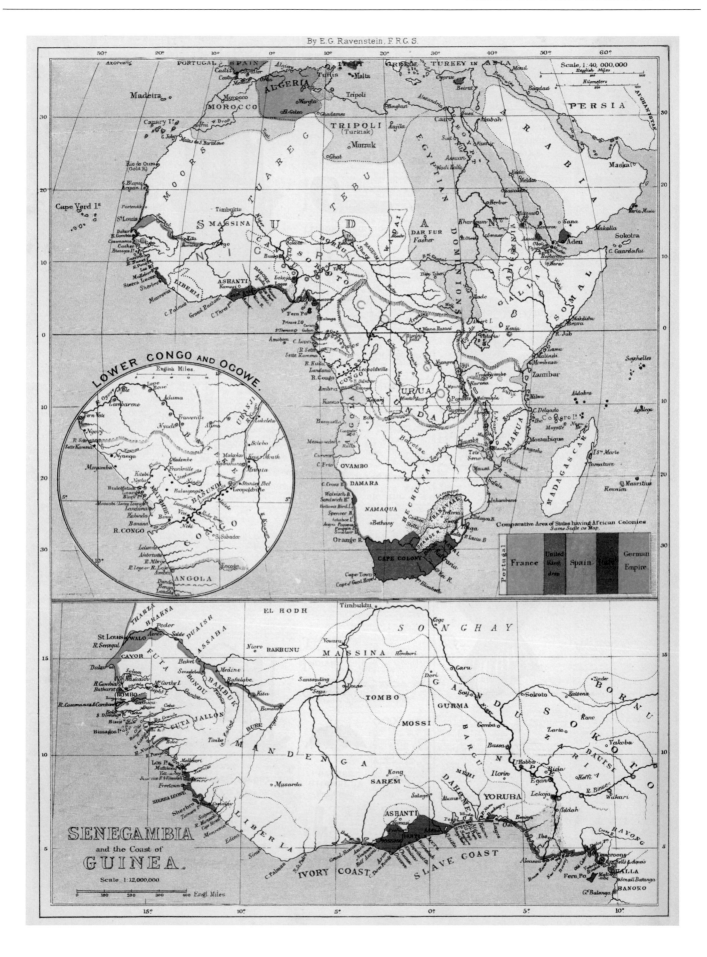

By E.G. Ravenstein, F.R.G.S.

In 1904, Sir Roger Casement (first left) who worked for the British consular service reported atrocities being committed in the Belgian Congo. Here he is with Congolese men who are holding the severed hands of men killed by Congo 'Free State' troops.

bush to save themselves and, when they returned, had found the dead bodies of their relatives lying about.

'While the men were in the forest trying to get rubber, their wives were outraged, ill treated and stolen from them by the sentries. In the light of all they have suffered at the hands of their oppressors, one wonders they do not hate the very sight of white men. We missionaries sometimes feel that our message of salvation [through Christ] must seem like a mockery to them.'

The uproar that first arose in Britain when news of the Congolese atrocities broke spread to Germany where, in 1899, a damning report was published in a Cologne newspaper, the *Kölnische Zeitung*. In this

report, Achille Fiévez, commandant in Sultanate of Zemio, a Free State protectorate, was charged with no fewer than 1308 mutilations, most of them the severing of hands.

> they had fled into the bush to save themselves and, when they returned, had found the dead bodies of their relatives lying about.

A BARRAGE OF CRITICISM

By this time, at the turn of the twentieth century, Leopold found himself under fire from virtually all sides as a man responsible for some of the most fearful atrocities it was possible to commit. Not all of it was true. There were exaggerations, outright lies or highly

It was reckoned that, since the advent of the Free State in 1885, the population of the Congo had declined by 70 per cent, from around 30 million to 9 million.

King Leopold, who had posed as a benefactor of the Congolese, was universally condemned for the near-genocide he permitted in the Congo.

coloured speculation. Nevertheless, the valid evidence was sufficient to establish the fact that an appallingly savage state of affairs had developed in the Congo, where innocent people were being maltreated and murdered in the name of commercial profit. The scale of these abuses was appalling. It was reckoned that, since the advent of the Free State in 1885, the population of the Congo had declined by 70 per cent, from around 30 million to 9 million. With this, the mask of good intentions, humanitarian concern and civilizing purpose which King Leopold had cultivated for so many years at last fell away.

ATROCITY AND ABUSE

When charges of atrocity and abuse were first laid against the Congo Free State around the turn of the twentieth century, Leopold felt deeply hurt. As the attacks escalated to nearly worldwide proportions, however, he thought he could see the reason behind them: he believed it was a British plot, backed by King Edward VII and powered by malicious jealousy, all of it designed to destroy the Congo Free State and, with it, the great achievement of his life and effort.

This conspiracy theory intensified in Leopold's mind in 1903, when Sir Roger Casement, British consul to the Congo, was sent to the Free State to investigate the situation. Casement discovered a litany of horrors, including one young man whose 'hands had been beaten off with the butt

KING LEOPOLD III (1901–1983)

The sons of hero-kings have always had a hard time matching the renown of their fathers, and King Leopold III, who succeeded to the throne of Belgium in 1934, was certainly one of them. His father, Albert I, had made himself a national hero in Belgium during World War I. As his son and successor, Leopold III never managed to live up to his father's shining example. Instead, his reign was marked by painful controversies. The last of them cost him his throne.

In 1926, Leopold married the beautiful Princess Astrid of Sweden. Astrid was instantly popular in Belgium, for her informality, her grace and her refusal to follow strict royal protocol and so hold herself aloof from the adoring masses who flocked to her every

On 16 July 1951, the unpopular King Leopold III of Belgium (third from left), signed an instrument of abdication in favour of his son, Baudouin (far right).

public appearance. Leopold and Astrid had a daughter and two sons, and were expecting a fourth child in 1935. On 29 August of that year, Leopold was driving along a narrow, winding road near their villa on the shores of Lake Lucerne in Switzerland. Without warning, he suddenly lost control of his car. The vehicle veered off the road and plunged down a ravine before crashing into the lake. Astrid, aged 29, was killed and her unborn child with her.

The effect on the people of Belgium was comparable to the response in 1997 to the death of Diana, Princess of Wales, who was also killed prematurely in a car crash. The mourning crowds were inconsolable in their grief as Astrid was buried in the royal vault at the Church of our Lady in Laeken. Her tomb became a focus of pilgrimage for many years afterwards. In a sense, the Belgians never stopped grieving for Astrid and laid the blame for her death on her husband. Leopold became seriously unpopular in Belgium and was never able to repair his reputation.

ACCUSED OF COWARDICE

This hostility came home to roost after the forces of Nazi Germany invaded Belgium in 1940, soon after the commencement of World War II. The Belgian army was totally outmatched by the German Blitzkrieg – lightning war – but they nevertheless managed to keep the invaders at bay for more than two weeks. The Belgians were prevented from fighting to the finish by King Leopold, who realized that his people were likely to be slaughtered and their towns and villages pulverized if the hostilities continued. Leopold capitulated to the invaders and, although he refused to cooperate with them, he was still accused of cowardice and treason by British Prime Minister Winston Churchill and Churchill's French counterpart, Paul Reynaud.

The mud stuck. The Belgians were convinced that Leopold had betrayed them, and their attitude was reflected by his government ministers, who fled to London to escape the invaders. There, they set up a government-in-exile, but refused to accept Leopold's rights as their king.

Leopold spent the rest of the war as a prisoner of the Germans. Then, on 11 September 1941, he created

The Belgians never forgave Leopold III after his beautiful Swedish wife, Queen Astrid, was killed in 1935 in a car accident while he was at the wheel.

yet another controversy, this time by marrying again. His second wife, Liliane Baels, afterwards created Princess Liliane, became a hated figure in Belgium, where her marriage was regarded as an affront to the late, still lamented Astrid.

The war ended in 1945, but Leopold did not immediately resume his reign in Belgium. The Germans had moved the king and his family to a fort in Saxony in 1944; a few months before hostilities ended, they were moved again, this time to Salzburg in Austria. After being liberated by the US Army, the king chose not to return to Belgium immediately. Instead, he removed to Switzerland, where he remained for the next six years until his position in Belgium was sorted out.

In 1946, a special Commission of Enquiry found Leopold not guilty of treason, but his loyalty to his country remained in doubt and the intense bitterness against him failed to diminish. In 1950, a referendum was held to decide whether the Belgians wanted their king back or not. The results looked hopeful: around 57 per cent of Belgians voted for him to return, but the story was quite different after Leopold arrived home. He was greeted with strikes and vociferous protests in which several demonstrators were killed. Civil war seemed about to break out between Leopold's supporters and his enemies. Rather than divide the country and damage the monarchy, Leopold decided to abdicate in favour of his eldest son, Baudouin, who succeeded to the throne on 16 July 1951. Leopold died in 1983, aged 82.

ends of rifles against a tree'. In another village, three small children, a youth and an old woman had had their right hands cut off at the wrist.

'I visited two large villages in the interior,' Casement reported. 'I found that fully half the population now consisted of refugees … I saw and questioned several groups of these people … They went on to declare, when asked why they had fled [their district] that they had endured such ill treatment at the hands of the government soldiers … that life had become intolerable, that nothing had remained for them at home but to be killed for failure to bring in a certain amount of rubber, or to die from starvation or exposure in their attempts to satisfy the demands made upon them …'

Casement had intended to probe further into the interior of the Congo, but by November 1903, six months after his arrival, he had seen and heard enough. He returned to Britain to present his report to the Foreign Office.

With the Casement report, another similar opinion from Evelyn Baring, 1st Earl of Cromer, who also visited Free State territory in 1903, and the conclusions of a British commission of inquiry in 1905, the evidence against Leopold was piled too high for him to be saved by any denials, protests or obfuscations.

THE GOVERNMENT INTERVENES

This far, the Belgian government had remained in the wings. But the scandal of the Congo and the

This document, signed by King Leopold II in 1906, ended his control of the Congo and allowed the Belgian government to annex the territory that he believed was his private possession.

exploitation and maltreatment that had taken place there were so abominable that it could no longer afford to stand aside. There was talk of removing the Congo from the king's jurisdiction and annexing it to Belgium if he could not or would not introduce fundamental humanitarian reforms to put the situation right. No one seriously believed that the autocratic Leopold would backtrack as far as this, if at all. It would not be an easy task to prise his private colony from his grasp, as Leopold registered a furious reaction to a motion passed in the Belgian parliament in 1906 to examine the legal framework for annexation

'My rights over the Congo cannot be shared,' the king announced. They are the fruit of my own labours … the adversaries of the Congo are pressing for immediate annexation. These persons no doubt hope that a change of regime would effectively sabotage the work now in progress and would enable them to reap some rich booty from the wreckage.'

Leopold had underestimated his liberal-minded enemies in the Belgian parliament. They wanted him out of the Congo forthwith. A similar debate in the British Parliament four months later reached the same conclusion and for the same reasons. There had been no real sign that any reforms were going to be introduced in the Congo or that the condition of the native inhabitants would in any way be mitigated. Then, on 13 December 1906, Leopold suddenly changed tack and announced that he was in favour of annexation and wanted it to take place soon.

> The scandal of the Congo and the exploitation and maltreatment that had taken place there were so abominable that it could no longer afford to stand aside.

This sudden about-turn was largely due to news that the United States might soon intervene in the Congo affair. Leopold had always valued the approval and support of the United States, and, in an effort to make sure of it, he invited American millionaires, such as Daniel Guggenheim, to invest money in the development of a stretch of territory covering more than

one million hectares at the mouth of the River Kasai, a tributary of the Congo River. By this means, Leopold hoped to tie up the wealth of the Free State in foreign companies, invest in those companies and, through them, retain control of the Congo's money supply. If, however, the Americans were to side with his European enemies, it would destroy Leopold's plan.

LEOPOLD LOSES HIS HOLD

The plan failed anyway. Once again, Leopold had underestimated the strength of the opposition to his Congo policy. The Americans, like the British and also the Germans, were horrified at the cruelties and abuses that had taken place in the Congo and refused to support Leopold. With this powerful united front ranged against him, Leopold knew the end when he saw it. On 14 December 1906, the Belgian Prime Minister, Baron Beernaert Smet de Naeyer, announced that his government was now committed to the annexation of the Congo. For a while, Leopold kept up the fiction that only he had rights over the Congo, but it was a fantasy that soon faded when, on 18 October 1908, he was obliged to sign the Treaty of Cession which finally took the Congo away from him and made it a Belgian colony.

Belgium was now the imperial power Leopold had wanted it to be, but the price, for him, was a new status as a pariah. He was detested by the Congolese and spurned by his government and people, by public opinion abroad and by his fellow monarchs and their ministers, diplomats and parliaments. On a personal level, Leopold was also estranged from his wife and two of his three daughters.

Only one person in the world, it seemed, wanted to know the King of the Belgians. Blanche Delacroix, who became Leopold's mistress in 1900 and later gave birth to his two sons, brought him some happiness, but their affair also incurred resentment among the Catholic Belgians, whose strict morality had no room for irregular liaisons.

DESPISED EVEN IN DEATH

Leopold was nearly 75 years of age when he lost the Congo Free State. It was a traumatic experience that he did not survive for long. In early December 1909, he became seriously ill with an intestinal blockage. No drugs or other treatment succeeded in shifting it and Leopold realized that he was dying. He summoned his

Belgium was now the imperial power Leopold had wanted it to be, but the price, for him, was a new status as a pariah. He was detested by the Congolese and spurned by his government and people.

priest, Father Coorean and married his mistress Blanche Delacroix, whom he had created Baroness de Vaughan. A few days later, Leopold died and Blanche, who had stayed with him to the end, was led away in floods of tears.

A month before his death, Leopold had given instructions that his funeral should be a simple affair, without pomp or show, and no procession following his cortège. It was feared, though, that a humble burial would be interpreted as an insult to the dead king and a last cruel barb from his successor, his nephew Albert, and his government.

Instead, Leopold's wishes were ignored. He lay in state for two days at the royal palace in Brussels and was afterwards given the full state funeral that was appropriate for his high position. All the same, the hostility and disgust Leopold had aroused played its part in the ceremony. His enemies among the crowd watching his funeral procession were determined to have the last word. Some onlookers booed as his cortège passed by, and others, it was said, spat at his coffin. No one could have been more detested than that.

Leopold II was so detested by his subjects in Belgium that some of them booed and spat at his coffin during his funeral procession in 1909. This illustration shows him on his deathbed.

KING ALBERT II AND HIS ILLEGITIMATE DAUGHTER

For at least half a century after the scandals and controversies surrounding King Leopold III, the Belgian royal family carefully cultivated a respectable, even staid, image that made them too dull for sensational media interest.

Then, in October 1999, a sex scandal broke with a story that King Albert II had sired an illegitimate daughter, born in 1968. There was widespread television coverage and, in Britain, *The Times* splashed the news across its front page.

'This is an earthquake for royalty,' one newspaper editor commented. 'For the first time in our history, the Belgian media has looked through the keyhole of the royal palace.'

If it were an earthquake, then the Belgian royal family did their best to fend off the aftershocks and prevent too many media revelations. Nevertheless, the press did discover enough to identify Albert's illegitimate daughter as Delphine Boel, a sculptor and artist living in London's Portobello Road. Delphine's mother, the Belgian aristocrat Baroness Sybille de Selys Longchamps, married a wealthy industrialist after Delphine's birth when her rumoured royal father was heir to his brother, the late King Baudouin. Albert succeeded him in 1993.

After the first burst of publicity, however, everyone involved – Baroness Sybille, Delphine herself and the Belgian royal palace press office – remained very close-mouthed about the affair. The palace dismissed the story as 'malevolent gossip' and King Albert denied that Delphine was his daughter. There has been no formal proof, and no paternity test has ever been carried out. But the rumours, as rumours always do, persist.

Delphine Boel (right) the illegitimate daughter of King Albert II of Belgium, on a shopping trip with her mother the Baroness Sybille de Selys Longchamps (left) in 1999.

THE GRIMALDIS OF MONACO

The Grimaldis of Monaco – Prince Rainier III, his wife, the former Hollywood film star Grace Kelly, and their three children – formed another royal family who have kept rumour mongers and the popular press well fed with salacious gossip, innuendo and sensation.

✦

When it was not the romantic adventures of Rainier and Grace, it was the antics of their two daughters, Caroline and Stephanie, both of whom became pregnant first and married afterwards. Either that or the spotlight was on their brother Albert, the present ruler of the tiny Mediterranean principality, whose sexual orientation was considered suspect as he aged, but remained unwed.

Left and above: Prince Rainier and actress Grace Kelly at her parents' home after their engagement was announced on 5 January 1956. Kelly gave up her successful Hollywood film career when she married Rainier in 1956.

The irony of the Grimaldi story derives from the convincing but false snow-white image that Hollywood manufactured for the beautiful blonde Grace Kelly, who was a star turn of Tinseltown during the 1950s. She was presented as a virginal Roman Catholic who was far too scrupulous to 'play around' and a young woman who avoided all the temptations, sexual and otherwise, offered by the glamorous movie capital. Before Grace married Prince Rainier in a so-called 'fairytale' wedding in Monaco, her record was apparently checked for any scandals, affairs or less than respectable boyfriends. Anything untoward might have ruined Grace's chance of marrying Rainier: as a reigning prince, he could not afford a wife, the future mother of his heirs, who had a suspect past. But nothing incriminating was discovered, or so it was reported, and the wedding duly took place in Monaco on 19 April 1956.

THE TRUTH BENEATH THE IMAGE

Subsequently, the report turned out to be one of the greatest cover-ups of all time. The truth about Grace's life before Rainier came from an incontrovertible source – her mother, Margaret Kelly, who provided the press with the low-down on her daughter's affairs. So many lovers were involved that there was enough information for a 10-part series, entitled 'My Daughter Grace Kelly – Her Life and Romances', which appeared in newspapers right across America. There was no shortage of famous names: the cast list for the series included almost every male star in Hollywood, married or single, who made films there in the early 1950s.

> Her mother, Margaret Kelly, provided the press with the low-down on her daughter's affairs. There was no shortage of famous names: the list included almost every male star in Hollywood, married or single…

Gary Cooper, Bing Crosby, William Holden, Ray Milland, Frank Sinatra and David Niven were among them. So was Clark Gable, whom Grace seduced during the making of the film *Mogambo* in 1952. 'What else do you do when you're alone with Clark Gable in Africa?' she reputedly commented. Cary Grant had an on-again, off-again affair with Grace for seven years. Alfred Hitchcock, the renowned director of Hollywood thrillers, was also in love with Grace. He lived a mile away from her home in Laurel Canyon, Los Angeles, and provided himself with a powerful telescope so that he could see Grace undress next to a window left open for the purpose.

Other 'dubious' characters were also listed as Grace's lovers. One was the French film star Jean-Pierre Aumont, who, Grace came to suspect, wanted to promote his own career by appearing with her in

THE NEED FOR HEIRS

Rainier was in the United States when Margaret Kelly's revelations appeared in the American press. He arrived late in 1955, ostensibly to have a medical check-up. In reality, Rainier wanted to see Grace and meet her family. It was already well known that the 32-year-old prince was looking for a suitable wife for political as well as personal reasons: if he failed to marry and died without a legitimate heir, Monaco would be absorbed by France in accordance with a treaty signed in 1918. This was a fate that Rainier believed it was his duty to prevent. He had hoped to marry the French model and actress Gisèle Pascal, but was forced to break with her on learning that a physical examination showed she was unable to bear children. The diagnosis proved incorrect when Pascal gave birth to a child in 1962. Rainier was heartbroken, but by then it was too late. Rainier had already been married to Grace Kelly for five years.

'sensational' paparazzi-style photographs. Another was the fashion designer Oleg Cassini. Shortly after they first met in 1955, Grace and Cassini announced their decision to marry and were obviously in a hurry to do so. It transpired that the reason for their haste was that Grace was pregnant. Grace's parents did not approve of Cassini, who was sixteen years older than their daughter and had already been married and divorced twice. Grace bowed to parental pressure and, instead of marrying Cassini, she had an abortion. Afterwards, Cassini always refused to talk about it. 'It's too delicate a matter,' he would say. 'Let people think what they want to think.'

THE HUNT FOR A SUITABLE BRIDE

In 1955, there were several names on Rainier's list of potential brides, but Rainier believed that Grace Kelly filled the bill best – for her looks, her elegance, her fame and her fertility, which was proved by a routine test.

Right: Grace Kelly dancing with the singer and film star Bing Crosby in her last Hollywood film, *High Society*. Crosby was allegedly one of Grace's numerous lovers.

Rainier and Grace first met in September 1955, when she was attending the Cannes Film Festival. Rainier was surprised that, instead of the hard-faced glamour queen he expected, Grace was a pleasant, ladylike young woman with excellent manners, but without the demanding temperament usually associated with film stars. His opinion was confirmed by their meetings in the United States, including several days which Rainier spent on the film set where Grace was making her last movie, *High Society*. Besides Grace, the film starred two of her former lovers, Bing Crosby and Frank Sinatra, but it seems that Rainier had been so completely taken in by Grace's virginal 'made in Hollywood' persona that he noticed nothing to suggest that they were more than her fellow film stars.

> MGM could do nothing to prevent the Kelly series appearing in American newspapers, but it did manage to get hold of all the copies intended for Europe. The articles were heavily edited to excise any coverage of sexual or other misdemeanours.

Jack Kelly, Grace's tough, outspoken father proved harder to take. Basically, Grace's parents did not approve of Rainier, who, though royal, they considered not quite good enough for their daughter. Jack also believed that Rainier was after Grace's money and later went ballistic when the prince asked for a dowry of US$2,000,000 . In addition, Jack Kelly was under the impression that Rainier was Prince of Morocco, not Monaco, and became alarmed at the thought that Grace meant to marry a man from this Muslim country in northwest Africa.

'I don't want any broken-down prince who's head of a country that nobody ever heard of marrying my

On the face of it, Grace Kelly lived up to the reputation for purity which her studio, MGM, had created for her. But the face of it was deceptive.

daughter.' was how Jack Kelly put it. He eventually calmed down and paid the $2,000,000 dowry because a royal, even a 'broken-down prince', went one better as a son-in-law than had been managed by other socially ambitious families in the snobbish world of American high society.

A HASTY COVER-UP

Of course, Margaret Kelly's series of articles might have wrecked the whole arrangement and, even though he was not directly involved, the publicity placed Rainer too close for comfort to a potential scandal. He soon departed the United States, heading for Monaco and leaving Grace, her family and Metro-Goldwyn-Mayer, her studio, to try to repair the damage. This was achieved by some fast thinking on the part of MGM executives, who fortunately did not have to contend with international television and radio, computer links, Internet websites and other means of rapidly spreading scandalous news around the world. MGM could do nothing to prevent the Kelly series appearing in American newspapers, but it did manage to get hold of all the copies intended for Europe. The articles were heavily edited to excise any coverage of sexual or other misdemeanours. They were then dispatched across the Atlantic to convince European newspaper readers that Prince Rainier's bride was as she should be: *virgo intacta*.

THE ARRIVAL OF CHILDREN

Any fallout from this close shave with the truth vanished shortly after the wedding, when it was announced that Princess Grace of Monaco was expecting her first child. The Monagesques celebrated as never before, as an heir for Prince Rainier meant freedom from French laws and, above all, French taxes. The couple's first daughter, Princess Caroline, was born on 23 January 1957, and was followed on 14 March of the ensuing year by a son, Prince Albert. In two years, Rainier and Grace had managed to produce 'an heir and a spare', and the first purpose of their marriage was accomplished. So were other, social, purposes. The former film star became president of the Red Cross of Monaco and the Garden Club of Monaco, and created the Princess Grace Foundation, which worked to involve young people in the creative arts and set up scholarships for suitable students.

Grace gave birth to a third child, Princess Stephanie, on 1 February 1965, but by then, it appears, her marriage to Rainier was already in trouble and had been for some time. In 1960, when Grace went home to Philadelphia to be with her father, who was dying of stomach cancer, Rainier was seen out on dates with one of her ladies-in-waiting. When Grace returned, she demanded to know what had been going on. Rainier denied everything. The lady-in-waiting was dismissed, but that was not enough for Grace. She invited a former film star lover, Cary Grant, to Monaco, and saw to it that photographers were at the airport to see the two of them kissing. From the shots that appeared in the newspapers, it seemed clear that Grace was doing much more than welcoming an old friend. Rainier fired back and banned cinemas in Monaco from screening *To Catch a Thief*, which featured Grace and Grant in steamy love scenes.

> Grace ... invited a former film star lover, Cary Grant, to Monaco, and saw to it that photographers were at the airport to see the two of them kissing. From the shots that appeared in the newspapers, it seemed clear that Grace was doing much more than welcoming an old friend.

After this, the marriage of Rainier and Grace gradually became a game of scoring points, one over the other, to show which of them had the upper hand. Grace had become extremely popular and greatly loved in Monaco. Rainier began to feel that he was playing second fiddle and grew jealous. Friends noticed that he tended to push her into the background, where before he had consulted her on matters to do with the government of Monaco.

A MARRIAGE UNRAVELLED

A spate of rumours arose, suggesting that the 'fairytale marriage' was on the rocks. Rainier and Grace were sleeping in separate bedrooms. There was talk of 'his and hers' love affairs. The children, it appeared, took up so much of Grace's time and attention that she had little or none left for Rainier. He resented this. It was true, though, that Grace began to spend more and more time away from Monaco on visits to her family or to Paris with the children. Before long, Grace's trips to Paris were no longer just visits: she was living in the French capital for long periods of time while Rainier remained in Monaco and made a life of his own there. It seems that in Paris, Grace, now in her late forties, was 'supplied' with young men around 10 or 15 years younger than herself.

Paris was not the only place to find these 'toy boys', as Grace's friends called her youthful lovers. While in New York, Grace met a Swedish actor named Per Mattson, 33, who was at once invited to her hotel room and, apparently, remained there until 5 a.m. next morning.

After little more than 20 years of marriage, the relationship between Rainier and Grace had unravelled so far that communication between them was virtually nonexistent. Grace had become a saddened figure, drinking too much, eating too much and growing fat. In the spring of 1978, she was staying at an Oxfordshire farmhouse owned by the English author Gwen Robyns, where the two of them were co-writing Grace's *Book of Flowers*. To Robyns's amazement, Grace made a startling relevation. 'I have begun to feel quite sad being married to Rainier,' she said. 'It's not what I'd hoped for.' Asked why she felt that way, Grace replied, 'He's not really interested in me.'

A UNITED FRONT

There was, though, one situation where Rainier and Grace, so distant in other ways, worked as a team, and that was where their children were involved. In 1978, the couple were faced with the sort of situation all parents dread: their elder daughter, Caroline, now aged 21, wanted to marry a man who, her parents were convinced, would be disastrous for her. Caroline had always been a 'wild child', headstrong and rebellious. She smoked in public, drank heavily and was frequently pictured in nightclubs and bars with rock stars or raffish young men of dubious respectability. Rainier and Grace scanned the royal families of Europe, desperate to find a prince capable of reining in

Right: Rainier and Grace with their 14-month old daughter Stephanie in 1966. Stephanie was their third child, following Princess Caroline, born in 1957 and Prince Albert, born 1958.

their wayward daughter. Charles, Prince of Wales, was one suggestion, but he was not interested. Unsurprisingly, as Caroline was obviously too hot to handle. Nor was anyone else.

PLAYBOY BANKER

Caroline, meanwhile, had been making her own arrangements. She had fallen for a Paris *boulevardier*, the wealthy playboy banker Philippe Junot, whom she met in 1976. Junot, 17 years older than Caroline, was still 'playing the field' at age 36. In addition to womanizing on a grand scale, he was interested in fast cars and racehorses, the typical pastimes of the pleasure-seeker. Rainier and Grace were aghast. They tried separating the couple by sending Caroline to the United States. But out of sight was not out of mind. Junot followed and the romance resumed. Next, Grace delivered an ultimatum: 'Leave or marry this man who is not for you!' she told Caroline. The effect was nil. Then Caroline was pictured – topless – on a yacht with Junot. Imagining, correctly as it turned out, that Caroline and Junot were already sleeping together, her parents finally gave up in despair. Rainier confessed to Grace that he was heartbroken. 'I know this marriage will end in tears,' he said.

Rainier and Grace scanned the royal families of Europe, desperate to find a prince capable of reining in their wayward daughter.

And so it did. Married on 28 June 1978, Caroline and Junot were divorced just over two years later. The trouble had started on their honeymoon in the Polynesian Islands, after Caroline discovered that her new husband had invited press photographers to join them. Junot intended to sell the pictures to the world press, which was avid to print them. The trouble continued when it became clear that Junot had no intention of letting his marriage get in the way of the 'good time' he had been enjoying for years. The paparazzi photographers were soon nosing out the haunts where they could take pictures of Junot romancing other women. Before long, Caroline was having assignations of her own and, again, the

paparazzi were there to provide the pictures. Husband and wife accused each other of adultery, and the marriage finally ended in mutual recrimination on 9 October 1980.

GRACE'S SUDDEN DEATH

Some two years later, on 14 September 1982, Princess Grace died, aged 52, after suffering a cerebral haemorrhage. She was driving back to Monaco along a winding mountain road that led from the royal retreat at Roc Angel. Grace's younger daughter, Stephanie, aged 17, was with her when she lost control of their car. It left the road and plunged more than 30 metres

down the mountainside. Stephanie was injured, but survived, although in later years the long-term effects of shock and grief seem to have increased the 'wild child' tendency she shared with her elder sister.

Despite the chill that had lain over their marriage for some years, Rainier was devastated at the unexpected death of his wife.

'My life will never be the same again,' he said. 'Without Grace, none of it matters to me now. It's all meaningless. My God, it's all meaningless.' And he hid his face in his hands and wept. He never really recovered and 20 years later confessed that he still felt the same about Grace's death as when he had first learned of it.

In 1978, Princess Caroline, 21, married the first of her three husbands, the playboy Philippe Junot, 38. The marriage did not last long. The couple were divorced in 1980.

Rainier, who survived Grace by 23 years, aged rapidly after she died, becoming a white-haired old man before he reached the age of 60. He never remarried, nor was he ever likely to.

THE PRINCESS MARRIES AGAIN

In contrast to her father, Caroline *did* marry again, on 29 December 1983. Her second husband, Stefano Casiraghi, was the heir to an Italian oil fortune.

Casiraghi was three years younger than Caroline, but he was a strong personality who, at long last, managed to keep the princess in order. Caroline was already pregnant when she married Casiraghi, a fact which pained her conventionally minded father. After the Philippe Junot fiasco, however, it was a relief for Rainier to know that here was a husband who truly cared for his daughter. It was said of Casiraghi, who was created Duke of Monaco after the marriage, that Caroline felt 'safe' with him. He was certainly the love of her life. But tragedy was not yet done with the

Prince Rainier, shown at Princess Grace's funeral in 1982, never recovered from the shock and pain of losing her and aged rapidly in the years that followed.

Grimaldi family, who were said to be subject to a curse that meant they would never have long marriages.

On 3 October 1990, close on seven years after he had married Caroline, Casiraghi, a world powerboat champion, was taking part in a race near Cap Ferrat when his boat foundered and sank. Casiraghi, aged 30, was killed. Caroline, who had left for a visit to Paris the previous day, became distraught when she heard the news. She returned to Monaco immediately. Rainier was scarcely less affected: he collapsed in tears and virtually went into shock on hearing of the death of the son-in-law he had come to regard as a son.

Caroline mourned her young husband for many years, but she still had three young children to care for. Years later, she explained how she faced up to the task.

> Despite the chill that had lain over their marriage for some years, Rainier was devastated at the unexpected death of his wife.

'Strength comes when you're in a very narrow valley and have no way of turning back,' Caroline explained. 'You just have to choose to live your life. I had to go on.'

STEPHANIE NOW THE 'WILD CHILD'

Caroline, by now aged 33, had obviously matured well beyond the tempestuous rebel she had been in her youth. Her sister Stephanie, however, eight years younger, was misbehaving in ways that made the Caroline controversies seem mild. Stephanie had been profoundly affected by her mother's death. The broken bones she suffered healed soon enough, but the emotional trauma remained. She was, after all, in the car with Grace when it crashed, and subsequent rumour suggested that she had been driving. This made her appear guilty, something that Stephanie resented, yet at the same time seemed to believe.

Like many people who escape

Stefano Casiraghi, Princess Caroline's second husband, was a successful businessman and sportsman. The couple, who married on 29 December 1983, had three children. Casiraghi was killed in 1990 in a boating accident.

Tragedy was not yet done with the Grimaldi family, who were said to be subject to a curse that meant they would never have long marriages.

death in dramatic circumstances while others die, Stephanie seemed to lose all sense of self-preservation – a process usually known as 'living life to the full'. She did not bother about her own wellbeing or the feelings of her family, and became unmindful of the future. She frequently appeared drunk in public. She took drugs. She dated several 'undesirable' young men and, in 1985, signed a modelling contract with a model agency in Paris and another in the United States. Rainier was in despair. He took the old-fashioned view that princesses should not stoop to modelling, but Stephanie went ahead anyway, and posed for fashion pictures that appeared *Vogue, Rolling Stone, Elle* and other international publications.

Next, complaining of the pressures that went with her new job, Stephanie checked in to the Belvedere Clinic in Paris, which specialized in detoxifying its clients.

Rainier, Caroline and her brother,

Princess Caroline, photographed on 20 March 2004, attending the Rose Ball a charity event, in Monte Carlo. In 1999 she had married again: her third husband was Prince Ernst of Hanover.

Albert, descended on her and persuaded her to give up modelling.

Stephanie went on to design swimwear, then became a recording artist. Her single, entitled 'Irresistible', scored immense success in Europe, especially in France, where more than a million copies were sold. The recording fully exploited Stephanie's 'bad girl' image and went with a video that Rainier considered 'provocative'. What it also exploited, of course, was Stephanie's royal status, something which, ironically, she was trying to shed. She went on trying, causing shock waves with her personal life. In 1987, while on holiday in Mauritius, she was photographed topless while embracing her current boyfriend, Mario Oliver, a convicted rapist.

Princess Stephanie tried several times to separate herself from her royal status and make a life of her own. One of her attempts was becoming a pop music star: here she is on 14 October 1985 recording a song called *Irresistible*.

The two of them were soon living together in Hollywood, in a mansion in Benedict Canyon. Stephanie had marriage in mind, but as soon as he heard of it Rainier put his foot down at last. He threatened to deprive Stephanie of her royal title if she dared to marry Mario. As things turned out, Rainier need not have bothered. By mid-1988, Stephanie's romance with Mario was over, and all she had to remember him by were his initials tattooed on her bottom. The initials were removed the painful way, by laser surgery.

RUNNING OFF TO JOIN THE CIRCUS

Far from being cured of her excesses following the failure of her marriage to Daniel Ducruet (see box), Stephanie went on as she had begun. In 1998, she gave

Princess Stephanie, aged 25, photographed in 1990 when she was still creating one scandal after another with her outrageous behaviour.

> Like many people who escape death in dramatic circumstances while others die, Stephanie seemed to lose all sense of self-preservation – a process usually known as 'living life to the full'.

birth to her third child, a daughter, again out of wedlock. She refused to reveal who the father was, but gossip and suspicion picked out Jean-Raymond Gottlieb, another security guard at Rainier's palace. In 2000, Stephanie announced a fresh romance; the new man in her life was Franco Knie, who co-owned the popular Circus Knie. Stephanie met Franco while on royal duty, presenting him with the Silver Clown Award for the Best Animal Trainer at the Circus Festival. The twice-married Franco, 47 years old, left his wife for Stephanie. For a year, the princess lived in a trailer with Franco and her three children, following the Circus Knie from one engagement to the next. Stephanie even allowed her elder daughter, Pauline, aged six, to perform with elephants in the circus ring while her eight-year-old brother Louis learned to be a juggler.

FINAL ACCEPTANCE

Stephanie had long wished to live her life as someone other than a Princess of Monaco, and her year with the Circus Knie gave her the chance. But as so often with Stephanie, it did not last long. By 2002, her affair with Franco was at an end. For a while, she remained in the circus world by marrying one of the Circus Knie acrobats, Adans Lopez Perez, in 2003. This marriage also foundered and, after it ended in 2004, Stephanie returned home to live in Monaco. She was now aged 37 and, after some 20 years of trying to escape her royalty, it seems that she had at last accepted it. Rather late in the day, but very welcome to her long-suffering father, Rainier, she was prepared to settle down, do her duty and leave her 'wild child' image far behind.

'I've stopped trying to change the game, stopped trying to change people,' Stephanie admitted. 'You build your own way in life with everything that is thrown at you, and make what you can from it.… I don't look back any more and I don't have any regrets.'

THE PRINCESS AND THE BODYGUARD

Stephanie's two liaisons following her abortive relationship with Mario Oliver, one of them to a man who had been jailed for fraud, were similarly brief. She then met Daniel Ducruet, a palace guard hired by Rainier to guard his son, Albert. Ducruet was a tall, dark-haired and handsome athlete and bodybuilder, covered in tattoos. He had been previously married and, in 1991, had a son by a former girfriend. The

same year, Rainier chose him to guard Stephanie during her tour to publicize her record album.

It was not a good idea. Stephanie and Ducruet began an affair and she gave birth to two children, in 1992 and 1994. Significantly, neither Rainier nor Caroline, nor her brother, Albert, visited her in hospital on either occasion. But they were there when Stephanie and Ducruet married in 1995. For a while, the couple seemed happy, and Stephanie declared in an interview, 'He really loves me for myself. He has proved to me that I am the one who counts.' Her family had some hope that Stephanie, now 30 years old, was starting to settle down at last.

The hope was brief. In 1996, Ducruet was photographed enjoying a poolside 'sex romp' with Muriel 'Fifi' Houteman at Villefranche-sur-Mer. Ducruet claimed that he had been entrapped by Houteman – who had been Miss Bare Breasts of Belgium in 1995 – one of her lovers and a photographer. They had 'spiked' his drink with drugs, making it that much easier for Miss Bare Breasts to seduce him.

'My mistake has destroyed me!' Ducruet declared. 'I curse the day I met her,' he said of Houteman, but neither remorse nor the suspended prison sentences later handed down to the three conspirators was able to save him. Stephanie at once filed for divorce and the marriage ended before the year was out.

Daniel Ducruet, a tall, handsome athlete, was hired by Prince Rainier as Stephanie's bodyguard. He later became the father of her two children, born in 1992 and 1994. Stephanie and Ducruet married in 1995, but divorced the following year.

THE GOOD SON

Prince Albert, Rainier's only son and heir, had always been a total contrast to his sisters, with their riotous behaviour and flamboyant social life. Albert was the 'good boy', pleasant, polite, widely touted as the most eligible bachelor in Europe, but seemingly uninterested in girls or the high life, and therefore hardly worth space in the gossip columns. The one thing about Albert that sparked press interest was his persistent failure to marry.

By 2002, when Albert was 44 and still showed no signs of taking a wife, Rainier decided he must secure the succession or risk Monaco returning to the jurisdiction of France. In that year, the Principality's constitution was changed to name Caroline as her brother's heir and, after her, her three children by her second marriage to Stefan Casiraghi and her then three-year-old daughter by her third marriage, in 1999, to Prince Ernst August V of Hanover.

Stephanie with her second husband, Adans Lopez Perez, circus acrobat. Married in 2003, the couple divorced in 2004.

Three years later, on 6 April 2005, Prince Rainier died, aged 81, and his son succeeded him as His Serene Highness Prince Albert II of Monaco. Almost at once, Albert made public two secrets he had been keeping for several years: he revealed that he had two children. The first was a daughter, born in 1991 to an American waitress, Tamara Rotolo. His other child was a son born in 2003 to Nicole Coste, a flight attendant who met Albert on an Air France flight in 1997. Neither of these children was eligible to succeed to the throne of Monaco, as both were illegitimate. But around the time of his coronation on 12 July 2005, Albert promised to that he would marry at some time in the future, so that a legitimate male heir of his own was, at least, a possibility.

A HAPPY ENDING?

This may or may not happen, of course. But with the unspectacular Albert in charge and his once untameable sisters calmed down and more mature, the time when Monaco was persistently embarrassed by its royal family could be at an end. For the Grimaldis, Albert's reign could also add a happy ending after so much trauma and tragedy in a 'fairytale' gone wrong.

The Grimaldi family on Monaco's National Day, 19 November, in 2006. The picture shows (left to right) Princess Caroline, her third husband Prince Ernst of Hanover, her brother Prince Albert, her elder son Andrea Casiraghi, and Princess Stephanie.

MAP OF KEY LOCATIONS

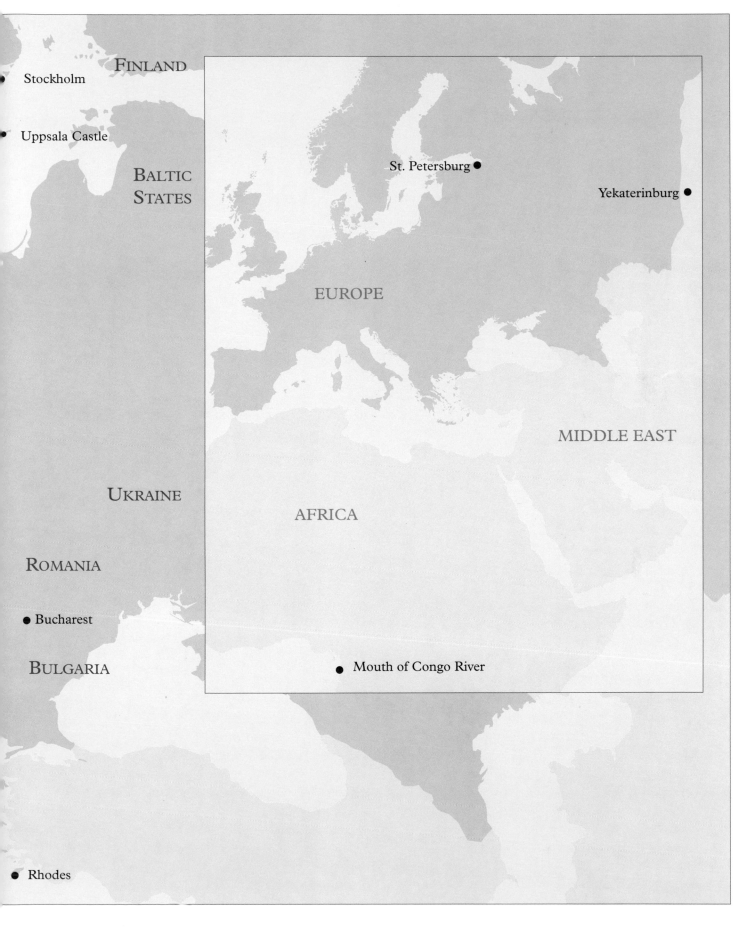

Stockholm

FINLAND

Uppsala Castle

BALTIC
STATES

St. Petersburg

Yekaterinburg

EUROPE

MIDDLE EAST

UKRAINE

AFRICA

ROMANIA

Bucharest

BULGARIA

Mouth of Congo River

Rhodes

INDEX

Page numbers in *italics* refer to illustrations

abdication 71–2, 154–5, 197–8, 200, 203, 209, 212

acromegaly 140

Albert II of Belgium, King 231

Albert of Monaco, Prince 237, 245, 247, 248, *249*

Albert of Saxe-Coburg-Gotha, Prince 165, 166

Alexander VII, Pope 155, 157, *157*, 159

Alexandra of Greece, Princess 194

Alexandra of Russia, Tsarina *166*, 168–9, 170, *170*, 171

Alexis, Tsarevich *165*, *167*, 168–70, 171

Alfonsito of Spain, Prince 171, *174*, 175

Alfonso XIII of Spain, King 168, 171, *173*, 175, 176

Alfred, Prince 165

Alice, Princess 165, 168

Amsberg, Claus-Georg 205–6, 207, 208, 209–10, 212

Antoinette, Marie 57

Antonescu, General Ion 189, *189*, 190, *190*, *191*

Arthur, Prince 165, 166

Astrid of Belgium, Queen 226, 227, *227*

Azzolino, Cardinal Decio 161

Baels, Liliane 227

Barbara of Spain, Queen Maria Teresa *144–5*, 147, *147*

Baring, Evelyn 228

Bathory, Elizabeth 27–38, *27*, *36*

Bathory, Stephen *26*, 27, *29*

Baudouin of Belgium, King 227, 231

Bavaria 59–93

Beatrice, Princess 165, 166, 173, 175, 176, *176*

Beatrix of the Netherlands, Princess 197, 205, *207*, 208, *208*, 209–10, 212, *213*

Bécu, Marie Jeanne 55, *55*, 56, 57

Beneczky, Katarina 38

Benicka, Katarina 37

Bernhardt of the Netherlands, Prince *197*, 198, *198*, 199, 200, *202*, 203, 204–5, 209, *209*, 210, *210*

Boel, Delphine 231, *231*

Boniface VIII, Pope 10, 19

Bourbon, House of 140, 145, 168, 171, 172

Braganza, House of 147

Bratianu, Ion 185, *186*

Calinescu, Armand *188*, 190

Carlos II of Spain, King *130*, *136*, 137–40, *137*

Carlos III of Spain, King 146, *146*

Carlos IV of Spain, King 146

Carlos, Don *130*, 131–7, *130*, *134*

Carol II of Romania, King *178*, 179–95, *179*, *181*, *183*, *188*, *192*, *193*

Caroline of Monaco, Princess 237, 238, 240, 241, *241*, 242–3, *244*, 247, *249*

Casement, Sir Roger *224*, 225, 228–9

Casiraghi, Andrea *249*

Casiraghi, Stefano 241–2, *243*, 247

Castle Berg *74*, 75, *76*, 90

Castle Cachtice 29, *30–1*, 34, 35, 37, 38

Catholicism 66, 69, 154, 157, 159, 161–2, 203, 204, 205

Charles I of Spain, King 128, *128*, 129, 132

Charles II of England, King 44

Charles, Prince of Wales 240

Christian IV of Denmark, King 152

Christina of Sweden, Queen *148*, 149–63, *148*, *149*, *152*, *156*, *158*, *159*, *160*, *162*

Churchill, Winston 195, 227

Clement V, Pope 10, 21, *24*

Codrianu, Cornelius 187, 189

Columbus, Christopher *123*

Communism 178–95

Congo, Belgian 215–29, *216–17*, *220*, *221*, *224*

Coste, Nicole 248

Crosby, Bing 234, *235*, 237

Crusade, First 1095–1099 11

Czewucka, Countess 100

dark arts 29–38, 47, 68, 137

Darmstadt, House of 168

d'Aubigné, François 47

de Champagne, Comte 11, 13

de Charnay, Guy 10, 18

de Courtarvel, Jacques 44

de Floyran, Esquin 21

de Folliaco, Jean de 21

de Fonseca, Juan de 119, 121

de Goneville, Geoffroi 10

de Guiche, Comte 45

de la Vallière, Louise 44, 45, *45*, 46, 48

de Laval, Gilles 22–3, *22*, *23*

de Ludre, Madame 47

de Mailly-Nesle, Marie *51*

de Molinos, Miguel 161, 162

de Nnaeyer, Baron Beernaert Smet 229

de Nogaret, Guillaume 19, 21

de Pairaud, Huges 21

de Payens, Huges 11, 13, 16
de Pompadour, Marquise Jeanne Antoinette Poisson 43,
    51, 52–3, 55–6
de Rairaud, Hugues 10
de Toledo, Fernando Alvarez 135
de Troyes, Etienne 21
de Valdo, Bernard 18
Delacroix, Blanche 229, 230
Descartes, René *160*
d'Etoiles, Jeanne Antoinette 51, 52–3, 55
drugs 29, 47, 243
Du Barry, Jean Comtesse 43, 55–6, *55*
Duc d'Orléans, Philippe 44, 54, *54*
Duchesse de Fontanges, Angélique de Scorraille de
    Russille 48, *48*
Ducruet, Daniel 246, 247, *247*

Edward II of England, King 24
Edward VII of England, King 171, 185, 225
Edward, Duke of Kent 166
Edward, Prince of Wales 165
Eleonora, Queen Maria 149, 151
Elizabeth I of England, Queen 132
Elizabeth of Parma, Queen 143
Enriquez, Fadrique 126
Erik XIV Vasa of Sweden, King 163, *163*
Ernst August V of Hanover, Prince 247, *249*
Eugenie, Empress 85

Farnese, Elizabeth 140
Fedele, Luigi 157
Ferdinand II of Aragon, King 114, *114*, 117–18, *117*, 121,
    121, 122, *123*, 124, 127–8
Ferdinand of Romania, Crown Prince 179, 180, 182, 185
Ferdinand VI of Spain, King *140*, *142*, 143–4, *144–5*, 146,
    146, 147
France 43–57
Franco, General Francisco 204, 205

Gaveston, Piers 24
Gaydon, Mildred 175
gender confusion 148–63
George III of England, King 166
George V of England, King 179
George VI of England, King 192
Gilbert, Marie Dolores Eliza Rosanna *see* Montez, Lola
Gonzalo, Prince 175
Gottlieb, Jean-Raymond 246

Grace of Monaco, Princess *232*, 233–4, *233*, *235*, *236*, 237,
    238, 240–1
Grant, Cary 234, 238
Green, Mary 180
Gregory IX, Pope 21
Grimaldi family of Monaco *232*, 233–48, *233*, *235*, *236*,
    239, *240–1*, *242*, *243*, *244*, *245*, *246*, *247*, *248–9*
Grinda, Helène 211, 212
Guggenheim, Daniel 229
Gustav of Sweden, King Karl 152–3, *153*, 155
Gustavus Adolphus II, King 149, *150*, 151, *151*

haemophilia 165–77
Hanover, House of 165–76
Hapsburg family 44, 131, 138, 139, 140
Harris, Reverend John 222
Heeckeren van Molecatan, Baron von 202
Helen of Greece, Princess 182, *183*
Hendrik of the Netherlands, Prince 198, 212
Henrietta Anne of France, Princess 44, 45, *45*
Henry VII of England, King 127
Hitler, Adolf 187, 198
Hofmans, Greet 199–201, 202, 203
Hohenzollern, House of 168, 180
homosexuality 54
Hornig, Richard 85
House of Hanover 165
Houteman, Muriel 'Fifi' 247
Hugo of Parma, Prince Carlos 203, 204, *204*, 205, 206, *206*
Hungary 27, 28, 29, 37

impotence 138
inbreeding/intermarriage 28–9, 131, 134
infidelity 44–6, 48–9, 51, 52–3, 55–6, 59–73, 95–110,
    179–86, 187
inherited disease 140, 165–77
Innocent II, Pope 14
Innocent XI, Pope 161, *161*
Irene of the Netherlands, Princess 203, 204–5, *204*, 206, *206*
Isabel of Portugal, Queen 113–14, *114*, 131
Isabella I of Castile, Queen 114, *114*, 118, *120*, 121, 122,
    123

Jo, Ilona 37, 38
John II of Castile, King 113
John III of Portugal, King 129
Josef I, Emperor Franz 76, 95, 96, *97*, 98, 99, 100, 105,
    107, 109

Juana I of Castile, Queen *112*, 113, *113*, 114–29, *125*, 140
Juarez, Benito 109, 110
Juliana of the Netherlands, Princess 197, *197*, 199, 200, 202, *202*, 203, 204–5, 209, 210–12, *211*
Junot, Philippe 240, *241*, 242

Kelly, Jack 237
Kelly, Margaret 234, 237
Kerensky, Alexander 171
Knie, Franco 246
Knights Hospitallers 11, 24, *25*
Knights of the Holy Sepulchre 11
Knights Templar *8*, 9–11, *9*, *11*, *12–13*, 14, *14*, 15–16, *15*, *16*, 17, 18–21, *20*

Lambermont, Baron Auguste 217
Lambrino, Iona (Zizi) 180, *181*, 182, 183, 186
Larisch, Countess 103–4
Lenin, Vladimir 171
Leo XIII, Pope 105
Leopold I of Belgium, King 109
Leopold II of Belgium, King 98, 99, *214*, 215–31, *215*, *222*, *225*, *226*, *230*
Leopold III of Belgium, King 226–7, *226*, 231
Leopold, Duke of Albany, Prince 165, *166*, 168, *177*
Linderhof Palace *92–3*
Longchamps, Baroness Sybille de Selys 231
Louis XIII of France, King 122
Louis XIV of France, King *42*, 43–9, *46*, 57, 85, 138, 140
Louis XV of France, King *43*, 49, *50*, 51–3, 54, *54*
Louise of France, Marie 138
Ludwig I of Bavaria, King *58*, 59–73, *63*, *71*, *73*, 76, 80, 88
Ludwig II of Bavaria, King 75–91, *75*, *76*, *77*, *78*, 84, *86*
Luitpold of Bavaria, Prince 89, 91
Lupescu, Eleana/Magda 183, 184–5, *184*, 186, 187, 190, *192*, 193, *193*, 195
Luther, Martin 69, 154

madness/mental derangement 28, 29, 75–91, 113–47
Magnus Gabriel de la Gardie, Count 153
magyari, Istvan 35
Majorova, Erszi 37, 38
Man in the Iron Mask 56
Mancini, Marie 44
Maniu, Juliu 185–6
Mansdotter, Karin 163
Manuela of Spain, Princess Maria 131
Maria Christina of Spain, Princess 175, 176, *176*

Maria Theresa of Spain, Infanta 44, *44*, 48, 49, 52, 140
Maria-Catherine Leszczynska of Poland, Queen 51, *51*
Marie Louise of Savoy 143
Marie of Romania, Queen *180*, 182, 186, *187*
Marie-Adelaide of Savoy, Queen 51
Marina Christina (Marikje) of the Netherlands, Princess 199, *199*, 203
Marquis de Montespan, François-Athénais 46, *46*, 47, 48
Mattson, Per 238
Maximilian II of Bavaria, King 77, *77*
Maximilian of Mexico, Emperor 109–10, *109*, *110–11*
Maximillian I, Emperor 114, 118, 123–4, *124*, 128
Mayerling tragedy 95–111
Mazarin, Cardinal Jules 44
Mazzini, Guiseppe 71
melancholy 96, 99, 113, 143, 146, 147
Michael I of Romania, King 190, *191*, 193, 195
misogyny 149
Molai, Jacques de *9*, 9–10, *12–13*, 16, 18, 20
Monaco 233–49
Monaldeschi, Marchese Gian–Rinaldo 157, 158–9
Montez, Lola 59–62, *59*, *61*, 63–5, *64*, *65*, *68*, 69–73, *70*, 80
Monvoisin, Catherine 47
Munich 63, 64, 66, 70, 72, *72*, 73, 80
murder 91, 95, 106–7

Napoleon III, Emperor 85, 109, 110
Nasady, Count Ferenc 27, 28, *28*, 29, *32*
Nazi Party 190, 192, 194, 198–9, 200, 204, 207, 208, 210, 227
Netherlands 197–213
Neuschwanstein Castle *74*
Nicholas II of Russia, Tsar *165*, 168–9, 170, *170*, 171

Oliver, Mario 245, 246, 247
Orange-Nassau, House of 197, 205, 210
Order of the Temple of Solomon *see* Knights Templar
Orders of Hospital of St John of Jerusalem *see* Knights Hospitallers
Otto of Bavaria, Prince 76, 77, *77*, 87, 88, 91
Otto, John Conrad 177

Parc au Cerfs 53, *53*, 55
Paul IV, Pope 205
Paul of Taxis, Prince 79, 83
Pavlovna, Queen Anne 198
Perez, Adans Lopez 246, *248*
Péron, Juan 199, 212

Peter II of Yugoslavia, King 194–5, *194*

Philip I of Spain, King 114, *116*, 117–19, *118*, 121, 122, 124, 126, 127

Philip II of Spain, King 132, *133*, 134–7, *135*, 143

Philip III of Spain, King 137

Philip IV of France, King *8*, 9–11, *10*, 14, *15*, 16–17, *16*, 19–21, *20*, 24, *24*

Philip IV of Spain 137, 140

Philip V of Spain, King *139*, 140, *141*, 142, 143, 145, 147

public execution *8*, *16*, *17*, *20*, 21, 28

Rainier III of Monaco, Prince *232*, 233–4, *233*, 237–8, *239*, 240–1, 242, *242*, 243, 245, 246, 247, 248

Rasputin, Grigori 169, *169*, 170–1

Reynaud, Paul 227

Robato, Edelmira Sampedro–Oeejo y 175

Romania 178–93, 195

Romanov, House of 168

Roosevelt, Franklin D. 192, *194*, 195

Rotolo, Tamara 248

Rudolf of Austria-Hungary, Crown Prince 95–6, *96*, 98, 99–100, *99*, *102*, 103–5, *106*, 107, *107*, 108, *108*

sacrifice, child 22, 23

sadism 28–38, 132, 134

Salvator, Archduke John 96, 98, 104

Scarron, François 48, 49, *49*

Scarron, Paul 48

Schloss Hohenschwangau *88–9*

sexual depravity 22, 154

Sophie Charlotte of Liechtenstein, Princess 84, *84*, 85

Spain 112–47

Sparre, Ebba 153, 155

Stanley, Henry Morton 220, *221*

Stephanie of Belgium, Crown Princess *98*, 99–100, *99*, 105

Stephanie of Monaco, Princess 238, *239*, 240–1, 243, 245, 246, *246*, 247, *248*, *249*

Stirbey, Barbu 185

Strubel, Milli 98

Sture, Nils 163

Sture, Svante 163

suicide 108

Sweden 148–63

syphilis, congenital 140

Szentes, Dorottya 37, 38

Szeps, Moritz 96, *96*, 98

Tampeanu, Lieutenant Ion 184

Thurzo, Count György 37, 38

Tito, Marshal 195

Titulescu, Nicholas 187

torture 9–10, 18, *18*, 19, *19*, 21, 32, 132
    as an interrogation method 18, *18*, 21
    star-kicking 33–4
    Strappado *19*
    water tourtue 33

Ujvary, Janos 37

Ulrich, Archduke 152

van Eetvelde, Baron 220, 222

Versailles 44, 47, 48, 52, 54, 55, 56, 85

Vetsera, Baroness Maria 95, *95*, 100, 104, 105, *106*, 107, 108, *108*

Vicky, Princess 165, 168

Victoria Eugenie (Ena), Princess 171, 172, *172*, 173, 175, 176, *176*

Victoria, Queen 165, 166, 168, 172, 176, 177, 178, 180

Vienna 95, 100

violence 28–38, 91, 95, 106–7, 132, 134, 135

Vlad III Dracul 27, 37, *39*, 40–1, *40*

Voltaire 53, 57

von Bismarck, Count Otto 79, *79*

von Bulow, Cosima 80, *81*, 83

von Donha, Count Christophe 154–5

von Gudden, Doctor 75, *76*, 90–1, *90*

Wagner, Richard 75, 78, 80, *81*, *82*, 83, 84, 85, 87

War of the Spanish Succession 140

Whitelocke, Bulstrode 153

Wilhelm I of Prussia, King 197–8

Wilhelm III of Prussia, King 198

Wilhelm IV of Prussia, King 78

Wilhelmina of the Netherlands, Queen *196*, 197, 198, 200, *200*, *201*, 202, 212

Wisniowiecki, Michael Korybut 161

witchcraft/occult 19, 22, 47, 68, 88, 137

Wittelsbach family 63, 64, 70, 71, 72, *75*, 76, 77, 83, 89, 91, 138, 140

World War I 171, 180, 226

World War II 190, 195, 198, 204, 208, 212

Yousoupoff, Prince Felix 171

Zaragoza *119–20*

PICTURE CREDITS